CW00542724

POLICING KENT

Guarding the Garden of England

1800-2000

Kent County Constabulary cyclists, *c*.1910.

POLICING KENT

Guarding the Garden of England
1800-2000

Roy Ingleton

PHILLIMORE

2002

Published by
PHILLIMORE & CO. LTD
Shopwyke Manor Barn, Chichester, West Sussex, England

ISBN 1 86077 233 1

Printed and bound in Great Britain by
THE CROMWELL PRESS
Trowbridge, Wiltshire

This book is dedicated to the men and women of the Kent County Constabulary
whose task it is to carry into the 21st century
the fruits of the labours of their forebears
and uphold their traditions and standards.

CONTENTS

LIST OF ILLUSTRATIONS

Frontispiece: Kent County Constabulary cyclists, *c*.1910

PREFACE

The past does not necessarily proclaim the future but one neglects the past at one's peril. In this book, Roy Ingleton sets out the past with admirable clarity and, in so doing, highlights the traditions of the Kent County Constabulary, the evolution of the force from a plethora of forces under local Watch Committees to the present day force of some 5,000 people, including civilians, supported by the Special Constabulary: a force that is vibrant and responsive to present-day demands.

I commend this book as compulsive reading for all those committed to the maintenance of law and order and suggest that the force could well adopt the motto of another venerable Kent body – the Buffs (Royal East Kent Regiment) – *Veteri frondescit honore* – ('With ancient honour ever green').

Sir John Grugeon
Chairman of the Kent Police Authority
1992-1998

List of Subscribers

Michael Abbott - Force No. 3791
Chas Alder
Adrian Allen, Kent County Constabulary
Nick and Daphne Allen
Peter Amey
Liza M. Andrews
Valerie Arrindell
John Avery
H. Baker
Carole A. Banks
John Barber
A.H.G. Barnes
Greg Barry
Colin Bates
Douglas J. Bennett
J. Blum, Hamburg, Germany
Dave De Boick, PC 8483, BSc (Hons)
Gordon Boozer
Stuart Bourner
Alan Bouruet
Mel Bowen, PC 5150
Bill Bowman
Iain Gordon MacCallum Braid, PC 10888
Colin S.B. Breed (retired D.C.I.)
Miss Mary A. Brett
Kevin Brigden
Fred Brisley
John and Mandy Brooker
John and Molly Brooker
Nick Brown
W.E. Browne
Brian W. Bull
John A. Bull, 2073 - 1951-1981
John R. Burden
R. Burns
David Burrows, PS 5313
Ex-Sgt. Jack Butcher (T2)
Brenda Butler, MBE
Andrew Callan
Betty Carman
Paddy Carpenter, Chairman - Police Vehicle Enthusiasts' Club
Lynn Castle
Colin M. Chandler
Anthony Chomiak
Bryan D.F. Clarke
Richard Clements
R. Cockram, Ex-Sgt
Peter David Coleman
Doug Constable
Colin Coomber
Sharon Cotter
Teresa Crane
Sgt Peter Crawley, 6467
Steve Cribbens
Martin J. Dale
David Davies
Mark Davies
Michael John Davis
Norah Dawes
Mr Brian R. Deacon (B.T. Police RTD)
Derek Dean
Ian Depledge
Tony Dewing, Ex-Inspector 4560
John D. Dibley, O.B.E.
Ted Dillon

Peter D. Doherty, PC 7136
Dr Roger Donaldson
Mick Donovan
Miss Barbara Duckworth, retired Ch. Insp.
George Dunk
David Charles Edwards
Gerry Edwards
R. Elwood
John D. Endicott
James Farrimond
Trevor Finbow
Mr Dave Finch
Paul Footman
Jeffery Stephen Foxley
P.R. Francklin
Annette Franklin
Brian C. Gamage, PC 4479
Ron Gamage
Mr Ian Ronald Gedge (PC 6026)
Andy and Judy Gent
Edward Arthur Gilbert (ex PS 2009)
Richard Godfrey
Garry Goodhew
Keith Grant
Eric Russell Green
Peter William Leonard Green
Harold Charles Gurney
Richard H. Hardy
J.G. Harman
Michael Haunschild, Hannover, Germany
Geoff Hayward
Adrian Herbert
Ali Herbert, PC 9767
Mr Ben Hicks
Barry Hilton
Nigel Holdstock
Detective Inspector Holl, 7800
John W. Hollands
Sean O'Sullivan Hollands
Alan and Barbara Hollings
Colin Neil Holman
Mark A. Holt
Ian F. Hubble
Sue and Chris Huke
Stanley James Humphreys
Brian Hunt
Don and Mary Ingleton
Bill Ireland
Colin Jackson
Ian Jackson
Ian Jarman, DC 9398
N. Jerome
Arthur Winston Jones
Sgt. Glen Jones
Levina B. Jones
Frank Jordan, Deputy Chief Constable 1979-82, Chief Constable of Kent 1982-89
Michael Stewart Kennedy
Kent Special Branch
Det/Supt David M. King
Peter Thomas King
Arthur H. Kubias
Trevor Lailey
Patricia Laing
John Laker, Sgt. 2960

Ernie Lane
David Leach
Richard Leahy
Nikki Lee, PC 10553
PC Lillicrap (Rtrd) 3824
John (Joe) Link, Ex PC 996
Dave 'Mad-Dog' Lloyd
K.H. London, J.P.
Sergeant R.C.W. Mackey
Alan Maitland
Richard J. Mallpress
Peter Markins, Sgt. 5900 (retired)
John Mason
Michael D. Matsell, F.F.S.
Mr S.A. McCabe
Bob McCaughan
John McCluskie
Terry McCormick, PC 5125, Thanet Police 1973-2003
Robin McIvor
Inspector Robert Mileham, Metropolitan Police
Michael and Janet Millen
Kevin Miller - Ex Inspector 4647
'Millsey' and Pauline
N.T. Minter
Alan Moody
Neil Mullett
Andy Mundy, PC 5628
Thomas Murphy
Paul Mutum
Marcel P. Nardin
I.D. Newman, PC 5771
Cliff Norrington, 5145
Clifford W. Norris
The Old Gallery Bookshop, Hythe, Kent
Det. Constable Andrew Orfila, 9178
June O'Connor
Michael John O'Rourke
Barry N. Pain, CBE, QPM
David William Painter
John Palmer, Chairman, Kent Police Authority
P. Parsons
Roger W. Pearce
Charles Edwin Pearson
Chris Phillips
Ray Pilbeam
Donald Pimp
John Neville Pitcher, retired Police Supt. Kent Constabulary
SO 16881 and Sc 17202 Plumridge
Guy James Friston Powell
Robert E. Prett
A.F.C. Pritchard
Sergeant Prodger 9181
Bill Pullinger
Mike Pursey
R. Quinnell, DS 2646
Paul Rason, Chairman, Friends of Met. Police Museum
Denise Rayner
Andrew Reid
David T. Richards
Roderick J. Richards
Peter Brian Richardson
Christopher Anthony Parry Richford (ex Sergeant 4446 Kent
      Constab.)
Tony Roach
G.A.F. Robbins, PS 4158
John S. Robertson, Ex D/Inspector 2485, 1956-86
M. Robertson
George H. Rogers
Irving Guy Miller Rogers
'John' Rogers, PC 5000
Ian P. Rudd

Arthur Ruderman
Maurice I. Russell
Peter J. Salt
Ronald Saunders
Keith Saunderson
Raymond Sayer
Maureen Scollan (ex Essex Police)
Les Scott, DC 3158 S.O.C.O.
David Seeney
Darren Sevket
G.A. Skinner BSc (Eng)
Harry Skinner
Mr Charlie Small
Kenneth Reginald Smith
Mark Smith, PC 9704
Mick Smith
Peter Smith, 2372
Robert Andrew Spicer, PC 6774
D.C. Dave Sprigg
Martin Stallion
Ian Standen, PC 7402
David Stanger
Raymond C. Stephens
John Stockham
Bill Stubbs
Mrs P.A. Sturgeon
Pat Sullivan
Bernard Swift, Ex Chief Superintendent
Peter Symes, 1967-1992
Peter Symons
Michael Bradley Taylor, Q.P.M.
Richard James Taylor, PS 4878, Rtd Kent
Hugh G. Tebay
Mr Rhodri Thomas
Mr S.W. Thomas
Eric Thomson, 2169
Roland Tolputt
John Henry Towner
'Tom' Tucker
S.F. Tully, Esq, M.B.E.
Alf Tunstall, Stoke-on-Trent
David Turner
Gay Turner
Alan Twyman
Mick Twyman
Superintendent (Retd) Julian Sendles Tyler
K.G. Usborne
David L. Valls-Russell
Peter and Vivien Vaughan
David Voice
Jon Ashley Warman
Dick Watchus
Paul Waterman
Jack Watson
Mark Webb
Frank Webster-Relf
Brian D. Weeden, 2031
Keith Wells
Ian Whitehead
Paul Whitehead 8627
Ex Chief Supt. M. Whitfield, BA
Anthony J. Whiting
Mr George Robert Whitlock
Mr Alan Whorlow
Det. Insp. Graham Wickens 4254 Rtd
Alan Wilkinson
Insp. Dave Wilkinson - Port of Dover Police
Neil Woods, PC 4932, R'TRD 05/03/02
Les Worthington
Marcus Wright
John Yarrow

IN THE BEGINNING

Identity is an important factor in a competitive environment and is no less so in the context of the police. A former Inspector of Constabulary, Sir Geoffrey Dear, is quoted as saying, 'Identity should seek to distinguish an organisation from its competitors, subtly setting it apart. It should embrace product, people, pride, history, ethics and standards'. Sadly, as we enter the new millennium, it is a commonly held view within the police service that history is of little consequence. The task of compiling this book was made all the more difficult by the fact that so many of the force's records have been destroyed in recent years on the principle that history is irrelevant to today's policing and because of lack of storage space.

This is in complete contrast to the attitude of the armed forces. Their recruits are taught the history of their particular regiment, squadron or ship from the very start. This is not done for sentimental reasons; it is designed to instil unashamed pride. The fact that the weapons and tactics of the past have little in common with present-day warfare is of no consequence; the courage, pride, ethics and standards are unchanged. And so it should be with the police service. Of course the work of the present-day police officer has changed from that of a century or more ago but the essential *raison d'être* remains the same; to serve the public. The principles laid down by the first Commissioners of Police in 1829 are still valid: the prevention and detection of crime and the maintenance of public order.

Much is talked today of 'Best Practice' and readers will find between the covers of this book a great deal which might serve them in their search for this elusive goal.

In the Beginning …

There have been 'policemen' of one kind or another in Kent since at least the times of the Saxons, when families were grouped in tens (*tithings*), each being mutually responsible for the other with one member of each family taking it in turn to act as *tithingman* or *borsholder* and see that the laws and customs were observed and to bring offenders before the lord of the manor. The Norman invasion brought with it the original office of *Constable* who was in fact a senior military officer of the King's court.

By the 13th century this system had largely evolved into one in which each *hundred* (ten *tithings*) appointed a High Constable with Petty (later Parish) Constables responsible to him for the good behaviour of his parish. (In some places, including part of Kent, the latter retained the title of *borsholder.*) A series of royal writs in that century ensured that any substantial town had a system of watchmen whose main duty was to close and guard the city gates at night but this was soon extended to include lighting the lamps, calling the hours and watching for fires. The 1285 Statute of Westminster codified this system of social commitment and provided that (a) it was the duty of every citizen to maintain the King's peace and arrest any offenders; (b) the unpaid, part-time constables had a special duty in this respect, assisted in the towns by the watchmen; (c) if the offender was not caught *in flagrante delicto*, a hue and cry must be raised; (d) all persons were expected to bear arms and to join in the hue and cry if required to do so; and (e) the constable had a duty to bring the offender before the court.

In 1361 an Act of Parliament introduced the office of justice of the peace, a post usually occupied by the lord of the manor or a substantial landholder. These soon supplanted the High Constables and the parish constables became answerable to these local dispensers of justice. All this time the parish constable remained a temporary and usually part-time job. Every householder was liable for constabulary duty for (usually) a year – even criminals and other unsuitable persons. He was frequently appointed '… *without his knowledge or consent and decidedly against his will*'.[1] However, some delegation was permitted and the more wealthy appointees merely employed someone else to perform their period of service. That they did not always choose wisely may be seen from the fact that, in 1598, some two dozen Cranbrook men were indicted before the assizes for contempt, having elected one William Sheafe as the constable, 'although they knew him to be an infirm man incapable of discharging the office'.[2]

Much has been said and written about the illiteracy and general inefficiency of many of these constables but it must be remembered that this was in a period in which literacy was something only the fortunate few could aspire to. His jurisdiction was confined to the parish and there was a notable lack of contact or collaboration with his counterparts elsewhere. Nevertheless, William Lambarde (1536-1601), a justice and legal scholar, was so disturbed by the ignorance and lack of diligence shown by the parish constables in Kent in the 16th century that he wrote and published a handbook for them, *The Duties of Constables, Borsholders, Tythingmen, and such other low and lay ministers of the peace.*

In the years prior to the introduction of an organised and paid police service in the 19th century, the great majority of the population worked and lived in rural areas and the policing system was equally pastoral. It was far from perfect but, whatever its faults, for most people the English system was preferable to the despised and centralised 'French' system, with its nationally directed *maréchaussée* and paid spies.

With the population living in small communities, local offenders soon became known and the main problem was therefore the many itinerants who passed through the town or village. Many of these were tinkers, hawkers, pedlars, knife-grinders – others were penniless vagrants who relied on begging and charity, making them a drain on the parish resources. Consequently, it is not surprising that, as early as the 14th century, laws were passed to control and punish beggars and vagabonds.[3]

The extent to which these wandering people were responsible for criminal acts is uncertain but in a statute of 1572 '… rogues, vagabonds and sturdy beggars' were blamed for '…murders, thefts and other great outrages'.[4] Beggars could be jailed, whipped, bored through the ear, branded on the shoulder and even executed. The main purpose of these ancient Acts was to get the penurious population off the parish in which they were discovered or sought relief and return them, parish by parish, back to their place of settlement (where they were born or had lived for at least a year).

Where laws were passed somebody had to enforce them and the control of these travellers and, to a greater or lesser extent, the poor in general, became a policing task from the very earliest days until the end of the 20th century. The 1824 Vagrancy Act (5 Geo.IV, c.83) repealed and consolidated all previous legislation on this subject and parts of this statute – such as those dealing with prostitutes behaving riotously or indecently, begging, fortune telling and sleeping out – were still in force as the 20th century drew to a close.

As the population became more mobile, so footpads and highwaymen appeared to ambush travellers and, although not suffering quite as much as some counties, Kent had its share of these merciless and vicious robbers. Totally unable to cope with such criminals, the essentially local, sparse and untrained system of parish constables was also unable to deal with any form of serious disorder. Public order had been the province of the justices of the peace ever since the days when they were knights commissioned by Richard I in 1195 to keep the peace. Although they had the power to swear in special constables, this took time and most justices preferred to resort to the military in times of disorder. Three main avenues were open to them : the militia, the yeomanry or the regular army.

The militia has long historical roots but largely fell into disuse until the middle of the 18th century when it was reinforced to foster British ambitions in Europe. Property holders were compelled to join but, like the parish constable system, they could offer a substitute. The general impression of the militia is that it was not very effective in public order situations and often created more trouble than it quelled. In Whiggish Kent there was considerable opposition to the formation of a local militia in the early 1800s, consisting as it would be of artisans, retailers, unskilled men and servants – in other words, the 'lower orders'.

If the Whigs had little regard for the militia, they had even less for the Yeomanry. This was a territorial force (and was the origin of today's Territorial Army), created in 1794 to counter the possibility of a Napoleonic invasion. It consisted of armed, well-trained tenant farmers and small landowners, officered by the local gentry and aristocracy. They were only paid when they had been mustered but most owned their own horse which aided their considerable mobility. The reputation of the yeomanry was regrettably tarnished by the so-called Peterloo massacre in 1819 and, although seen by many as a wholly Tory creature, Yeomanry units were nevertheless formed in Kent. However, in 1838 this body was felt to be too expensive for the government to maintain, especially as the Napoleonic threat had long been dissipated and the Metropolitan Police was nearing its first decade. Troops in Cobham and Tonbridge were disbanded and there were mass resignations in Dartford and Sevenoaks.

For the justices of the peace, the advantage of the regular army was the fact that it did not have to be paid out of local funds. The drawbacks were its lack of mobility and the fact that the Home Secretary had to approve any call for its use. However, with no efficient police force, the army 'did a far better job that any other body … was able to perform at the time'.[5]

This then is what passed for policing in Kent as the church bells rang in the new century.

One

The Early Days
1800-1857

The End of the Old System

The turn of the 18th/19th centuries was a significant period in English history which affected Kent like most counties. Although the Revolutions in France and America caused unrest and discontent among the poorer classes in England, aggravated by the draconian Poor Law, this was not enough to provoke a full-scale revolution here. The intermittent war with France had led to galloping inflation so that, even with twice the wages, the working man found himself worse off in 1815 than he had been in 1793. The economic depression was sharply felt in rural Kent. And, in the course of his famous 'Rural Rides', Cobbett found: '… the labourers' houses all along through this island [Thanet] beggarly in the extreme. The people dirty, poor-looking, ragged but particularly dirty'. A situation he ascribed to the use of horses and machines to do work once performed by labourers.

By this time it was clear that the parish constable and watchman systems could not cope with the burgeoning population and increasing crime and mob violence. There were a number of protagonists for a 'police' force, whose task of preventing and detecting crime would be divorced from that of the administration of justice. These included Patrick Colquhoun (1745-1820), whose pamphlet, *Police of the Metropolis*, was published in 1795. Another was Sir Edwin Chadwick, whose treatise on the formation of a preventive police force was also read with great interest. But proposals to introduce such a police system were routinely thwarted by powerful vested interests.

But were these, and other policing proposals, visions held by far-sighted men or were they, as some revisionist historians claim, merely an expression of the need for the ruling class to keep the new industrial working class under its thumb?[1] If the latter is the case, it may help to explain why Kent was so slow in introducing a county police force; there was little industry and the county retained its largely rural character throughout the 19th century.

And what of the population? What sort of people were the Kentish Men and Men of Kent? The first official census was taken in 1801 and showed the population of the county to be just over 300,000. Most were employed on the land, where they were poorly regarded by their 'betters'. At the end of the 18th century, one farmer described them as: '… being of a race the most low bred and illiterate … [that] do often turn out the most unprincipled and profligate; and though perhaps they may not have attempted the commission of the most atrocious offences, yet in the low arts of deception, the country ploughman is inferior to few'.[2]

The 'New Police'

In 1822, Sir Robert Peel, as the Tory Home Secretary, told Parliament that the country should have 'a vigorous system of police',[3] and set up a Parliamentary Committee, whose Report formed the basis of Peel's 1829 'Bill for improving the Police in and near the Metropolis'. Once passed, the 1829 Metropolitan Police Act heralded the end of the old, fragmented and ineffectual system of parish constables and the dawn of a whole new era of policing. Firstly, policing was to be preventive, the primary means being conspicuous patrols by uniformed police officers. Secondly, command and control were to be maintained through a centralised, quasi-military organisational structure. Thirdly, the police were to be patient, impersonal and professional. Finally it made it clear that the authority of the English constable derived from three sources: the Crown (not the political party in power), the law and the consent and co-operation of the citizens.

Peel made it clear he was not looking for 'all the virtues under heaven'.[4] He refused to enrol 'gentlemen' or commissioned officers as superintendents and inspectors because he was '… certain they would be above their work'. He felt 'a Sergeant of the Guards … is a better man for my purpose than a captain of high military reputation'.

The Police in the Provinces

But this new police force only covered the capital and outside London the old system continued as before. When depression and extreme poverty gave rise to what was known as the Last Labourers' Revolt in August 1830, there was no effective police force to deal with it. The uprising broke out at Hardres, near Canterbury, where around 400 farm workers destroyed threshing machines and caused other damage. Further uprisings followed throughout September of that year when farm machinery was damaged and ricks were set on fire. By October, the revolt had spread to the Dover area and the unrest then spread to the Maidstone and Sittingbourne areas; the situation was becoming serious.

The problem was how to deal with it; an efficient police force would no doubt have been able to cope but no county force was to be formed for another three decades and it would be four or five years before the first of the small 'borough' forces would be created. In extreme cases where public order had broken down, the justices of the peace could call upon the military and this is precisely what the Maidstone magistrates did on 30 October 1830 when they went out with a troop of soldiers to meet a mob of some 400 people just outside the town.

The 1833 Lighting & Watching Act was the first attempt to establish a paid police throughout the country but it took the passing of the Municipal Corporations Act in 1835 to really get things moving. This required all the new incorporated boroughs to appoint town clerks and treasurers and, under Clause 76, to appoint a Watch Committee and set up a police force.

The response to the Act was patchy and, as late as 1837, less than 55 per cent of the boroughs had formed a police force. In Kent, nine forces were established between 1835 and 1837; Tunbridge Wells (1835), Canterbury (1836), Deal (1836), Dover (1836), Folkestone (1836), Gravesend (1836), Maidstone (1836), Ramsgate (1836), Rochester (1837). There were also police forces of sorts in Ashford, Faversham, Hythe, Sandwich and Tenterden but these were usually little more than 'one-man bands'.

The man in charge (and it always *was* a man in those days) was known by a variety of titles but usually Inspector or Superintendent. Only later was the title of chief constable introduced. The non-statutory nature of the office meant that the chief officer in a borough was an employee of the Watch Committee who could be hired and fired at will – and many indeed were. The Committees generally looked for someone who would carry out their instructions faithfully rather than competence as a policeman. Indeed, even as late as 1919, one of the HMIs, giving evidence to the Desborough Committee, stated that he thought that chief constables were appointed, '… not on their merits as policemen, especially in the smaller boroughs'.[5]

Once local police forces had been formed, the rural parish constables were frequently issued with a uniform similar to that worn in the towns. This, in turn, was based on that worn by the Metropolitan Police. In the earliest days, the 'Peeler' wore a navy-blue swallow-tailed coat with a raised leather collar or stock (as a protection against garrotting), together with navy trousers in the winter and white ones in the summer. The white trousers proved impracticable and were soon dispensed with while the swallowtail

1 London police uniform as copied by most early police forces.

coat was later replaced by a tunic that came almost to the knees. The ensemble was topped off with a stovepipe hat.

'No man is an Island, entire of itself', wrote John Donne 400 years ago, and this adage has always held good for the police. The police forces which were formed in the first half of the 19th century could call upon each other for aid in times of difficulty or, in extreme cases, call upon the military to lend a hand. There were also the special constables.

The origins of the special constabulary go back to 1673 when Charles II passed an Act which laid down that any citizen might be sworn in as a police officer for a year to deal with threats of great disorder. However, the Act was seldom invoked in the South as the incidence of major disorders was low. When the Metropolitan Police was formed in 1829, it was soon apparent that the force could not hope to deal with serious disorders on its own and the system was revised. A Special Constables Act was passed in 1831 under which the justices of the peace could swear in as many men as necessary to deal with 'tumult, riot and felony' and, although amended over the years, this Act still forms the basis of today's special constabulary. In addition, in the boroughs, lists were kept of special constables who were appointed annually under the Municipal Corporations Acts.

2 Contemporary drawing of an early 19th-century watchman.

3 Charles Roose (1785-1880) – one of the last watchmen.

The Kentish Boroughs

Ashford was never an incorporated borough and so was not subject to the Municipal Corporations Act. Nevertheless, it made some valiant attempts to police itself. It employed watchmen to patrol its streets by night and a parish lock-up behind the Forge Lane workhouse was available for their use. In 1829, one of the watchmen was dismissed for assaulting a colleague and it is indicative of the problems facing the town authorities that, a year later, he had to be re-employed as there were no other applicants for the job. In 1840 the authorities appointed their first constable, Walter Smith from the Canterbury City Police, but he resigned two years later after being charged with being drunk and in possession of a loaded pistol while on duty. The strength was later increased to two constables and, in 1855, Superintendent Fawcett was in charge of this minuscule force. In 1857, when the Kent County Constabulary was formed, Ashford was absorbed into the new force and was placed under the command of Superintendent Dewar, who had been the superintending constable in charge of the parish constables in the Ashford area.

The early records for the City of **Canterbury** show that in 1787 there were nine watchmen, including two supernumeraries. Watch houses were set up successively in the Corn Market (1777-1800), Iron Bar Lane (1800-20) and White Horse Lane/ Westgate (1820-36). Their task was laid down as calling the hour and the weather, examining and securing property, raising alarm of fire and apprehending wrongdoers. In 1829, three of the watch were so senile and infirm that they were incapable of performing their duties and were replaced.

By now the need for change was obvious, labourers working 12 hours or more a day could hardly be expected to police the city at night. There was no watch in the day time and the hue and cry had fallen into disuse.[6] In December 1835 a Watch Committee was formed and, in February the following year, it appointed a superintendent, two inspectors and 15 constables to police the city in uniform. Unusually, this force was created without recourse to the Metropolitan Police and all were local men. Most of the new men were labourers, including one of the inspectors, whilst others were shoemakers, lime burners, grooms, tailors, butchers and gardeners.

This creation was not without opposition, a local newspaper viewing it with 'hostility and suspicion' and complaining of the 18s. a week being wrung by taxes from the pockets of the inhabitants: 'Six policemen we think would have been amply sufficient to maintain order and execute the civil business of Canterbury.'[7]

The 'New City Police' went on duty for the first time on 7 March 1836. The *Kentish Gazette* for the following day reported:

> Yesterday this 'great first cause' for imposing a Borough rate, assembled opposite Mr. Payn's slaughterhouse in Crown Alley and having been duly inspected by the municipal authorities, made their debut on the city stage before a crowd of anxious persons congregated ... to witness the 'interesting' spectacle. On enquiry at a late hour last evening, we have the pleasure of stating that not one misdemeanour had been committed ... The consolation the economising liberals, out of office, will receive will arise from seeing their protégés listlessly parade our quiet streets in their livery.[8]

Of the 18 proud young men who paraded that day in their spanking new uniforms, half would be gone within the next four years (three resigned, six dismissed for misconduct). By the time the force reached its tenth anniversary a further four had left (Inspector Andrew Plank, aged 37, died in 1841, two constables were dismissed and one resigned). The second inspector, William Bradley, was dismissed in March 1846. The first superintendent, John Clements, however, soldiered on until May 1860 when he retired after 24 years' service.

A number of men were taken on over the years as 'supernumerary' constables, usually two at a time. They followed their own occupation but turned out for police work as and when required, for example to assist at special occasions, to cover sickness, suspensions, vacancies. They were sworn in as special constables and issued with a uniform and paid 2s. 6d. for every day's duty performed. These men formed a major source of recruitment over the years (31 per cent).

The 'Rules and Regulations for the Government and Instruction of the Police Force of the City and Borough of Canterbury' (based on those of the Metropolitan Police) provided that 'the main objects of a police force are these: first; the prevention of crime; second; its detection; third the apprehension and punishment of offenders.'

However, they had many other mundane tasks to perform such as enforcing the height of shop blinds, dealing with nuisances and rubbish, reporting broken gas lamps, opening/closing the Westgate urinal, apprehending vagrants and beggars, maintaining order and supervising processions.

Canterbury had long been a garrison town as well as an ecclesiastical one, its military strength varying between 100 and 2,000 soldiers. The officers were, as one might expect, generally wealthy, fashionable young men from 'good families', but there were several reports of their 'outrageous' behaviour' – drunkenness and riding their horses across fields and damaging crops. Although the army only represented some 10 per cent of the population, soldiers accounted for 25 per cent of the cases brought before the magistrates.

Disciplinary powers were shared between the Watch Committee and the justices[9] and the early records show that those policemen dismissed or otherwise punished had committed the usual misdemeanours of the time: drunk/asleep on duty, leaving the beat, neglect of duty. Most cases were dealt with by way of reprimand with the added threat of dismissal for a subsequent offence. The number of dismissals in the early days of the Canterbury force is indicative of the calibre of recruits, their lack of training and the public opposition to their existence. Of the 104 men who left the force in the period between 1836 and 1888, one third were dismissed.

Familiar images of dallying policemen are conjured up by the instruction that members of the force would be severely punished if found engaged in conversation with female servants or other women. The threat of disciplinary action did not always deter them and Jesse Manuel, who served in the Canterbury City force from 1847 to 1885, told of being disturbed by the 'Missus' whilst being administered to by a kindly cook during the early years of his service. He beat a hasty exit but, in doing so, upset the dish and had to complete his tour of duty with a large gravy stain on his otherwise spotless white trousers.[10] Perhaps remembering his own indiscretions, when Manuel was made sergeant he would roll a stone towards a sleeping policeman to warn him of his approach, thus avoiding having the report the man.

The new police force was initially housed in a disused abattoir in Crown Yard/Stour Street. In 1850 part of the old city workhouse (the Poor Priests' Hospital) in Lamb Lane was converted to provide six cells, an office and accommodation for the superintendent's family. The cells were probably those previously described by the Municipal Corporation Commissioners as 'very small and close, presenting very insufficient means of ventilation'. Although steps were taken to alleviate complaints by the provision of WCs and palliasses, the smell that emanated from these facilities was extremely offensive and the superintendent complained bitterly about it. Nevertheless, despite their very obvious disadvantages, these premises remained the City police station for 15 years.

Deal was incorporated as a borough in 1699, having previously been a dependency of Sandwich. In the 18th century it was a thriving little town of some 7,000 souls, with a Town Sergeant and 12 parish constables to police it, aided by a number of watchmen. On 1 January 1836 a Watch Committee was appointed which chose George Hoile, a native of Deal and formerly a butcher, to be the inspector of watchmen with five men under him, working from 10 p.m. to 5 a.m. The new police force was initially housed in the Town Hall, where the gaol was also situated.

So successful was this arrangement that it was decided to create a day police as well, consisting of the town sergeant and two constables, all to be dressed in the same fashion as the London police. The town sergeant declined the police role and so two of the nightwatchmen were promoted and another man was shortly added to their number. All these were Deal men. In fact, during the whole existence of the force – some fifty years – only one man was ever appointed who was not from the area. Being responsible for both day and night branches, the inspector found he was unable to give the men the degree of supervision they needed and, in July 1839, the night watch were found accepting beer from a prisoner and were all fined a week's pay. Three of them promptly resigned and were replaced. Shortly afterwards it was decided to amalgamate the two groups with an increase in pay. The men who had just resigned were prompted by this to re-apply for their old jobs but were rejected. The force now consisted of an inspector, a sergeant and five constables together with three watchmen who only worked at night but, a fortnight later, the three watchmen were dismissed in order to save money. This increase in establishment led to a building adjoining the gaol being purchased to act as a watch house.

In December 1841, money was again a problem and so the last three constables to be appointed were dismissed and there was talk of disbanding the police altogether. The following November (1842), Queen Victoria arrived to take up residence at Walmer Castle, then just outside the borough boundary. Because of this, two of the recently dismissed policemen were re-employed as night-watchmen and were gradually re-absorbed into the force. One of these was Henry Redsull, who later became the chief officer.

In 1848 it was agreed that a thorough re-organisation of the force was necessary and a new Inspector of Police should be appointed. The Committee decided that candidates should be between 30 and 40 years of age, be married and have previous police experience. Before the advertisement appeared in *The Times*, Sergeant Boyd of the City of London Police applied for the post and was appointed. Mr. Hoile, who was now around 69 years of age, retired but, shortly before he did so, demonstrated his considerable physical strength and courage by overpowering and arresting three violent thieves.

The new broom swept very clean and made a great many changes in the organisation of the force, with Constable Redsull being appointed sergeant. Inspector Boyd did not last very long, however, being dismissed in 1850 for slackness following some very pointed comments by the Government inspector. The gaol was closed, the post of inspector and gaoler abolished and Sergeant Redsull was put in charge of the force.

Prior to the passing of the Municipal Corporations Act, policing of the town and port of **Dover** was in the hands of watchmen employed by the Paving Commission who were provided with watch boxes at various points throughout the town in which they could take shelter. The local youths delighted in overturning these boxes, trapping the watchman inside. Immediate supervision was by the parish constable for whom a tower was built (roughly where the *Britannia Inn* now stands) for the '…constable of ye night to keep ye watchmen to their duties'. In 1831 the Paving Commissioners decided to appoint a uniformed chief constable and two assistants, although the night-constable was to continue with nine watchmen. The day police worked from 7 a.m. to 10 p.m. and their duties included being present when passengers were boarding or disembarking from the Channel packets, supervising the scavenging and watering of the streets, reporting nuisances, dealing with vagrants and seeing that the various Acts of Parliament were observed. They were under the general instructions of the justices of the peace.

With the passing of the Municipal Corporations Act, Dover promptly formed a proper police force in January 1836, consisting of 15 men made up of three sergeants and 12 constables. The latter included Richard Crosoer, the late 'chief constable'. A police station was erected in Queen Street, Dover in 1838 which the Government Inspector later found to be 'well-constructed but requiring some appliance for promoting warmth in cold weather'.

The members of the new force were required to devote all their time to policing the town and were not permitted to follow any other trade or calling. Discipline was strictly enforced with the main disciplinary offence, drinking on duty, being punishable by instant dismissal, although a good man could apply to be reinstated. When different classes of constable were introduced, a reduction in grade was another favoured punishment.

In February 1836 a Henry Crosoer (brother of Richard?) was appointed the inspector in charge of the force but, in November the following year, he was warned that, unless there was a marked improvement in the force, he would be dismissed. Crosoer managed to hold on to his job for a while but, perhaps as a result of his apparent lack of control, a Superintendent (Edward Correll) was appointed over his head in March 1839. Inspector Crosoer did not last much longer and was dismissed the following January for drunkenness.[11] Drunkenness was not the only misdemeanour committed by the senior ranks; in 1847 Superintendent Correll was accused of ordering bread for prisoners when there weren't any, of harbouring an acquaintance at the station who was burning coals at the expense of the Borough, and of failing to make the required twice-weekly night visits. The Superintendent denied these accusations and said that he often visited the men without their knowledge in accordance with a system of supervision that he had developed. The Watch Committee was not convinced and Mr. Correll's resignation was accepted.

Dover's run of bad luck continued, however, with the promotion of Sergeant Laker to succeed Superintendent Correll and, in 1850, the former attempted to commit suicide. He expressed a desire to return to his duties but was regarded as unfit to continue in the post and was dismissed. Applications were received from a wide variety of candidates for the resulting vacancy. These included three superintendents, another police officer, a prison warder, several local men and soldiers. The Committee finally appointed John Rofe, lately chief of the Walsall police, who took charge in 1850 but resigned the next year to take an inn in Walsall.[12] He was replaced in April 1851 by John Coram, a sergeant in the Metropolitan Police who had been the second choice when the previous interviews were held.

The Dover Police were also responsible for fire brigade duties and a fire engine was kept in the Town Pound in Queen Street. The superintendent was also the captain of the fire brigade and was paid an allowance for each time he turned out to a fire. The two constables detailed for permanent fire-brigade duties lived over the fire station for much of the time and were aided by other policemen when necessary.

Faversham was one of the smaller municipal boroughs with a population of just over 4,000. The earliest reference to police in the borough records is dated 22 August 1836 where mention is made of a certain James Craig and a William Waters who were convicted of assaulting the Superintendent of Police. In September of that year the Borough finance records refer to the sum of £15 4s. 0d. being paid to the superintendent 'for Watchmen's and Police wages for 4 weeks'. It is reasonable to assume that the borough followed the common system of having watchmen on the streets at night with a couple of day constables patrolling during the daylight hours.

There is no record of who was in charge in the early days; there is a mention of a Constable Orpin in 1842 who was referred to as the superintendent in 1857. However, in the same year, a Thomas Burrough is referred to as 'the newly-appointed superintendent'.

Folkestone also had a population of around 4,000 when, at a meeting of the new Watch Committee held on 14 January 1836, it was resolved that 15 constables be appointed for the borough. It may be assumed that these were special constables who were appointed for one year as was the usual arrangement and expected to combine certain policing duties with their normal trade or calling. They were not required to perform any regular duties apart from two men who were to watch the borough 'from 6 p.m. to midnight by the church clock', for a week, another two taking over the next week after which the first couple came back on duty and so on. They were paid 2s. per night and their engagement was on a month-by-month basis.

Although referred to as constables, these four men were in fact on a par with the old town watchmen. They were not issued with any kind of uniform but, in June of that year (1836), it was re-

4 Faversham Guildhall.

solved that there should be a regular policeman, paid 18s. per week and issued with a coat, trousers, waistcoat and hat of the same pattern as the London Police as he would be required to give his whole time to the office. In September a second constable was appointed, to work every day of the week from 10 a.m. to 11 p.m. It was also resolved that the services of two of the night-constables be dispensed with.

In January 1837, the earlier appointments expired and another 12 men were appointed. These included the gaoler, a baker and a labourer (three of the retiring constables), together with four butchers, another baker, two bricklayers, another labourer and a fish carrier. Their addresses included Upper Tree Row, Broad Street, Fancy Street, Queen's Place and Butchery Road – names that seem to have long disappeared from use. At the time of their appointment these new constables were instructed '... to give notice that parties beating carpets, removing manure and emptying vessels in the public streets ... would be proceeded against ...'.

These constables continued to provide police cover until 1847 when a further six constables were employed 'to watch the Borough at night' from 10 p.m. to 5 a.m. They were accommodated in the central watch house until around 1852 when they moved into the Sessions Hall in the (Old) High Street, adjacent to the Bayle steps.

Although these measures provided a form of policing in the borough of Folkestone for some two decades, they were really no great improvement on what had been the system for many years. In 1850, however, an advertisement was placed in the local newspapers calling for applicants for the new post of superintendent of police (referred to later in the same advertisement as 'Inspector') and James Steer of Gosport was appointed.

Steer soon had problems with some of his men and, in June 1852, he had to report Constable Gilbert, stating:

> I respectfully beg leave to report Constable William Gilbert for neglect of duty in taking a glass of rum from a Mr. Martin, landlord of the Fountain Public House, High Street, on the pretence of taking William Ottway home, who was at the time in a state of intoxication and leaving him in the street whereby his life was endangered.

Gilbert was soon in trouble again and in January 1856 he was dismissed for being absent from his beat for about an hour, during which time three door-knockers were pulled off houses in Guildhall Street.

Superintendent Steer did not stay much longer, however, and resigned in July 1857, apparently under something of a cloud since there was talk of his being prosecuted for appropriating certain property that had come into his possession following a burglary. Following exhaustive discussions between the mayor and Government officials, an information was laid with a view to Mr. Steer's arrest but the Folkestone Bench, on the advice of their clerk, refused to issue a warrant.

At the beginning of the 19th century, **Gravesend** was patrolled by two watchmen, one in Gravesend itself and one in Milton. They received no pay but relied entirely on voluntary contributions for their services and, in at least one case, pursued another business activity in the daytime. From 1816, following the passing of a local Act of Parliament, the arrangements were put on a more professional basis with the watchmen receiving a fixed wage from the town rates and being supplied with greatcoats and rattles. A third watchman was appointed the following year and, from 1827, a further two watchmen were appointed for the winter months only.

In 1833 William North was appointed inspector of the watch, which now consisted of six men (two of whom acted as day-constables on an alternating basis for an extra 3s. per week), plus two day-constables who worked 10 a.m. to 11 p.m. With the introduction of the Day Police more interest was given to clothing and equipment. Frock coats were issued bearing the initials G and MP together with blue trousers and an extra heavy coat for night duty, sometime referred to as a Foulweather or Fearnought coat. This dress was topped off with the usual high hat with an oilskin cover for wet weather and a waterproof cape. Cutlasses and handcuffs were also issued, staffs following two years later.

The following extract from a letter published in the *Gravesend and Milton Journal* of 6 September 1834 gives a good indication of the attitude of local businessmen to the newly formed police:

> Sir,
>
> There is one great nuisance in Gravesend, that ought to be speedily removed, as it throws a censure upon the powers that be – is very unpleasant to the inhabitants, and injurious to the shopkeepers of the place. It is the congregation of half-grown youths and others. ... the pathway is so much occupied, that the passengers ... [are] ... in danger of being run over by every passing vehicle. Independent of this, the disgusting language heard, tends to exclude every

respectable person from the place. ... and we consider it equivalent to robbery, that we should pay for the support of that from which we receive no benefit. I allude to the police establishment who, in the foregoing matter, show the greatest negligence. In fact, the whole of ... the force ... is occupied by looking for refugee deserters and criminals, (from the committal of which they receive a bounty), while the order and comfort of the town, from the inhabitants of which they receive a permanent pay, is shamefully neglected.

I am, Sir, Yours respectfully,

A Shopkeeper.

One can but speculate to what extent the citizens of Gravesend, nearly two centuries later, would empathise with this shopkeeper's comments.

With a population of around 9,500, Gravesend formed a Watch Committee in January 1836 to which Will North reported that each watchman (including himself) had a watch coat, sword, stave, pair of handcuffs, rattle, whistle and a cape; the day policemen had a coat, pair of trousers, greatcoat, high hat and waterproof cover. There was no watch house, station or watch box for their use and he considered that a station house and three lock-ups were needed. He claimed that the watchmen were efficient, although two of them were 'a little deaf'. The watch committee resolved that all the men should become watchmen under the control of an inspector with the day policing divided amongst them. Two additional watchmen were appointed together with four (unpaid) constables and Will North was formally appointed inspector of police by day and by night. One of the original watchmen, Will Penman, was appointed assistant inspector, making a total of nine men. These men had very little time to themselves as the whole force had to be on duty from 11 p.m. to 5 a.m. and day duty was performed in rotation, i.e.:

> No's 1, 2 and 3 from 10 a.m. to 3 p.m.
> No's 4, 5 and 6 from 3 p.m. to 8 p.m.
> No's 7, 8 and 9 from 10 p.m. to 5 a.m.
> (no watch between 5 a.m. and 10 a.m.)

A station house was erected in Gravesend in July 1836, forming part of the Town Hall in the High Street, and served as the town's police station for many years.

In October of 1836 the Watch Committee recommended that 24 special constables (12 for Gravesend and 12 for Milton) be appointed and these were duly sworn in. The Borough also adopted the usual practice of appointing 'supernumerary' constables who were only paid if they were called out to cover for absent regular officers. Unfortunately, this practice was not without its difficulties and two of these supernumeraries were reported for 'persistently refusing to turn out when required' but, as they pointed out, they 'could not leave a Master who regularly employed them in order to obtain uncertain employment as a supernumerary constable'.

Gravesend had its share of disciplinary problems with two constables being reprimanded for being found asleep on the steps of the National School in 1836. At a meeting of the Watch Committee on 10 January 1837, Assistant Inspector Penman was fined 5s. for being drunk and two day-constables were disciplined, one being reprimanded for 'violence of temper' while the other was discharged. Inspector Penman was later dismissed for persistent drunkenness and Edward Taylor was appointed in his stead despite Penman 'craving to be reappointed'. Following complaints from the worthy citizens of Gravesend, the Watch Committee issued an instruction in December 1838 that the men were not to go round the town asking for Christmas boxes which effectively cut off a valuable source of income for some of the more brazen constables.

In some cases the Watch Committee seems to have extended considerable leniency towards members of the Borough Police. For example, Constable North (the son of the inspector in charge of the force) committed 16 offences and was fined a total of 56s. over a period of three years. He was eventually dismissed for a third offence of failing to report for duty. A sergeant had a variety of convictions against him including three cases of drunkenness, sleeping on duty, using insulting language and behaviour, careless and slovenly entries in account books and allowing a prisoner to escape. His questionable conduct with a prostitute at the Maidstone Assizes had resulted in his reduction in rank from inspector to sergeant but, in spite of his record, he remained in the service of the Borough Police for a considerable number of years.

In July 1839 Mr North's post was renamed 'Superintendent' and in 1841 Josiah Oxley was appointed inspector while William Penman (whose cravings had apparently borne fruit) was appointed sergeant. Mr Oxley was subsequently replaced by Inspector Denyer.

In 1848 the Committee set up a formal Superannuation Fund into which the constables paid 8d. a week and the superintendent ¼d. In addition, any money received for the service of summonses or the execution of warrants was paid into the fund. Consequently, when Superintendent North retired in 1851 he was granted £1 a week out of the Fund, plus a further 6s., from the Borough Fund and another £10 in view of his length of service and loss of office. Unfortunately, the pensions paid out soon exceeded the sums paid in and it was decided to make use of a clause in the Municipal Corporations Act by means of which the Watch Committee could make an allowance to those who became worn out through length of service. At that time the Fund was only paying out £1 per week to ex-Superintendent North and 17s. per week shared between two retired constables but it was unable to sustain even this level. The three pensioners, therefore, had no option but to accept a reduced pension (12s. for ex-Superintendent North and 7s. and 5s. respectively for the other two). This enabled the Superannuation Fund to build up its funds to meet future commitments.

The untimely death of Inspector Denyer in December 1850[13] gave the Watch Committee the opportunity to reorganise the force. It was decided that Superintendent North should be superannuated 'as being worn out by length of service'. The Commissioners of the City of London and Metropolitan Police were asked to recommend some fit and proper person for the post of Superintendent of the Gravesend Borough Police at a salary of £65, plus gaol fees. Commissioner Harvey of the City force replied that he had a recommendation to make but considered the pay too low. The Watch Committee decided to increase the offer to £80 which, with the emoluments offered, would amount to £120 p.a. As a result, 14 applications were received and Frederick White, a family man of 35 years of age with 11 years' police experience in London, was selected for the job. He took up his duties on 1 April 1851, the force at this time consisting of the superintendent, two sergeants and 14 'privates' for a population which had grown to just under 17,000.

Mr. White promptly set about reorganising the force, laying down new beats and issuing printed 'Rules and Directions for the Instruction and Guidance of the Police Force for the Borough of Gravesend' to each member of the force. These booklets followed a general and familiar pattern, instructing the men what they must do (report promptly for duty, work their beat properly, obey instructions, etc.) and must not do (drink on duty, enter licensed premises, incur debts, etc.) and gave a layman's guide to the criminal law, as well as setting out the more common minor offences. An idea of a constable's duties in the first half of the 19th century may be gleaned from these Instructions:

> … Constables are to pay attention to uninhabited houses on their beats as robberies are often effected by entering such houses. The Serjeant will inform new Constables that they are to make a mark upon the doors and windows of unoccupied houses which will enable them to ascertain at any time whether any entry has been made during their absence … Constables will note the times the Gas Lamps are lighted and extinguished, also any lamps or glass broken during the night … particular attention must be paid to persons conveying parcels and bundles or the removal of goods … at unreasonable hours or under suspicious circumstances … Attention is directed to persons who go from house to house collecting bottles, rags and refuse of similar kinds from servants at an early hour as many opportunities are then given for committing felonys [sic] and enabling servants to dispose of the property of their masters … The attention of Constables is directed to coal holes, trap-doors or other places on or near the footpaths; such conveniences should be secured …

Prior to this the Gravesend Pavement Commissioners had criticised the force for failing to attend to offences committed under the Pavement Act and instructed constables to observe: '… every kind of nuisance, stench, obstruction or annoyance arising from accumulations of offensive matter, any defect of drainage or neglect in the cleaning of the streets within their beats …'.

Gravesend had something of a reputation for disastrous fires and conflagrations were a fairly regular occurrence. The timber construction of the closely packed buildings made any fire likely to spread extremely rapidly. The Gravesend Improvement Act of 1833 authorised the Commissioners to provide fire engines and other equipment and employ a number of firemen. These were placed under the control of the police Inspector. By 1845 the fire service had become a separate unit with 15 men under their own Superintendent but this was not entirely efficient so, in 1854, the Watch Committee decided that the fire engines should come under police control once more. The firemen were issued with a low-crowned glazed hat with the word 'Fireman' and the man's number painted on it and three years later it was agreed to provide three fire helmets and thick coats.[14]

The early history of the **Hythe** police is somewhat hazy. It appears that in 1830 John Friend was appointed the parish constable for the town and in 1834 he was named as chief constable. At the same time he was carrying on his bootmaking business which employed several hands but in 1844 the Town Council offered to make it worth his while to give up his business and become a full-time policeman, to which he agreed. Although given the title of chief constable, Friend was in fact the only police officer, although there may have been some night watchmen.

A gaol and accommodation for the gaol keeper had been built on a piece of land in Stade Street, opposite Oaklands, around 1794[15] and was used by the town's police as a lock-up but the 'police station' seems to have been whatever house the head constable or superintendent occupied.

Prior to the Municipal Corporations Act, the peace officers for the county town of **Maidstone** consisted of a high constable and four borsholders who were appointed by the justices of the peace at the Court Leet. These were usually local tradesmen who wore no uniform but carried a baton bearing the borough coat of arms as a symbol of their authority. There was also a watchman to patrol the streets at night and call the hours. A small borough police force was established under the 1819 Improvement Act but over the years it became increasingly ineffectual.

By the 1830s crime had become a major source of anxiety; according to the mayor, there were in the town: 'a great number of bad characters who … had no other mode of getting a living than that of plunder', adding that there was 'no one thing in Maidstone wanted more than an efficient police'.[16]

And so a police force, modelled on the newly formed Metropolitan Police, was created for this town of 17,000 inhabitants and came into operation on 18 April 1837. It consisted of Thomas Fancett, aged 53, as superintendent, a former drum-major as inspector, two sergeants and a body of 12 men. These were each furnished with a greatcoat and it was decreed that 13 truncheons painted with the king's arms and 'Maidstone Police' be supplied. A set of 'Instructions and Conditions' was printed and issued to all the constables very similar to that issued to the Gravesend and other police forces and, in 1836, a building was provided in King Street (almost opposite the entrance to Church Street) but this was condemned in 1868.

There were subsequent claims that 'a great change for the better has taken place in the streets; prostitutes and other disorderly and bad characters are deterred from pursuing their former annoying and disgusting conduct ... [and] … government of the town is greatly improved'.[17]

How far this improved state of affairs was effected through the phenomenon of displacement is not easy to determine. Since the force only operated within three-quarters of a mile from the Town Hall, for which the inhabitants had to pay an additional rate, it seems likely that many criminals simply turned their attentions to property outside the borough boundary which was to remain without a police force for another two decades. In fact, the occupants of premises outside the town centre were in something of a limbo. In October 1851 Charles Neve of Shepway Court wrote to the Town Clerk complaining that, although he contributed to the borough rates, the town's police did not patrol beyond the top of Upper Stone Street. He had applied to Mr Dunne, the superintending constable for the local county district, who had told him that the parish constables under his command were not authorised to patrol within the borough. Poor Mr Neve was therefore excluded from both the borough police and the existing county system.

In 1854 Thomas Fancett had reached the ripe old age of 70 and decided to retire. Seven candidates, all with police experience, were selected for interview and John Blundell, a superintending constable from Pembroke and a former detective sergeant in the City of London Police, was selected to lead this force, now consisting of an inspector and 14 constables.

Although not incorporated as a borough until 1884, **Ramsgate** had a police force of some kind for many years before this. In 1816 a body of night-constables was formed and 20 years later a sergeant was appointed to take charge of them. The 1838 Ramsgate Improvement Act provided the basis for a true police force and the Improvement Commissioners formed a Police and Lighting Committee. James Livick was appointed to take charge of this body of men which, by 1844, consisted of four or five constables, plus a couple of 'night-constables', who appear to have been simply watchmen, working alternate weeks. The constables were issued with the usual police uniform of the day (swallow-tail coat, high hat, etc.) but the night-constables only had a greatcoat, a cape and boots and it was common practice for the night-constables to transfer to the uniformed police when a vacancy arose. The 'Station House' about this time appears to have been located at the Town Hall.

In 1845 it was agreed that 12 (later 25) supernumerary constables should be appointed, to work as and when required, being paid only when called out at the rate of 2s. 6d. per half day and 'the sum usually paid to special constables', if working longer than this. They were issued with a staff and an armlet but no uniform. In addition to the Town Police, five constables, employed by the Board of Trade, were sworn in by the justices in May 1855 to police the royal harbour. They were appointed as watchmen under the Ramsgate Improvement Act and, being sworn, were empowered to assist

5 Ramsgate Borough police station.

the local police if so required. They had an office and a cell in the Harbour Yard, near the clock tower, and were equipped with a boat. But their main occupation was dealing with the drunks leaving the many public houses in the harbour area and preventing them from falling into the water.

By modern standards concern for the welfare of the man on the beat was lamentable. At first there were no paid rest days or annual leave and when Constable Farley of the Ramsgate Borough Police wanted to take four days' leave of absence in 1846 to visit his relatives in London, permission was granted on condition that he got one of the night-constables to substitute for him, at his own expense. Not until June 1859 was permission given for the chief constable to grant up to three days' leave each year.

The Ramsgate Police were not originally responsible for the town's fire engine, although Timothy Terry, one of the so-called 'night-constables', was also the 'Super-intendent of the Fire Engine'. When he gave up his police job in January 1845 to take the licence of the *Ship Inn*, he retained his fire brigade post. In 1848, the Police Committee considered that there should be a 'Chief Officer of the Fire Brigade' in addition to the 'Superintendent of the Fire Engine', with full control of the engine and the men in that department, and recommended that James Livick should be appointed. The personnel under his command were all volunteers and consisted of three of the four 'night-constables' together with three other Council employees who were required to turn out when called upon by a runner. After they had attended a fire, a bill was sent to the individual owning the property or his insurance company and the proceeds were distributed among those attending the fire. Nevertheless, in August 1856 the superintendent reported that, apart from one man, the fire brigade had become extinct.

In accordance with the Municipal Corporations Act, **Rochester** City Council formed a Watch Committee in 1837 which resolved that the City area, with its population of some 13,600 souls, should be patrolled and watched. For this purpose it proposed that a constabulary force would be needed, consisting of a superintendent, two inspectors and 21 (later increased to 22) 'Constables or Police-men'. It later decided that the existing gaol and gaoler's house should be used as the Watch and Station House for the constabulary force and one Edward Newman was appointed Station House keeper.[18]

In September 1837, Thomas Cork was appointed as superintendent of police with Joseph Anderson and John Tuff as the two inspectors. Twenty-two men were sworn in as constables, plus a further four supernumeraries, and the force commenced its duties on 2 October 1837. As early as 1840 the Watch Committee recommended the formation of a River Guard to watch the warehouses and wharves on the banks of the River Medway but there is no record of this proposal being pursued.

In July 1842, Superintendent Cork found himself in trouble. One of his jobs was to collect the tolls at the cattle market and pay them over to the treasurer but, having performed the first task, he omitted to do the second. When chased for the money (nearly £40) he was unable to pay the sum due but paid over £18 and offered to pay the rest at £1 a week. This was accepted but, as he failed to pay the weekly instalments, he was suspended from duty.

About the same time further pressure was being exerted on the Watch Committee to reduce the cost of policing the city and a sub-committee was formed to see 'what (if any) practical alterations should be made to render the police more efficient and less expensive'. The sub-committee came up with a string of ideas, including dispensing with one of the inspectors and reducing the number of constables to 14 and reducing their pay to 20s. per week. The ten men on permanent night duty should perform their tour of duty (9 p.m. to 6 a.m.) without a break and the three day duty men work 6 a.m. to 8 a.m. and 9 a.m. to 1 p.m. and then 4 p.m. to 9 p.m. The gaps would be covered by the 14th constable, designated as the superintendent's assistant.

Superintendent Cork's disgrace facilitated the implementation of these changes and he was dismissed in December 1842. Inspector John Tuff was appointed superintendent in his stead while Inspector Anderson remained as the solitary inspector. The 'surplus' constables were summarily dismissed. In February 1843, because of the difficult hours they were required to work, the day-constables complained they were unable to attend divine service on Sundays. It was therefore resolved that the force be united once more and that the men take day and night duty in turns.

By July 1844, Rochester City was in serious financial difficulties, 'chiefly from payment having been withheld to a very great extent of their Due on Coals imported into this City ...'.

This meant that it was again necessary to reduce the cost of the police. The inspector was therefore dismissed, together with four constables (although another constable was taken on shortly afterwards). Not surprisingly, this greatly reduced force had considerable difficulty in keeping crime under control and in February 1848 it was claimed that the City, the population of which was now around 16,000, was infested with thieves. To combat this, six more constables were to be employed for just three months but, with only the superintendent to exercise supervision, discipline became very lax and a number of men were punished for being found asleep on duty or other offences. To combat this, it was ordered that each of the night-constables in turn should act as a sub-inspector and visit all the beats to make sure that men were awake and alert. The post of Station House keeper was not a very happy one since Constable James Vine was dismissed in September 1850 for allowing a prisoner to escape, emulating the fate of his predecessor, Edward Newman. Vine's replacement was in turn dismissed in May 1857 for drunkenness.

Despite constantly complaining about the cost of policing the City, the Council was very quick to join the outcry against the proposed Police Act in 1856 and promptly sent a petition to Parliament, objecting to the idea that the police functions should be assumed by a new county force. As will be seen, this was successful.

Under a charter of 1462, four jurats were elected each year for the ancient Cinque Port of **Romney** who, together with the bailiff, exercised the office of keepers of the peace and coroners for the year. The position of these justices was fully investigated by the Municipal Corporations Commission in 1833 when the Romney Marsh police consisted of five (parish) constables appointed at the Michaelmas Sessions. At this time the gaol at New Hall was still in use.[19] The Commission left the administration of justice in the Marsh untouched so that, when the Kent County Constabulary was formed in 1857, its area of influence did not initially extend to the Romney Marsh.

Like Dover, Hythe and Romney, **Sandwich** is one of the Cinque Ports (the fifth being Hastings in Sussex) and so enjoys special corporate status. The Municipal Corporations Act of 1835 therefore applied to this small town and a Watch Committee was duly appointed which reported in March 1836 that there was no permanent police force, 24 parish constables being sworn in to act whenever called upon and who could be supplemented by special constables '… if ever there were occasions of extraordinary excitement'. The Town Council recorded in the Minutes of 31 March 1836 that a permanent police force and police station were regarded as an unnecessary and expensive burden on the town.

With the introduction of Government inspections under the County & Borough Police Act of 1856, Sandwich was subjected to careful scrutiny by the inspector of constabulary who reported that the town's police was very inefficient. The town council demurred and held that the existing arrangements were 'quite sufficient' but, a few months later, it received a letter from the Home Secretary regretting that:

> … the Council do not appear to have put into force the provisions of the Municipal Corporations Act which requires within the Borough of a sufficient number of fit men to act as Constables … In Sandwich, only one police constable is employed who receives annually a suit of uniform clothing. The duties are undefined and the Constable occasionally follows his trade as a hairdresser.

It proposed a properly organised police force of one sergeant and two constables '… which is necessary for a town the size of Sandwich … and which, at the time of the census in 1851, had a population of 2,966 persons'.

Sandwich, therefore, had to climb down and create a professional police force. The first sergeant (known as the head constable) was J.D. Warren who was also the inspector of weights and measures and served from 1856 to 1868.

In 1824 the **Tenterden** Association for the Prevention of Depredations organised a night watch consisting of around half a dozen men who patrolled the streets at night and noted who was abroad. This continued until around 1831 and, four years later, the newly formed Watch Committee organised Tenterden's first police force consisting of a high constable and three constables. These were attired in similar uniforms to those worn in London at the time. The first superintendent appears to have been a James Barns who was appointed in 1856. A shopkeeper, he continued to follow his trade at the same time as he supervised the other three constables.

To begin with the force does not appear to have had a police station as such. There was a lock-up at the Tollgate House on the corner of Church Road and the police presumably worked from their homes.

The Report of the Local Act Committee, dated December 1832, refers to the policing of **Tunbridge Wells** in the following terms:

> The question of Nightwatching and Day Police have been separately considered … It appears by the evidence that burglaries and robberies on an extensive scale are not common in this place, but that other depredations are of frequent occurrence and much complained of, as well as wanton mischief, such as breaking of windows, defacing and destruction of fences, continual noise and disturbance at night, occasioned by persons leaving public houses … These are evils which … an effective Nightwatch … would greatly prevent. On the subject of Day Police, there appears to be some diversity of opinion. It is agreed that the present number of Parish Constables and those of the hundred would be sufficient, if they were effective, but they are found to be not sufficiently under the appointment or control of the magistrates to be rendered efficient … and some force therefore seems necessary, differently constituted.

As a result of this Report, the Tunbridge Wells Improvement Act was passed in 1835 and in the August of that year the Tunbridge Wells police force was formed, consisting of a superintendent and five constables. As the town had not been incorporated as a borough (it had long been a subsidiary of the town of Tonbridge) the force was not constituted under the Municipal Corporations Act but under the local Act; in fact, the town did not become a borough until 1889. There was, therefore, no Watch Committee, the police being controlled by a Police and Lighting Committee which, in August 1835, resolved

> … that the police force be clothed in a uniform consisting of a blue coat and trousers with the letters TWP and a number (of white cloth) sewed on the collar and with a hat partly glazed, similar to the London Police, and that the Superintendent or Inspector have a similar dress except that on the collar of the coat, a crown only should be sewed instead of the numbers and letters. That each policeman be also provided with a great coat of dark grey cloth with a similar distinction on the collar and all the other articles as provided for the use of the London police.

The uniform, therefore, followed the usual pattern and later went through the various phases of frock-coats and tunics as the other forces in the county.

Anxious that the new police force should be effective and efficient, the police committee asked for a sergeant from the Metropolitan Police to be attached to the town temporarily, to advise on its proper organisation. A Sergeant Sillwood arrived in 1835 and gave the committee valuable advice, including a recommendation that the men should not call the hour at night, since this will

> … completely destroy the efficiency of the night police … because it prevents the detection of offenders. … and in a place like Tunbridge Wells, where there are so many places for thieves and other offenders to hide themselves, it is more necessary than in London for the movements of the police to be as secret as possible.

Based on the advice it had received, the police committee wasted no time in issuing a 'Police Instruction Book' to the members of the new force which by the end of 1838 had added a sergeant and another constable.

The first superintendent of the Tunbridge Wells Police was John Alexander Thompson who was appointed around October 1835 but appears to have quickly become unhappy with his excessive workload. He went so far as to resign from the post and the committee considered seeking a replacement from London but Thompson subsequently asked to withdraw his resignation '… in consequence of the contemplated appointment of a Serjeant'.

The committee recorded that it

> … did not feel satisfied with his conduct so far as respects the sincerity of his motives assigned by him for resigning but that they had been induced again to appoint him to that situation in consequence of the zeal, steadiness and unremitting attention which he had hitherto displayed in the performance of his duties …

As promised, one of the men was promoted to sergeant, whose task was to supervise the men on night duty and take charge of the Station House in the daytime whenever the superintendent was absent on his rounds, which no doubt made the superintendent's job a lot easier.

In November 1840 Superintendent Thompson gave in his notice, having been appointed a superintendent in the newly-formed East Sussex force. He was replaced by Thomas Barton, aged 39 from Hadlow, who left after four years to take the licence of the *White Bear Inn*. Next came William Plumb from the East Sussex Constabulary who died in harness in May 1847. The Tunbridge Wells police force had, by this time, evidently become something of a plum since the next man in charge had been the superintendent in charge of the Cambridge City Police, one Captain Charles Bailey, who took over in June 1847. However, in October of that same year he was allowed leave of absence 'in consequence of the expected death of a beloved daughter' but failed to return and was therefore summarily dismissed.

The committee wasted no time in replacing Bailey and on 25 October 1847 William Morten, who had been a sergeant in the Metropolitan Police, was appointed, taking up his new post early the following year. Mr. Morten gained an excellent reputation in Tunbridge Wells as a thief-taker and, when he applied for the superintendency of Nottingham City, he was supplied with numerous glowing testimonials as to his 'promptitude, activity, sagacity, courage and general good conduct' from the borough and county worthies. For reasons which are not known he apparently withdrew his application for this new post and, shortly afterwards, was given a number of rewards for his action in arresting 'the Sussex burglars' and others. However, in April 1853, Mr Morten was reported as absent from duty. His absence prompted numerous complaints from the men under him to the effect that he had defrauded them of money due for their attendance at court. Morten was removed from office in his absence and apparently emigrated to Canada shortly afterwards where he changed his name to Martin, possibly to avoid any pursuit.

The Morten case gave the police committee cause for concern and the Commissioner of the Metropolitan Police was asked for assistance and he sent one of his inspectors to investigate the present state of the force. It appears the committee was right to be concerned since, in May 1853, Inspector Robert Bray duly reported: 'I find every department connected in a very disorganised state, no one properly understanding his position. …. Clothing and appointments [dirty and in a poor state of repair] … the Police Station filthy and having more the appearance of a lumber room than a Police Station.'

The town now had a population of some 12,000 and Inspector Bray suggested the force should consist of an inspector (in place of the superintendent), two sergeants and 10 constables. He closed by saying: 'I attribute the whole of the imperfection to the negligent and very loose manner in which the late Superintendent [Morten] conducted the force'.

Consequently, the advertisement for Morten's replacement called for an 'inspector' rather than a superintendent and the successful candidate, Cyril Winnington Onslow, 37, a parish constable from Chatham, was duly appointed. Although he was described as inspector in June 1853, the post was renamed superintendent four years later and, in February 1860, in response to a letter from the Home Office, chief superintendent.

The new police force was initially housed in a building on the corner of Mount Pleasant Road and Grove Hill Road but, when a prisoner escaped by simply demolishing a brick wall, it was agreed that something better was needed. In May 1847 the new Town Hall was available with accommodation for the police and a number of cells. At the same time, the County justices readily agreed to a proposal that the superintendent in charge of the Tunbridge Wells Police should also act as the superintending constable for the area and undertook to pay him an appropriate stipend for looking after the parish constables.

Recruitment

The early policemen met with a very mixed reception. Although parish constables and watchmen had been in existence for many years, the concept of a professional, paid police force was not always welcomed. The wealthy, land-owning gentry already had their own private 'police' consisting of gamekeepers, stewards, bailiffs and other servants and they did not see why they should pay for a force to look after other people. The lower social orders, too, quickly realised that they would be the centre of attention for such a police force, especially as most criminals came from their peers. Only the newly burgeoning commercial and industrial sectors generally welcomed the idea. They were suffering from thefts, industrial unrest and malicious damage and quickly saw that a paid, professional police force would be better than some lackadaisical parish constable.

Given this widespread opposition to a professional police force, what sort of man was going to offer his services? Many chief constables looked to the agricultural labourer to fill the ranks of his force. They were strong and comparatively healthy and many were looking for a more secure life than could be found on the farms, where they could be hired and fired on a whim. But the precarious economic and employment situation encouraged many from other trades and callings to apply – bootmakers, carpenters, blacksmiths, bakers, ostlers and grooms were all represented. But labourers of one kind or another made up a large proportion of the recruits to both town and county forces. Young, single men were generally preferred and some forces expressly excluded married applicants. Others, like Deal, found married men much more reliable and loyal.

The chairman of one watch committee stated, it was 'simply a question of wages'[20] but this view was perhaps overly simplistic. A variety of factors encouraged young men to apply: stability of employment, regularity of pay and various fringe benefits. There was also the fact that a trained policeman was often sought after by other employers and, later on, the attraction of a pension.

Therefore, despite public opposition, there was no great difficulty in attracting recruits. Retaining them was, however, quite a different matter. Of the 3,400 men who joined the Metropolitan Police when it was first formed only a quarter remained in post four years later.[21] This trend was reflected in most of the early police forces. The demands of the job, both physical and mental, were considerable; the discipline was high – unacceptably so for many – and even one's private life was strictly controlled and monitored.

The early borough forces in Kent tended to employ local men, many of whom were farm labourers or brewery workers. The officers in charge, by whatever title they were known (usually superintendent) were often recruited from the Metropolitan or City of London forces.

Crime and Punishment

The 'General Instructions for the different ranks of the [Metropolitan] Police Force', published in 1829, make it clear that '… the principal object to be attained is the Prevention of Crime …'.

One form of crime prevention is the punishment of those convicted of crime, the ultimate form of prevention being capital punishment which ensures that at least that criminal will commit no more crimes. As a discouragement to others, the evidence is less clear-cut; certainly some on the fringes of criminality are deterred by the thought of punishment, be it execution, flogging, imprisonment, fines or even just the disapprobation of one's peers, but history shows that many who suffered flogging and other severe punishments were not deterred from committing further crimes.[22]

At the beginning of the 19th century death by hanging was the punishment for over 200 felonies, including petty theft. Although it was not unusual for the death sentence to be commuted to life imprisonment or transportation, many a wretched criminal met his death on Penenden Heath just outside Maidstone. A total of 37 prisoners was condemned to death at the Spring Assizes in Maidstone in 1801, having been convicted of crimes ranging from sheep stealing and burglary to highway robbery and murder. Of these 18 were reprieved, four were hung at Shooters Hill while the remaining 15 were executed before a roisterous crowd at Penenden Heath. The last execution on Penenden Heath took place in December 1830 when three young men were hanged for arson.

Although much maligned, the old parish constables were on occasions very effective, as in the case of the murder of 13-year-old Richard Taylor. In March 1831, Richard walked from Rochester to Aylesford to pick up his father's parish relief grant of nine shillings which he collected but never returned home. The parish constable was called and, as a result of enquiries, questioned two boys Richard had been seen speaking to – John Any Bird Bell, aged 14, and his 10-year-old brother, James.

Despite an extensive search Richard's body was not found until some eight weeks later when a man stumbled across it in some woods near where Rochester airport now stands. Although badly decomposed, it was clear that the boy's throat had been cut. The Bell brothers were again interrogated and the younger boy tearfully related how his brother had cut Richard's throat with the latter's own knife and stolen the money. James was released and John confessed to the crime, adding that he had returned the knife to the dead boy's jacket in which he had by now been buried. The constable obtained permission for the grave to be opened and, when the coffin lid was removed, ordered the boy to clamber into the grave and retrieve the knife from the pocket of the coat worn by the putrefying corpse. Incredibly he did so without a murmur and was returned to Maidstone prison. There, an equally unfeeling warder gave John Bell his meal of bread and cheese and told him to use the bloodstained murder weapon to cut it. This proved to be the last straw and the boy refused to eat. There was no sympathy for Bell and he was one of the first victims of the gallows erected outside the new Maidstone prison. A crowd of at least 4,000, mostly women, surrounded the gallows to watch the boy's execution in the summer of 1831.

As well as dealing with crime, the new policemen waged a constant war against drunkenness and associated disorders. It was as a result of such an incident in 1844 that Constable Couchman of the Dover Borough Police was beaten to death by Thomas Clark, a drunken chimney sweep, who used his brush rods to fatal effect during a serious disturbance between two feuding families at Charlton, to the north of the town. The lack of communication between the few police forces at that time no doubt explains why the fugitive murderer was never caught.

The Rural Constabulary Act, 1839

The success of the Metropolitan Police led in 1836 to the government forming a 'Royal Commission for the purpose of enquiring as to the best means of establishing an efficient constabulary force in the counties of England and Wales'.

The Commission consisted of Edwin Chadwick, Colonel Charles Rowan (one of the Commissioners of the Metropolitan Police) and Sir Charles Shaw Lefevre (representing the county magistrates) and submissions included statements that: '… the leet constables […] are all connected by family or some other way, they are of no use; we could never get a protecting force from the neighbourhood [in Lancashire]'.

Parish constables were said to be unable or unwilling to put a stop to unlawful popular recreational activities such as cock-fighting, drunkenness, prize fights and it was quite common for the local constable simply to refuse to turn out to deal with brawls and other disorders.

Chadwick, the driving force behind the Commission, saw this as an opportunity to further the points he had already made in his essay *Preventive Police*.[23] Indeed, it has been suggested that the *Report* was merely 'a gigantic sequel' to this essay.[24] The Commission accordingly recommended that forces be formed in the boroughs and counties, controlled centrally by the Commissioner of the Metropolitan Police. This was widely opposed, the press in particular being strongly in favour of forces under local control, and the ensuing debate proposed that the justices and an elected body be in charge of any county forces.

Because of the weight of the opposition Parliament passed a 'permissive' Act – The Rural Constabulary Act of 1839 which:

1. Left the boroughs which had been incorporated under the 1835 Municipal Corporations Act, or which had a separate court of quarter sessions, in control of their own forces.
2. Allowed magistrates in quarter sessions in any county in which the majority had expressed a wish for a police force to be formed, to appoint a chief constable in order to create a county police force.
3. The whole cost of the force to be met out of the county rate.

It was largely this latter proviso which formed the stumbling block and many counties declined the opportunity to create (and pay for) a police force of their own. It was felt, as Henry Worsley wrote in his work *Juvenile Depravity* in 1849: '... there is a difference in the quality of crime between the professionalism of London and the feckless offenders of the countryside. Poaching and petty larceny, rather than the metropolitan sophistication of forgery or housebreaking characterizes rural crime.'

Nevertheless, in Kent a proposal to form a rural constabulary in 1840 was defeated at quarter sessions by a majority of only three votes. In the light of this, the Kent magistrates set about improving the old system of parish constables, imposing stricter conditions and making proposals for head or superintending constables to oversee them. Between 1841 and 1852, five measures, all originating in Kent, were brought before parliament to this end.[25] Some of these ideas were incorporated in the Parish Constables Act of 1842 and the Superintending Constables Act of 1850.

In a letter to an unknown person dated 11 October 1850, Sir Edwin Chadwick re-stated the need for a nation-wide police system, adding:

... the landed gentry whose houses have outer walls and porters' lodges, and are, as it were, garrisoned by servants, ride out attended by grooms and feel and see no real danger to person and property, whilst they feel a strong objection to increased rates.... On the other hand, the Corporations of the towns were content with their own wretched constabularies, tenacious of patronage and ready to raise a yell against the slightest interference ...[26]

Despite the obvious difficulties and costs, a number of counties did set about forming a county force. The initial problem for those that adopted the Act was the selection of the chief constable. Where the borough forces often selected a local tradesman or possibly a member of the Metropolitan Police as the man in charge, the counties looked for a different type. He would have considerable independence and exercise extensive powers, the justices having little control over him other than the ultimate sanction of dismissal. This meant that most benches endeavoured to select men of good social standing, often with local family connections and preferably with distinguished military careers. Some forces looked to the Metropolitan Police which had now gained a decade of policing experience but the Commissioners were none too happy with this and tried to forestall a number of proposed appointments. As was pointed out, the Metropolitan Commissioners could not be expected to run a training school for aspiring chief constables.

The Parish Constables Act, 1842

Many counties preferred to retain the principle of universal obligation and adopted the 1842 Parish Constables Act. Despite the fact that it was much troubled by the Swing and anti-Poor Law disturbances, Kent was included amongst these. The county justices were so pleased with the workings of the superintending constables system that a motion raised at quarter sessions to introduce a rural constabulary in 1849 was roundly defeated and it remained foremost among the counties calling for a revitalised parish constable system. This was presumably because the county magistrates wanted a police force under their orders but did not wish to pay for it.

The justices could provide a lock-up (at their own expense) in which case they had to appoint a 'superintending constable' to take charge of the lock-up and the constables in the area it served. The superintending constable came under the exclusive directions of the local justices and was paid out of the county rates. Unlike the men under their command, the superintending constables were professional policemen, often appointed from London or another of the new county forces, and had considerable difficulty in motivating the part-time parish constables under their command. There also arose a problem of parochiality. The justices sometimes refused to see the wider picture and jealously guarded 'their' police. In the summer of 1853, when the superintending constable at Tonbridge, on the directions of his local magistrate, asked his counterpart at Ashford for assistance because of a riot, the Ashford magistrates refused to allow the superintendent to cross the petty sessional division boundary.[27]

In July 1850, the Kent Court of General Sessions appointed a Constabulary Committee[28] to report on the duties of the superintending constables, the districts covered by them and the salaries and fees due to them. This committee made its first report on 7 April 1851, recommending that a superintending constable should be between the ages of 25 and 45 years and literate. Whilst so employed he was not to follow any other occupation and had to reside where instructed by the Court. He was not allowed to leave his district except in an emergency and was to keep in contact with the other superintending constables, informing them of any robberies, etc. He was to visit his constables at least once a month and visit all public houses in his district. He was to be notified of all serious offences and should attend the scene to investigate. His pay was to be £85 a year plus a £25 horse allowance and £6 towards the upkeep of a cart and harness (which he had to provide himself). Vacancies were to be advertised in *The Times* and the relevant local newspaper.

There were 12 petty sessional divisions outside the municipal boroughs to which the following superintending constables were appointed in October 1850:

No.	Division	Lathe	Name	Population
1.	Ashford	Lower division of Shepway	Robert Gifford[29]	24,926
2.	Cranbroook	Lower division of Scray	Marcus Rigg	24,121
3.	Bearsted	Eastern division of Aylesford	John Dunne	20,515
4.	Dartford	Upper division of Sutton-at-Hone	Christopher Brandon	17,008
5.	Elham	Upper division of Shepway	Thomas Link	11,808
6.	Faversham	Upper division of Scray	Joseph Boyd	36,416
7.	Home	Western division of St Augustine	William Walker	19,256
8.	Malling	Upper South division of Aylesford	George Hilton	24,216
9.	Rochester	North division of Aylesford	Thomas Everist	44,226
10.	Sevenoaks	Lower division of Sutton-at-Hone	James Handley	24,448
11.	Tunbridge[30]	Lower South division of Aylesford	Richard Gilbert	27,683
12.	Wingham	Eastern division of St Augustine	James McGregor	26,495

Each superintending constable was given a staff bearing the number of his division, a pair of handcuffs, a sword and belt, cartouche and box. Double-barrelled pistols and a holster were issued later, as were bull's eye lanterns.

Superintendent Dunne left in 1851 to take up a position as superintendent of the Norwich City Police, finally ending up as Sir John Dunne, DL, JP, the Chief Constable of Cumberland and Westmorland, while Superintendent Boyd was dismissed in 1853 for inefficiency with regard to a robbery. Superintendent McGregor was dismissed in April 1852 as lacking the necessary qualities for the efficient discharge of his duties.

The Court of General Sessions sent a circular to the justices in the various divisions on 21 March 1851, setting out the conditions for the employment of parish constables:

> Constables to be appointed for one year only under the Parish Constables Act of 1842, by the justices who will select 'the most efficient men' in their Division from the lists sent in by the parishes of men who are *liable* to serve, as well as those who are *willing* to serve.
>
> When a parish has determined to have a *paid* constable, the justices should take especial care to appoint the best man and to inform him that, in consideration of the salary paid, he will be required to perform all such business as appertains strictly to his own parish, such as serving summonses and warrants for non-payment of rates, apprehending vagrants, etc.
>
> All Parish Constables will come under the control of the Superintending Constable for their respective division.

Although these appointments give the impression of an organised police force, it must be remembered that the constables and their supervisor were all appointed locally by the justices of the peace and most of the constables were unpaid. Nevertheless, the supervisory posts were much sought after, by both experienced policemen and others. For example, when the Faversham post came vacant (following the dismissal of Boyd) and that for Cranbrook (resignation of Rigg), the advertisements attracted 60 applicants, of whom 10 were short-listed, including:

Thomas Mapleston Green	Sub-Inspector, East Suffolk Police (selected for Faversham)
Richard Dance	Sergeant, Gloucestershire Police (subsequently selected for Tunbridge)
Thomas Hazle	Sergeant, Gloucestershire Police (selected for Cranbrook)

The County & Borough Police Act, 1856

By 1853 there were police forces in 22 counties and parts of seven others – mostly those where the Chartist unrest was strongest. The majority of these had been created and developed along curiously – even dangerously – original lines by former army and navy officers. Meanwhile the question of a nationwide policing system continued to excite its proponents and opponents and, following a motion raised by E. R. Rice, the MP for Dover, amongst others, a further select committee was appointed in April 1853 'to consider the expediency of adopting a more Uniform System of Police in England and Wales and Scotland'. In giving evidence before the committee, Sir Edwin Chadwick proposed (as he had done before in the 1836 Report) that all the police should be supervised from London. All the counties that adopted the Rural Constabulary Act, as well as the boroughs therein, should be an extension of the Metropolitan Police Force and supplied by that force with a nucleus of trained men and supervisors. He thought it would eventually be necessary to direct a national police force from several district centres, each centre comprising several counties.[31]

Perhaps because of Kent's known preference for the existing superintending and parish constable system, no one from the county was called upon to comment on that type of policing. Although E.R. Rice chaired the committee, he was an advocate of a new constabulary system and was not likely to sing the praises of the 'old' system. Although evidence was heard from one former Kent superintending constable, John Dunne, he was a veteran of the Manchester Police and the Essex Constabulary and was now the head constable of Norwich. He spoke of the Kent system in very disparaging terms.

Much of the discussion in the committee focused on the value of a professional constabulary in suppressing vagrancy and it was convinced that the new constabularies had contributed to a decline in this as well as 'to the maintenance of order and the improved habits of the population'.[32] The select committee presented its Report in 1853 which resolved:

> That the efficiency of all the existing Police forces is materially impaired by the want of co-operation between the Rural Constabularies and the Police under the control of the authorities of the Boroughs or other local jurisdictions ... your Committee are of the opinion that the smaller Boroughs[33] should be consolidated with Districts or Counties for Police purposes and that the police in the larger Boroughs should be under a similar system of management and control to that of the adjoining District or County and (where practical) under the same superintendence ...

The boroughs were strongly opposed to the proposals and a very large and influential meeting was held in London on 2 February 1854. Delegates included deputations from Canterbury and Faversham, while a letter of support was sent from Rochester. The meeting, chaired by the Lord Mayor of York, resolved: 'That the contemplated measure for the consolidation of the Police of Counties and Boroughs is a most unjustifiable attack upon the rights and liberties of Municipal Corporations and an unconstitutional interference with their privileges and independence.'

A deputation was formed which went immediately to the Home Office and made it clear that they saw the proposals as favouring the establishment of a National Police and were concerned that the select committee had heard little or no evidence from the boroughs. On their return, a specimen petition was sent to all the boroughs in the country which they were urged to send (adapted as necessary) to their Member of Parliament, protesting at the proposals. Maidstone Borough was one which duly obliged.

For various reasons, partly because of this concerted resistance on the part of the boroughs, partly because of the volatile political situation, the Bill was left on the table for two years. In 1855 another Kent MP, William Deedes, made a further proposal to develop the parish constable system, a proposal which received considerable support but was eventually withdrawn after Mr Deedes had had lengthy discussions with the new Home Secretary, Sir George Grey, on a new government bill.

Grey's bill was introduced in parliament in February 1856 with the object of 'providing an efficient police force, both for counties and boroughs, as is possible under the existing system of local management' and, in 1856, the County and Borough Police Act received the Queen's Assent. Unlike the 'permissive' Rural Constabulary Act, this was a 'mandatory' Act which required the establishment of a police force in all counties of England and Wales, embracing those boroughs which had not created their own force as well as the rural areas, towns and villages. The government would pay one quarter of the total expenditure on pay and uniforms in all counties and boroughs. Smaller incorporated boroughs with fewer than 5,000 inhabitants could either (a) continue to provide their own force but with no government support or (b) amalgamate with the surrounding county. In this way much of the opposition to the earlier Bill was overcome and, as they were able to retain control of their police force, the vast majority of boroughs were satisfied. The 1856 Act also introduced the concept of three inspectors of constabulary who would visit all police forces in receipt of the government grant and report on the numbers of men employed and their discipline. If they felt that the force was not being efficiently run they could recommend the withholding of the grant.

It was this Act in particular which removed policing from the parish pump level. It did not go as far in producing a central, national police force as the government would have wished but it was a step in that direction and was not so violently opposed as the latter course of action would have been. By this time two-fifths of the counties in England and Wales (including Kent) still relied on the parish constable system and, like Kent, had no option but to form a constabulary force. At the Annual General Sessions for Kent, held on 21 October 1856, it was ordered:

> … that a committee of justices be appointed, consisting of the custos rotulorum[34] of the county, the chairman of the General and Quarter Sessions and one JP from each of the Petty Sessional Divisions of the county, to be named by the respective benches, to enquire into the probable number of men of all ranks required to carry into effect within the county the provisions of the Act 2 & 3 Vic. Cap 93 and subsequent Acts called 'The County Police Acts' and the rate of pay which it would be expedient to pay the Chief and other Constables and officers and other preliminaries and to report thereon to the next adjournment of the Court intended to be held on the third day of December next.

Wheels turned surprisingly quickly in those days and, on 11 November 1856, a meeting was held under the chairmanship of the Viscount Sydney, consisting of an impressive array of the great and good in the county at that time. It was reported that the population of Kent (outside the incorporated boroughs) was 334,115 for which it was recommended that the police should consist of a chief constable, 12 superintendents, 18 sergeants and 191 constables, making a total of 222 officers. It was further recommended that one of the sergeants should be designated the sergeant-major and another as clerk to the chief constable. The chief constable's annual pay was determined at £400, plus travelling and other expenses. A proposal made by the North Aylesford Petty Sessional Division that Chatham should be a separate, autonomous police district was not supported.

The main proposals made by this committee were agreed by the General Sessions, which ordered the committee to advertise and interview candidates for the chief constableship; 66 men applied of whom 29 were interviewed and 22 'short-listed'. These were nearly all military men – 12 captains, two majors, three lieutenant-colonels, one commander (RN) and only four civilians. In the end Captain John Henry Hay Ruxton, of Brenchley was duly appointed. As he was a Kent man, a justice of the peace and a member of the original 1851 Constabulary Committee the County authorities obviously wanted to keep things 'in the family'.

And so the Kent County Constabulary was born.

TWO

A COUNTY FORCE AT LAST
1857-1888

The Kent County Constabulary
Unlike the Watch Committees in the boroughs, county and shire police authorities tended to appoint former army officers as their chief constables, or persons '… who at any rate were men of education, with a knowledge of the world, accustomed to discipline and to the management of men and whose personal qualities were generally known to those making the appointments'.[1]

Kent was no exception and the justices of the County of Kent appointed Captain John Hay Ruxton to form and lead a new, county-wide police force – the Kent County Constabulary – from 1 April 1857. He was a Kentish man and knew the county well, being educated at Tonbridge before entering the King's Own Regiment as an ensign an 1834. Ruxton is described as possessing '… a tall, manly figure and a fine commanding presence … in the truest and best sense of the word, an English Gentleman'.[2]

The County justices' decision to appoint one of their number to this 'important and responsible office', was made despite the fact that, as a justice of the peace and one who lived more than two miles from the proposed headquarters of the force in Maidstone, he was in fact ineligible. In support of his application, Captain Ruxton suggested that it was an advantage, not a disadvantage, for him to live at Broad Oak, Brenchley since this was close to Paddock Wood railway station which would afford quick and easy access to most of the county. The Home Secretary agreed to waive these requirements and so Captain Ruxton resigned from the Bench and duly became the first Chief Constable of Kent, a position he was to hold for 36 years. True to his word, Captain Ruxton worked partly from his home and partly from the force headquarters in Maidstone, being at the latter location on Mondays and Thursdays. He instructed that all messages were to be duplicated and send to both places to ensure they reached him without delay. It is clear that he also spent a considerable amount of time travelling round the County, visiting his men.

The first General Order issued to the force read as follows:

> Captain John Henry Hay Ruxton, DL, JP, having been selected on 14th day of January 1857 by the Justices of the County of Kent in General Sessions assembled to fill the important and responsible office of Chief Constable and, subsequently to the removal of his name by the Lord Chancellor from the Commission of the Peace for the County, that appointment having received confirmation at the hands of one of Her Majesty's Principal Secretaries of State.
>
> Therefore in assuming the control of the Kent County Constabulary as Chief Constable, Captain Ruxton calls upon each and every person who may receive an appointment therein to carefully consider and recollect, that alone, by the individual exertion of each member of the Force and by his zealous and active co-operation with the Chief Constable and the Officers placed in authority over him, in maintaining the discipline and important character of the Service can the great aim and object of the County Constabulary be attained, viz. the 'Prevention of Crime and the Maintenance of good order.
>
> J.H. Hay Ruxton
> Chief Constable

The new chief constable was given premises at Wrens Cross, Maidstone, to use as his headquarters.[3] The accommodation included the office of superintendent in charge of the Bearsted Division and the quartermaster's stores. Additions were made over the years to extend the sparsely furnished barracks for recruits.

To begin with the chief constable had to appoint men to take charge of the various divisions of the new force. It was decided that the force should be divided according to the 12 petty sessional divisions within the County and the simple solution was to appoint the superintending constables responsible for the parish constables in these areas. This made sense as these men were intelligent and experienced policemen. Consequently, the original superintendents appointed to the new county force on 7 February 1857, were:

6 Capt. John Hay Ruxton, Chief Constable of Kent, 1857-1894.

Superintendent 1st Class William Turrall (Bearsted) – discharged on 24 October 1857 and replaced by Superintendent Maloney who was in turn dismissed in 1865
Superintendent 1st Class Thomas Everist (Rochester) – died July 1868
Superintendent 1st Class Thomas Maplestone Green (Faversham) – hurt on duty and pensioned off in 1868
Superintendent 1st Class William Stokes (Wingham) – retired 1879
Superintendent 1st Class David Dewar (Ashford) – moved to Elham in 1870

Superintendent 2nd Class Richard Dance (Tonbridge) – retired 1877
Superintendent 2nd Class George Hilton (Malling) – resigned 1875
Superintendent 2nd Class Thomas Hazle (Cranbrook)[4]
Superintendent 2nd Class William Walker (Home) – retired 1880

Superintendent 3rd Class James Handley (Sevenoaks Division)[5] – resigned 1862
Superintendent 3rd Class Christopher Brandon (Dartford) – retired 1870
Superintendent 3rd Class Edwin Robins (Elham) – resigned May 1857, replaced by Superintendent Colman

There was also a Reserve, or Headquarters Division but no superintendent was appointed to take charge of this until later. A sergeant-major was also appointed in the person of Lieutenant Edmund Weston. The chief constable gained such a high opinion of this old soldier that he was offered the vacant post of superintendent at Bearsted in October 1857 but declined the offer. He was instead appointed acting adjutant, moving to Elham to command that division in 1858. He resigned in 1861 to join the Kent Artillery Volunteers as captain and adjutant and his post in the police was taken over by Superintendent English.

Having formed his force, Captain Ruxton was not prepared to allow any 'outsiders' to take positions of authority in it and he informed a correspondent commending a certain captain in the army for a post as Superintendent in the force, that '… all promotions are made from within the force'.

Each division was to consist of two sub-divisions and each sub-division further split into two sections. The sections were then broken down into beats.[6] There were no Inspectors to begin with and a sergeant ran each sub-division, assisted by 1st class (or 'instructing') constables who supervised a 'section' consisting of about four 'beats', each of which was covered by the 2nd class and 3rd class constables. It was not until the end of 1859 that the first inspector was introduced as an assistant to the super-intendent for the Rochester Division. He wore the same uniform as the superintendent, his role being clearly laid down as '… the executive of the Superintendent, performing all the various duties in his name and by his authority'.

Certain physical standards were laid down for sergeants and constables, candidates having to be at least 5 feet 9 inches in height and under 40 years of age. (Special dispensation was obtained in February 1860 for the enrolment of James Hoare Steer who, at 45 and only 5 feet 5 inches, did not meet these standards but who was required to act as clerk to the force). Candidates had to be literate and were unacceptable if they were gentlemen, gentlemen's servants or had been employed as a gamekeeper, woodranger, bailiff or had any connection with the sale of alcoholic beverages.[7] As an indication of the strictness of the physical attributes imposed, one candidate was sent away in 1887 as being too short and fat and 'would take up the space of two men in the ranks'.[8] The next year another applicant was sent away as being so tall and thin as would make a good hop pole and was recommended a diet of beef and porter.[9] A letter from the chief constable in 1863 to a Mr Trafalgar Brattle of Chatham Dockyard referred to the latter's application on his brother's behalf for a position in the new force and stated, '… the trade followed by your brother of a higgler[10] is not a very good introduction to a police force [and he] … would need certificates of spotless character from the Superintendents of the Divisions in which he carried on this traffic'.

Bureaucracy was not slow to rear its head and in October 1860 the chief constable felt obliged to apply for an inspector to perform the duties of sergeant-major as well as an additional superintendent to act as chief clerk and be in charge of the Reserve (Headquarters) Division. The afore-mentioned James Steer was appointed to this latter post in April 1861 and simultaneously took on the role of deputy chief constable.

With the formation of the County Constabulary, 13 horses were made available, one for each of the 12 Divisions and one spare at Headquarters, whose role was to pull the superintendents' two-wheel carts. The horses, which were intended to double as mounts when the need arose, were mostly bay geldings, costing £35. The number of horses remained constant at least until the turn of the century.

One of the first things the justices had to do was to decide on the uniform to be worn by men of the county police force. A sub-committee met in London and decided on a uniform similar to that worn by the Metropolitan Police. In the event, the constable's uniform consisted of a greatcoat with cape, a blue frock coat with embroidered collar and badge (later replaced by a tunic), two pairs of blue trousers, a stock with a buckle

7 Uniform of the Kent County Constabulary
as worn in latter part of 19th century.

8 Constable Joseph Kadwill, Kent County
Constabulary, 1862.

and a waist belt with a German silver union clasp. The total cost of this outfit was under
£5 0s. 0d. but the superintendents' uniforms cost over £7 0s. 0d. each due to the
superior quality of the fine blue frock-coat and steel-grey greatcoat. The sergeant-major
and the clerk sergeant wore the same uniform as a superintendent.

The newly appointed men of the Kent County Constabulary were in place by
10 March 1857 but there were already problems. A contract had been placed for the
supply of the necessary police uniforms but these had still not arrived by 23 April. As
a result, the chief constable was unable to notify the towns when he would be able
to 'assume the charge thereof'. As he described in a letter to the contractors, the
Constabulary was '…complete in every detail but that of clothing and appointments'.[11]
Most of these items were received by the end of that month, although the force still
lacked '31 frock coats, 62 trousers, 121 greatcoats, 131 hats, 107 lanthorns and 47
belts'[12]

And so, on 10 May 1857, 222 constables were sworn in as a body and the next day
were drilled at Maidstone barracks. Drill parades and uniform fittings, the issue of
appointments and various administrative formalities formed the basis of their 'training' and, on 20 May 1857, the members of the force left Maidstone to take up their
duties at their various stations. The next day the chief constable wrote to the authorities in the towns which did not possess a borough police force that he would be ready
to undertake the charge of that area on 1 June 1857 and called for '… all Watchmen,
Watchboxes, Arms, Accoutrements, etc. provided for the constables or watchmen, be
delivered up to Superintendent … of the Kent County Constabulary'.

The county constables were allocated to areas on the 'threefold basis of Area, Assessment and Population', although no record has been found of the formula used in this calculation. For example, when a complaint was received from Ashford that the town was not properly policed, the chief constable responded that, with an acreage of 2,768, a population of 6,950 and a rating assessment of £26,550, the town was entitled to 3.6 constables, whereas it in fact had six.[13]

Conditions in some of the areas policed by the new force were far from ideal. When a farmer on the Romney Marsh, who had lost some of his sheep, complained in February 1860 about the lack of police cover at Brookland, the chief constable replied that 'the constables stationed at Brookland have so suffered from fever and ague that their services at that station were for a long time scarcely nominal'.

The original issue of hats soon proved unsatisfactory and they were quickly replaced by new tall ones of the 'London Police Pattern'. The superintendents' hats were originally intended to have a glazed leather crown, as worn by superintendents in London but these quickly proved unsuitable as the glazed crown made them very hot in summer and also meant they could be seen from a considerable distance. The initial uniforms soon needed replacing and a new type was introduced in April 1860 '... to establish a character for smartness and carriage'. Constables were instructed to keep their hair cut close following the introduction of shako caps, and the brass numbers, badges and buttons were to be kept polished and the white gloves regularly washed. When the new issue was made instructions were given to superintendents regarding the fitting of these:

> Superintendents are particularly desired to take care that the coats and trousers are an easy, loose fit and that in the former there is no confinement over the chest or under the arms, and in the latter that they are loose from the waistbelt to the knee. Superintendents will also take most particular care that the caps come well down over the forehead to within 1/2 inch of the eyebrow, the crown of the caps then to remain in a level line.

The shako caps were always worn straight with the chin strap down and placed under the chin. Oilskin covers for the caps were issued for use in wet or showery weather. In 1866, white cap covers were issued 'to be worn at the constable's discretion'. A General Order of 21 June 1877 specified that '... the oilskin cover with flap will be carried in the pocket and be worn in showery weather, with the flap neatly turned up underneath, in wet weather the flap will be worn down. The white cover with flap will be worn as [previously] directed ...'.

Later, an issue of a lightweight summer fatigue uniform was made, including a straw hat. However, the issue and wearing of this was subject to the officer purchasing three linen collars and a black bow at a cost of two shillings – about one day's pay. Sadly, no photographs appear to exist showing it being worn.

It has always been our proud boast that Britain has an unarmed police force, the members of which go out onto the crime-filled streets, armed with nothing more lethal than a short length of wood. But this is not, and never has been, the complete and true picture.[14] Cutlasses were certainly available to the members of the Kent County Constabulary in the latter half of the 19th century, although there is no record of their general issue or, indeed, for what type of incident such weapons were considered suitable. The chief constable, being a military man, had visions of his force being run on military lines and applied to the Home Office in 1860 for his men to be supplied with firearms. This application was promptly rejected, Sir George Lewis endorsing it: 'This gentleman has very grand ideas. I wish these constables would think more of their staves and less of rifles ...'[15]

In October 1860 leggings were issued and in 1867 an experiment was carried out with leather leggings. These proved successful and so more were purchased in 1869 and later issued to the whole force. They remained in use in the county force until October 1926. In 1903 instructions were issued as to the correct way to wear them, 'Trousers should be pulled up or tucked in the sock sufficiently high to allow them when turned over after the leggings are on, to come down as far as the third legging button from the top'.

One custom which disappeared as years went by was the wearing of black 'crape' armbands as a sign of mourning. Instructions to wear these were occasionally issued on the death of a senior member of the force (e.g. the deaths of Superintendents Dewar and Everist in July 1868 and March 1877 respectively, when the cap badge was also shrouded for 14 days after the funeral). Men could also wear them on a personal basis when a member of their family had died. The band was three inches wide and worn just above the left elbow.

As in the existing Borough forces, discipline (especially alcohol-related problems) was a constant headache for the newly appointed chief constable of Kent and his senior officers. Most of the policemen who were dismissed or suspended in the early days of the County force were, like their Borough colleagues, charged with alcohol-related offences. A General Order issued in December 1858 laid down that any constable '... suspended from Rank and Pay [was to be] ordered into the headquarters of the division by his Superintendent, to remain there during the period of his suspension and to be frequently paraded'.[16]

The following disciplinary cases, which all occurred in the summer of 1860, are typical of the early times:

P.C. George Kendrick, Tunbridge Division: drunk on duty – Dismissed from the force.

P.C. James Milton, Faversham Division: found on licensed premises – Fined 6 days pay and posted to another station at his own expense.

P.C. William Orpin, Tunbridge Division: Neglect of duty/Insubordination. – Fined 5/- and cautioned.

P.C. Samuel Tucker, Dartford Division: Under the influence of drink in a pub – Severely reprimanded

P.C. William Record, Home Division: Found smoking when on duty and with a prisoner waiting for an omnibus to Dover – Transferred to another station at his own expense.[17]

P.C. John Ealden, Rochester Division: Receiving a gratuity 'intended for a sixpence' from a gentleman – Dismissed from the force.

P.C. William Taylor, Faversham Division: (1) Drunk, (2) Absent from his beat between 7 p.m. and 12 p.m. (3) demanding money from the wife of a drunk for having brought him home. In view of the seriousness of this case it was dealt with by the magistrates who convicted him and fined him. He was subsequently dismissed from the force.

P.C. Edwin Winton, Tunbridge Division: Neglect of duty in failing to apprehend a man charged with cutting and wounding: Suspended without pay for one week.

P.C. Henry Sinden, Rochester Division: Inefficiency in not ascertaining the identity of three men seen on his beat at 4 a.m. and failing to check on hirings of rowing boats, knowing that in the past burglars had rowed from Kent to Essex. – Reduced from 2nd class to 3rd class constable.

P.C. Charles Martin, Sevenoaks Division: Drunk and incapable of duty – Reduced from 1st class to 3rd class constable.

The chief constable's involvement in discipline was limited to fairly minor cases; as seen in the case of Constable Taylor above, any complaints concerning an officer's 'neglect or violation of duty in his office' were brought before the Justices by way of a summons under the 1839 Rural Constabulary Act where he could be fined up to £10 or imprisoned, with or without hard labour, for up to one month.

So that it should not be thought that discipline offences were only committed by the lowly (and poorly-paid) constables, it must be mentioned that in May 1861 Captain Ruxton wrote, '... Sergeant Hodges as a gallant old soldier has always been a great favourite of mine and ... he has tried to do his "duty" in the strictest military sense of that term ... but was reported as being "flighty" while in the Tonbridge Division and has now shown further evidence of this'.

This 'particular favourite' was consequently dismissed from the force as there were considerable doubts as to his discretion.

Even the lofty superintendents were not above reproach and in the summer of 1858 Superintendent George Colman (Elham Division) arrested a man for nude bathing at Sandgate. The miscreant was handcuffed and marched through the streets of Hythe on a busy market day, presumably still in a state of undress. Not surprisingly he complained about his treatment and the superintendent was brought before the chief constable and transferred to Sevenoaks where one assumes nude bathing was an extreme rarity. Despite this salutary lesson, in November 1863, Superintendent Colman was once more in trouble and fined 20s. for neglect of duty in failing to report a possible case of arson until six days after the event. This neglect was undoubtedly aggravated by the fact that the chief constable learned of the incident as a result of an enquiry being made of him about the incident, of which he was totally ignorant. Similarly, Superintendent Brandon of Dartford was fined one week's pay for omitting a case of fowl stealing from his return to headquarters.

Another early innovation was the introduction of a Merit & Demerit Register. Whenever a felony was committed in a constable's area he was given a demerit mark and, for every case solved or arrest, he received a merit mark. He also received a merit mark if he discovered the felony himself, rather than had it reported to him. This was obviously designed to keep the men on their toes as they had to try to have more merits than demerits or at least a balance between the two. As a 'carrot' to the 'stick' of discipline, a system of Merit Badges, worn on the cuff of the right arm, was introduced. They were awarded, for example, to Superintendent Everist in June 1865 in recognition of his work in arresting a violent prisoner and to Superintendent Dance the following month. In March 1867 a special merit mark was awarded to Superintendent Colman of Sevenoaks 'for his meritorious exertions in the apprehension and conviction of Thomas King and Harold King for arson at Sundridge'.

The trial judge complimented the superintendent at the end of the case and said he would have awarded him a gratuity from the court but he would undoubtedly obtain a better one from the insurance company!

Despite his earlier failings, Superintendent Colman appears to have been a very zealous officer as he was awarded a further special merit mark in the spring of 1870 for the arrest of a burglar. The Merit Badges consisted of a silver chevron worn on the right cuff, the chevron being replaced by a star in 1879.

A notable exception to the area covered by the new County force was the Liberty of the Romney Marsh (Romney, Lydd, Romney Marsh) which had its own, separate commission of the peace and therefore its own justices. Consequently, there was some doubt as to whether this sparsely inhabited district came within the jurisdiction of the County Constabulary. Ultimately, the Queen's Bench Division held that the Liberty was subject to the provisions of the Acts and it therefore came within the county constablewick from the summer of 1860. A further sergeant and three constables were appointed to police this area which was allocated to the Elham Division.

The question of police stations soon became a pressing one. For many years parishes had provided lock-ups for their constables and watchmen, such as that in Herne Bay which occupied a vault under St George's Terrace.[18] A survey carried out in 1856 showed that there were parish constables in charge of lock-ups in Ashford, Chatham, Cranbrook, Dartford, Elham, Malling, Northfleet, Sevenoaks, Sittingbourne, Sheerness, Tonbridge, Wittersham and Wrotham. Consequently, when the County Constabulary was formed the next year, the new force took over all these lock-ups and then either used them or the policemen's houses as the point of contact for the public.

These lock-ups remained in use, in one form or another, for many years, especially those with living accommodation. In 1902 the old Sevenoaks lock-up, then used as accommodation for the groom constable, was deemed unfit for human habitation and was demolished, two cottages being erected on the site. Although there was a lock-up in Elham village, the Headquarters for that Division was originally located in Sandgate Castle but the justices ordered in January 1859 that '… a Lock-up House and Strong Room for the temporary confinement of persons taken into Custody by the Constables of the County be built at or near Sandgate'.

This was obviously prompted by the fact that the Elham Division was now responsible for policing the extensive military installation at Shorncliffe. Arrangements were therefore made for a police station to be built at Seabrook on the northern side of the coastal road. This included living accommodation for the superintendent, the lock-up keeper and the groom constable, as well as six cells, and was completed early in 1860—the first County police station. In 1862 a survey carried out by the Court of General Sessions revealed that, with the exception of the new Seabrook police station and the lock-up at Elham, none of the existing lock-ups were suitable for use as Station Houses and, apart from a small lock-up in Wittersham, none were suitable for conversion (lack of space, inconvenient situation, etc.). It recommended three classes of Station House should be provided:

Third Class = with cells and accommodation for the lock-up keeper and possibly a number of single men.

Second Class = as above but also with accommodation for the Sergeant in charge of the sub-division.

First Class = to act as the headquarters of the Division with quarters for the Superintendent and the lock-up keeper, stabling and accommodation for a number of single men and, where possible, a Petty Sessional courtroom.[19]

Ten first-class stations were needed at Chatham, Tonbridge, Ashford, Sevenoaks, Cranbrook, Dartford, Malling, Sittingbourne, Wingham and Canterbury.[20] Second-class stations were needed at Sheerness and Northfleet with third-class stations at

9 Whitstable police station, 1864.

Whitstable and Wittersham. It was proposed that all these should be built between 1863 and 1866 and they were in fact completed as follows:

1864: Chatham, Cranbrook, Sevenoaks, Tonbridge and Whitstable
1865: Ashford and Northfleet
1866: Dartford, Sheerness and Sittingbourne
1867: West Malling
1868: Canterbury (Kirby Lane), Sandwich

Police stations and lock-ups were exclusively for official purposes, as the chief constable pointed out in a General Order in November 1871:

> The Chief Constable has observed ... that the Magistrates' Retiring Room, being at the same time the Superintendent's Office, has been converted into a sort of family apartment. This is quite contrary to the intention for which these rooms were provided ... nothing is retained in these rooms for the future but furniture belonging to the County and the Books and Papers appertaining to the duties of the Superintendent.

The extension of the railway line to Sandgate seriously affected the new Seabrook police station and in 1874 it was damaged by a landslip, resulting in a claim against the Railway Company. It was suggested that the Railway Company should buy the police station for the use of the station master and railway staff which was accepted. A new station was built in 1878 on the opposite side of the road, beside the source of the Royal Military Canal, with living accommodation for the superintendent and six constables.[21]

10 Police station, Park Road, Sittingbourne.

The arrangements for prisoners consists of, first, a reception room where they are courteously received by the officer in charge and afterwards politely escorted to the cells, of which there are six in number. ... these are the most roomy and comfortable cells to be met with anywhere; they are most carefully ventilated and heated by means of hot water pipes ... A window at the end of the cell makes room for the admission of the balmy ozone of the ocean to fan the prisoner's brow ... Outside the prison is an exercise yard where prisoners are taken for an airing and a garden where Superintendent Maxted can grow sufficient vegetables to satisfy the most voracious family.[22]

Although the formation of the county force meant that the parishes no longer had to appoint parish constables after 25 March 1858,[23] the introduction of the County police force did not mean that they disappeared overnight. Many remained in post for some time and were often highly regarded by the populace, some of whom had little time for this new and expensive body. This situation is exemplified by an occurrence in May 1858 when Mr Delaseaux, HM Coroner for Kent, wrote to the chief constable complaining that he had instructed the local County policeman to warn a jury for an inquest to be held at Doddington. Instead, the constable got drunk and called a jury from Newnham, a mile away. The Coroner then had to employ the parish constable to get a jury:

... and when they had been sworn in and the business partly performed, the County Constable made his appearance but in such a state that, had I required his services, he could not have performed them.

The Coroner went on to state that he:

... regretted that the Magistrates have thought it right to take this service from the Parish Constable.

11 West Malling police station.

The chief constable apologised for this occurrence and the constable concerned was instantly sacked.

The coroner was not alone in his criticism of the new police force. In September 1858, R. Cobb, Esq. of Throwley wrote to Captain Ruxton complaining about the temporary removal of the constables from the parish for other duties. The chief constable replied that '… the only advantage of an organised police over the Parish Constable is in the power confided to the Chief Constable … of disposing of his men to the greatest advantage of the *General Public*'.

The main reason for such temporary postings was the influx of hop-pickers in the autumn – something that continued to apply for around a hundred years. There are also signs that the modern concept of 'tenure of post' applied even in these early days. In a letter to a Mr. Apps, dated 17 November 1860, Captain Ruxton referred to a 'memorial' submitted by gentlemen of the parish, asking that Constable Reuben Hilder be allowed to remain at his original post. This memorial '… only convinces me how necessary becomes the occasional removal of a constable to prevent him being almost considered Parish property'. He went on to say that Constable Hilder's good conduct had enabled his stay at his original station to be much longer than usual '… but now it is necessary for the good of the service, that he be removed'.

In 1863 an increase of 26 constables meant that the instructing constables could be relieved of their beat duties to concentrate on supervising the constables under their control. In 1874 permission was given for them to wear two stripes on their sleeves and they later became known as 'corporals'.

Constables were not expected to have much in the way of free time and Clause 172 of the Kent County Constabulary's Standing Orders and Instructions provided that: 'Every Constable, when his usual hours of patrol are over, will at once return to his own quarters to take necessary rest; and, unless his services are required elsewhere, which he is specially to report, he will be expected to be found at his Station until the hour for patrolling returns', although in a subsequent order the chief constable '… directs that Clause 172 … is not to be construed too literally but that as much liberty is to be accorded to Constables off duty as may be consistent with that clause not being entirely defeated'.

Up until 1869, constables had comparative freedom as to facial hair but an order in July of that year stated that, '… with a view to reduce the Medical Bills of the Force, [the chief constable] orders that the whole of the Constables allow the Moustache and Beard to grow'. It is not entirely clear what medical condition this order was intended to alleviate and it was rescinded in 1873.

Despite the support which continued in the county for the old system, Captain Ruxton was able to report to the Home Office in February 1862 that '… the employment of Parish Constables is merely nominal' and, in 1872, an Act of Parliament (35 & 36 Vic. Cap 92), entitled 'An Act to render unnecessary the general appointment of Parish Constables' was passed, ending an era that had lasted, in one form or another, for centuries; in future, policing would be the exclusive domain of professional, paid policemen.

From the earliest days, the Home Office insisted that an officer should be nominated to take command of the County force in the absence of the chief constable. At first this simply involved nominating one of the divisional superintendents, it being made clear that the nomination made no difference to the holder's rank or status. Accordingly, the first appointee was Superintendent William Walker, in charge of the Home (Canterbury) Division. It is not clear why this man was selected, especially as he was only a second-class superintendent and, in the event, he was relieved of this task in 1861, Superintendent Steer of the Reserve Division being nominated in his stead. As Steer was based at the force headquarters in Maidstone, this made much more sense and, in future, the deputy to the chief constable would always be a headquarters man. Superintendent Steer resigned from the force in 1864 and was followed by Superintendent Buckley who held the job for 17 years. In 1881 Superintendent (1st Class) Joseph Orrell took over but was suspended on one month's notice to leave the force. No details were given of the reason for his dismissal, which is especially intriguing as he had only been in post for one year. Superintendent Charles Johnson followed from 1882 until 1899.

Perhaps because most county chief constables had a military background, great emphasis was placed on foot drill as a means of instilling discipline and improving the bearing and demeanour of the men in the Constabularies. By 1878 the Kent County Constabulary was holding regular drill parades at the county headquarters, the men having to travel from all parts of the county to attend them. In fact, drill parades continued until as late as the 1950s.

Borough Police Forces
The existing borough forces in Kent were unaffected by the passing of the 1856 County & Borough Police Act. In addition, Margate received its charter in 1857

and promptly formed a Watch Committee and a police force as required under the Act.

So far as uniforms were concerned, the popular stovepipe hat continued in use in most Kent boroughs until after 1865 when the London police adopted the helmet and other forces quickly followed suit. There were probably mixed feelings amongst the men concerning the loss of the beaver hats since their sturdy construction meant they could be used as a seat to snatch a short 'doss' or form a useful step to help them look over high fences or into windows. Over the years, other changes were made to the uniforms and, by around 1860, tunics had replaced the tail dress coats. After 1857 most forces used the newly formed Kent County Constabulary as their role model, the Deal force even adopting the shako cap like the County police before changing to the helmet shortly after the Metropolitan Police adopted this type of headgear.

The borough forces were largely uncontrolled, except by the city fathers, until the 1856 Act introduced the system of financial aid from central government, provided the force was certified efficient by one of Her Majesty's Inspectors of Constabulary. Proud as the various Watch Committees might be of their police force, there were many that failed the first inspection, usually because of lack of spending on their force. In Kent, only Gravesend, Maidstone and Tunbridge Wells were given a clean bill of health at their first inspection.

Police work in the city of **Canterbury** had to be the full-time occupation of the man appointed.[24] He was considered to be on duty 24 hours a day and citizens were encouraged to call upon the nearest policeman whether he was officially on duty or otherwise. A varnished board bearing the constable's number was provided for him to hang outside his lodgings. An advertisement in 1858 for two sergeants and three constables required applicants to be (a) able to read and write, (b) aged between 25 and 30, and (c) at least 5ft. 7in. in height.[25] These requirements were more strict than hitherto because of pressure from Her Majesty's Inspector of Constabulary. Up until 1864 a constable worked seven days a week with just three days leave a year (the superintendent could take seven days).

A local newspaper stated that, 'It was one of the nightly sights to see the night duty section emerge from the police station … and parade up St Peter's Street in Indian file on the kerb edge "peeling off" at their respective beats.'[26]

The last man carried a stout walking stick to indicate that he was on the boundary beat which took him around the lanes and footpaths to the sanatorium. To prove he had reached the end of his allotted beat, he had to make a note of the names of all the patients there. Beats were worked on a fixed route basis with a conference point every 15 minutes, with no discretion as to timing or route. The locals soon learned to tell the time by the passing of the constable – as no doubt did some less worthy individuals! Despite this, the constables seem to have managed to visit various 'ports of call' where they would be welcomed with a cup of tea or perhaps something stronger. Tales are told of one constable who made it a point of honour when on nights to visit every one of the four breweries then existing in the city. The carelessness of another resulted in his helmet sailing across a vat of fermenting beer like a galleon in full sale!

One unfortunate Canterbury man was Constable Harry Culver who could never get the hang of Daylight Saving Time and was disciplined for turning up for duty an hour late, having failed to put his clock forward. The next year he was determined not to be caught out again, but turned up two hours late, having adjusted his clock backwards instead of forwards!

The harsh conditions prevailing in Canterbury at the time, and the fact that the men were working 12-hour shifts at a time when the nine hours worked in the Metropolitan Police was considered excessive, was a factor in the HMI's refusal to issue a certificate of efficiency in 1858. Poor discipline and insufficient numbers were also cited and Superintendent John Clements, who had been in charge of the force since its inception in 1836, resigned as an alternative to dismissal. The vacancy was widely advertised: '… [applicants] not to exceed 40 years of age and not under 27. Pay will be £100 p.a., official dress and accoutrements being found. The Superintendent is required to reside at the station house, fire and light being provided …' After interviewing suitable applicants, Robert Davies, a former sergeant-major, aged 39 years, was appointed the city's superintendent of police on 14 May 1860.

The Canterbury City force was eventually granted its certificate of efficiency but the HMI continued to find fault with the arrangements. In particular, in 1865 he described the cells at the police station as 'dark, badly ventilated and of inferior construction' but fortunately a solution was at hand. The city gaol at the Westgate towers (built c.1380) was sold for use as the police station and the force moved there in 1870 from their inadequate accommodation in Lamb Lane. These Pound Lane premises remained the city's police station until 1965. In 1880 the HMI recommended that heating be provided in the cells but Superintendent Davies told the watch committee that heating was unnecessary as no one was kept in the cells for more than 24 hours. Also, the prisoners were held in the station waiting room where there was a fire and they only went to the cells to sleep!

The early policemen were expected to be beyond reproach. A classic example of this may be found in the case involving two Canterbury constables, Banks and Bennett, who were dismissed from the force in September 1869 for 'misconduct'. They had been suspended from duty and charged on a vague report by the Superintendent that they were going to collect some stolen hops. The evidence before the magistrates mainly consisted of two inspectors saying that the constables were good friends and that of a witness who had to be arrested in order to bring him before the court. A more biased court would be hard to imagine and the two defendants had no opportunity to provide an explanation. The Grand Jury acquitted the men for lack of evidence but the Watch Committee had already dismissed the men 'without prejudging the case' according to the minutes of their meetings, and this action was supported by the local press: 'It is not necessary that a Constable should be actually convicted of a crime before he can be deemed to have forfeited the confidence reposed in him and to have merited expulsion from the force he has disgraced'.[27]

Superintendent Davies left little mark on the force and accepted the Watch Committee's control without question, turning his back on the increasing challenges and responsibilities to ensure a quiet life. By 1877 his slackness had become apparent to all and he was reprimanded for his laxity at a fatal fire incident and his general negligence. He was further criticised by the inspector of constabulary the same year

12   Canterbury City Police, *c*.1880.

for failing to keep a record of the Pedlars' Certificates issued and for pocketing the fees received. He resigned in 1881 as an alternative to dismissal.

He was replaced by 39-year-old James McBean, from the East Lothian Constabulary. In 1882, Superintendent McBean was successful in obtaining permission for each man to have one Sunday off in turn (i.e., once every six months) and seven days leave a year. Not until 1888 was each man given one day off a month and a half-hour meal break when on duty.

On his arrival in 1881, James McBean, 'a forceful leader',[28] set about cleaning-up the town and quickly fell foul of certain elements in the city. He was particularly strict on licensees who strongly objected and it is clear that there were certain vested interests which supported them. This may be deduced from the fact that the Mayor, acting in his capacity as an *ex officio* justice of the peace, dismissed a particular case brought before him, conveniently overlooking the fact that the defendant, a local licensee, was supplied by the brewery which the mayor owned!

Within a year of his appointment McBean was charged with exceeding his duty but the Watch Committee found that he had acted correctly. Only two months later, in September 1882, he was again accused of exceeding his duty and of drunkenness but once more it was held that he had acted correctly and was not drunk. A further charge of being drunk and disorderly in November of that year was similarly dismissed as being a 'vexatious and frivolous complaint'. It is clear that, despite upsetting many people, McBean generally had the support of his Watch Committee but he had many powerful enemies and rumours of his immorality were widespread. There is no doubt that this continued vendetta had an effect on him, especially when, bowing to pressure from licensees and other groups who were being targeted by the police, the Watch Committee eventually accused Superintendent McBean of over-zealousness and instructed him to tone down his 'zero tolerance' policy.

As a result, discipline collapsed and, in 1888, drunkenness within the force was so bad, tales of corruption so strong, and the supervision exercised by the superintendent so lax that the Watch Committee considered amalgamating the force with the Kent County Constabulary. It is intriguing to see that the force was still commanded by the man who had previously been castigated for being over-zealous! However, by this time McBean was no doubt feeling the effects of the campaign waged against him. His private life appears to have left much to be desired and, eventually, he was brought before the Watch Committee to answer charges of neglect of duty and gross immorality. The truth of these allegations was never established but this time there was no escape and McBean was given the 'opportunity to resign' in March 1888.

When he first inspected the **Deal** force, the HMI found there was 'no effective supervision of the constables taking the night duty' and the force was found to be lacking in other respects and was accordingly deemed 'inefficient'. Sergeant Redsull, the head of the Deal Police, died in post in 1858 and the Watch Committee decided to adopt one of the HMI's recommendations and appoint an inspector. Once again an internal appointment was made and Constable Thomas Parker was promoted to inspector but it was not until 1864 – the year the post was renamed superintendent – that the HMI was able to declare the force as 'efficient'. There appears to have been considerable stability of employment among the members of the Deal Police force in the mid-19th century and the policy of only employing married men may have had something to do with this.

Superintendent Parker died in service in 1874 at the age of 57. This time the appointment went outside the force although the successful applicant, 32-year-old William Thomas Parker, was the son of the late superintendent. This nepotism was widely criticised and many felt that there were better local candidates. However, William Parker could boast eight years' experience in the Essex Constabulary and his appointment was confirmed. Unlike his father, who served for 27 years, William Parker did not remain long. He was described as lazy and neglectful and, following complaints about his inattention to duty, resigned in 1877 after just three years in the job. His replacement, Sergeant Helder Ben Capps, of the Kent County Constabulary, appears to have been quite the opposite. He announced a complete reform of the force, upon which four constables resigned, and there were complaints that he was too enthusiastic in prosecuting licensees and he had to be cautioned against an excess of zeal.

Over the years the population of the town grew, exceeding 8,000 in 1881, prompting the inspector of constabulary to recommend an increase in the strength of the force. The Watch Committee again decided against a complete overhaul and merely agreed that there should be a superintendent, two sergeants and a total of six constables. The smallness of the force was a constant problem with the superintendent being too close to the men under his command. With only two men available for day duty, one of whom was permanently required to perform fatigues, there were numerous complaints about police inactivity which were met with a sudden spurt of summonses, causing the magistrates to comment on the triviality of the cases brought before them, such as small boys throwing snowballs and similar peccadilloes.

But the end was in sight; the 1888 Local Government Act removed the right of small boroughs to have their own police force and, in an endeavour to be able to claim the necessary population of over 10,000, overtures were made to nearby Walmer, but this independent parish was opposed to any amalgamation. All other attempts failed and on 1 April 1889 the Deal force was absorbed into the Kent County Constabulary with most personnel taken on at their existing rank. Superintendent Capps returned to the County Constabulary as an inspector, being promoted super-intendent in 1893 and retiring in 1898. The Deal force therefore had a history of some 60 years during which time it was responsible for no great initiatives; it was not involved in any serious or notorious cases and none of its members reached an eminent position. Like many another small town, Deal dealt with its own problems of watch and ward with diligence and success and took a pride in its tiny police force.

John Coram, a policeman from Fleet Street, took command of the **Dover** force in April 1851. By 1872 he was getting a little old for the job and, following a riot after the elections that year, the Watch Committee passed a motion: 'That the Committee feel it is necessary to record its sense of the want of efficiency which has lately been displayed in the superintendence of the Police Force', and Superintendent Coram was pensioned off as being 'incapable from infirmity of mind and body to continue to discharge the duties of his office'.

In advertising for his replacement, the Watch Committee ruled that applicants should be under 40 years of age and preferably with knowledge of the French language. The shortlist of 10 included James McBean (who was shortly to become the chief constable of Canterbury), and John Wilshere (who became the chief constable of neighbouring Folkestone). In the event, the job went to Thomas Sanders, also from London, who served for nearly 30 years. Superintendent Sanders was well thought of by the authorities and by the townspeople and was commended for his arrangements with regard to the visit of the Shah of Persia in June 1873.

The instructions issued to the Dover force[29] forbade the men from leaving the borough when off duty and from appearing in plain clothes without express permis-sion. This meant that they had to wear their uniform whenever they left their homes for any reason. They were also forbidden from smoking or drinking in the Station House and from smoking, carrying sticks or umbrellas when on duty. They were also forbidden to accept 'any description of drink' from a person in custody, from using unnecessary violence or using language 'calculated to provoke or offend them'. They were also reminded that, in taking persons into custody, they were 'not justified in doing more than is absolutely necessary for their security whilst they are being conveyed to the Station House'.

Dover's police wore stove-pipe hats until these were replaced by helmets in 1869. Whistles replaced the rattles in 1872 while in 1874 the sergeants were issued with chevrons to sew on their uniforms to distinguish them from the constables. The force remained unaffected by the Local Government Act although it was a near thing since

13 Dover Borough Police, *c.*1880.

the force was refused a certificate of efficiency from the Government Inspector on a number of occasions between 1857 and 1888. The main bone of contention seems to have been the number of officers deployed in the town. In 1881 the Dover police moved into the basement of the Maison Dieu building where they used some of the cells of the old prison there.

Dover was one of the first borough forces to appoint special constables under the Municipal Corporations Act and, in January 1868, the Watch Committee agreed to issue armlets and '… to provide 1,000 staves for Special Constables and to be made of billets of ash split'.

Little is known of the tiny **Faversham** force although the borough accounts in June 1857 refer to a Thomas Burrough as being the 'newly appointed Superintendent' and to 'three new constables'. No explanation is given for this apparent root and branch reorganisation of the little force. It appears that much of the superintendent's time was spent escorting prisoners to the prisons in Canterbury and Maidstone; he was also responsible for the local lock-up and supplemented his pay by washing the gaol bedding. In 1861 the chief constable of Kent lodged a complaint with the Faversham Watch Committee over the lack of co-operation in a case of burglary and the superintendent resigned. He was followed in 1862 by Charles White and in 1872 by M. Breary. By 1888 the town still had fewer than 10,000 inhabitants and the force was therefore disbanded as result of the Local Government Act.

In April 1857, the **Folkestone** Watch Committee applied to the Metropolitan Police for assistance in appointing a detective to serve in the town. The Commissioner

14   Folkestone Borough Police, c.1870.

recommended William Martin, a 38-year-old superannuated sergeant who 'appears to have recovered himself sufficiently to undertake the present duty'. Martin was appointed and, when Superintendent Steer resigned in July, he was replaced by the newly-appointed detective officer.

The force was inspected for the first time in August 1857 and the HMI advised that, in order to qualify for his certificate of efficiency, the establishment should be increased by one sergeant and two constables, which was grudgingly accepted. In 1859 a letter was received from the Home Office suggesting that the superintendent of police should be called chief superintendent, a suggestion which the Watch Committee agreed to adopt. The force was by now rapidly growing out of its existing accommodation and, when Folkestone Town Hall was completed in 1861, it incorporated a new police station in the basement.

Where uniform was concerned, the Folkestone Police followed the usual 'fashions'. By 1870 the men were wearing long tunics with a leather belt, to the left side of which the handbolts pouch was fitted while the truncheon was housed in a leather case suspended from the right side.

Towards the end of 1872 Mr Martin was taken seriously ill and died on 27 December, still in his early fifties. It was decided to appoint another replacement from London and, in 1874, John Moulden Wilshere took over. Mr Wilshere apparently had a reputation as a drinker, which may go some way towards explaining his death in July 1880 at the tender age of thirty-nine. In October of that year, Samuel Rutter came on the scene but appears to have got into some (unexplained) difficulties and only lasted three years; John Taylor took charge from 1883.

Soon after Superintendent White took over the **Gravesend** Borough force in 1853, he was instructed to procure a Tower Pattern cavalry sword and sling belt, together with a blue cavalry cloak.[30] He was later authorised to obtain pistols, similar to those issued to the Metropolitan Mounted Police,[31] presumably for use when parading on horseback. So far as the uniform of the other ranks is concerned, the force changed from frock coats and waistcoats to tunics in 1858/9 and received an issue of leather leggings in 1860. Helmets replaced the high hats in 1865.

In the 19th century, when the new mayor was elected, it was the practice to burn an effigy of him suspended from a lamp bracket and to set fire to a boat, filled with shavings or other flammable material, and drag it through the streets of the town. At the Parliamentary elections the successful candidate was hauled manually round the town in his carriage, from which the horses had been removed. The enjoyment of the spectators was much enhanced if the carriage met up with the burning boat as it passed through the streets, all of which increased the burden of the police, especially as it was also responsible for fire-fighting.

Nevertheless, the town of Gravesend was obviously a pleasant place to work since Superintendent White served there from 1853 to 1873 – a total of 20 years – while his successor, George Berry, appointed in 1873, remained in post for 19 years.

This was not the case in the tiny borough of **Hythe**. 'Chief Constable' John Friend was still in charge when the Government Inspector inspected the 'force' in 1860 and reported that there was just the one constable for a population of around 2,650. No changes had been made as a result of the Municipal Corporations Act and there was no police station, the cells being in the old town jail and '… badly conducted. The constable performs duty as he pleases and I consider the police arrangements to be altogether of an inefficient character'.[32]

The HMI's poor view of the force was shared by at least some of the locals and a correspondent to the local newspaper in July 1861 complained of the

> … insufficient police arrangements of this town, now containing nearly 3,000 inhabitants and in close proximity to a camp of 4,000 soldiers … We have one official styled 'Superintendent' without a single policeman to superintend. We have two borough constables liable to be called upon by the aforesaid superintendent when there is a row, to get their heads cracked for the handsome salary of £1 per annum each. Surely this is a mockery …[33]

Towards the end of 1862 an additional constable was appointed and, in October 1865, Mr Friend was referred to as the 'Chief Superintendent' and there was reference to a colleague. In February 1867 a complaint was lodged against Mr Friend by a local grocer whose shop windows were broken and who alleged that Friend did nothing to arrest the culprit. The committee decided that there was no wilful neglect but there was 'apparent neglect due to physical infirmity', Friend having admitted that he was incapable of running after the man. As a result of this admission, in July 1867, the town clerk wrote to the Court of General Sessions to make unsuccessful enquiries about the possibility of the town's police being absorbed into the county force. It must be borne in mind that, as the population of the town was less than 5,000, it did not receive any government grant towards its policing costs and it was a question of whether subjection to the County Police Rate would work out cheaper than the cost of its own force.

In July 1874 the Watch Committee recommended to the town council that the police be reorganised. It proposed that the aged and infirm Superintendent Friend

15   Maidstone Borough Police, 1906.

(the 'Chief' seems to have been dropped) be superannuated and that the new force should consist of a superintendent and three constables. Friend's place was thus taken by George Raymond, a 34-year-old from Dover, with Constables Aedy, Harman and Gauntlett under his command. Raymond appears to have been an unpopular man and there were frequent disputes between him and the men in his tiny force. Constable Harman lodged a complaint against the unpopular superintendent who in turn reported Harman and Gauntlett. The watch committee held an inquiry which showed :

> ... [a] state of mismanagement and insubordination in the Police Force utterly incompatible with the proper discharge of their duties and, without dwelling upon the strongly conflicting evidence ... they have determined to make an entire change and they therefor call upon the whole force to resign.

The committee apparently later repented and re-appointed Raymond and Aedy and, following a letter from him and a petition from the ratepayers, also re-appointed Gauntlett. The remaining post (vacated by Harman) was filled by Thomas Thompson who resigned after only four months. The reason for his resignation is made clear in a letter he wrote after Superintendent Raymond had reported him for neglect of duty:

> ... the neglect of duty referred to was my not having forcibly removed from under the Town Hall four men during heavy rain on Saturday night. Gentlemen, I beg to say that if I am to consider it my duty to use force in removing men who are not committing an offence against the law, I must under these circumstances tender my resignation. The men in question were sober and orderly.

16 Margate Borough police station.

Despite Superintendent Raymond's patronage of the town's licensed premises he was not universally popular with the landlords. One of these invited him for a day's coursing on Romney Marsh which involved much crossing of the dykes by means of narrow plank bridges. When the plank on one of these gave way and the policeman fell into the cold water, there were plenty of willing 'rescuers' to ensure that he was well soaked before he was finally extricated!

Apart from Constable Aedy, the men came and went with alarming regularity. Matters came to a head in February 1878 when Superintendent Raymond was himself reported for being drunk. He claimed that he had been drugged but, despite hearing witnesses called in his defence, the Committee were not satisfied and called for his immediate resignation. Superintendent Raymond was replaced by Constable Aedy with a further change of title to head constable, and he remained in charge until the force was forcibly absorbed into the Kent County Constabulary as a result of the Local Government Act of 1888.

Unlike certain other boroughs, **Maidstone**'s force was always certified as efficient. George Blundell remained in charge until 1866 when he was succeeded by a John Barnes. W. Gifford, the chief constable of Poole, was made the chief officer of the Maidstone Borough Police in 1869, followed by Henry Dalton in 1882.

Margate did not receive its charter until 1857 and, although there was evidently some kind of police force in the town prior to this, steps were taken to form a true Borough force the following year. The Watch Committee appointed as its first superintendent one Henry Saunders, who had 16 years' service in the Metropolitan Police. One of the existing local policemen was made sergeant and four existing constables were retained. On the question of uniform, the Watch Committee was able to benefit from the experience of other borough forces that had been in existence for some twenty years. The headgear was to be the high hat as worn in the Metropolitan Police while the sergeant's dress coat was to have two buttons on each cuff and two stripes on the right arm. From 1860, the constables' coats had metal letters and numbers

17   Margate Borough Police, *c*.1880.

and, in April 1862, the dress coats were replaced by tunics. In 1865 the sergeants began to wear three stripes instead of two and in 1866 the helmet was introduced for the constables.

The new force was inspected in 1858 and the Government Inspector recommended the appointment of an additional sergeant and three constables. This provided a force of 10 men in all, with a sergeant and three constables patrolling in reliefs between 6 a.m. and 9 p.m. and the whole section on duty from 5 p.m. to 9 p.m. One of the constables was promoted to fill the second sergeant post and he and the remaining four constables worked from 9 p.m. to 6 a.m. The role of the sergeants was clearly specified as 'visiting officers' who would visit the constables on their beats.

In November 1867 a discrepancy of nearly £26 in the superannuation fund was discovered and Saunders was required to resign, giving three months' notice. He was replaced the following March by Thomas Compton. It is not known where Mr Compton came from but he presumably had previous police experience since, when he was required to resign in 1876, following a vote of no confidence, he was awarded a pension. The next in line was the somewhat exotically named Robert Wilcox Romanis, a sergeant in the City of London Police.

Although essentially an agricultural county, the 19th century saw Kent becoming an increasingly important centre for the new-fangled craze for sea-bathing, and seaside resorts such as Margate grew both in size and importance. This development created additional, new responsibilities for the police. In 1873 a plain-clothes officer was detailed for duty on the Fort every Sunday between the hours of 9 a.m. and 1 p.m. to watch the bathing and look out for pickpockets. New bye-laws made six years later specified that male bathers were to wear 'suitable drawers or other sufficient dress ...' while females were to wear a 'suitable gown'. Soon afterwards a police boat was obtained and two men were sworn in as 'police boatmen' for the summer season. Their pay (30s. a week) was met by the proprietors of the licensed bathing machines. Two 'commissionaires' were appointed in the summer of 1876 to do police duty on the seafront for 17 weeks, presumably sworn in as special constables.

The attitude of the British police to foreign parts has traditionally been extremely insular. There were, however, some rare occasions when policemen ventured abroad on what might be described as goodwill visits, such as that made by constables of the Margate force who were invited to accompany the town's fire brigade on a visit to Boulogne in 1880. This was not an unqualified success; it appears that some or all of the policemen were left behind when the packet sailed for England – possibly due to a surfeit of hospitality. Superintendent Romanis later criticised the town crier for '... crying a notice which [the superintendent] considered was likely to bring the officials of the town into disrepute, viz. with reference to the members of the police who were left behind at Boulogne ...'. The superintendent obviously worked on the basis of 'least said, soonest mended'.

The force does not seem to have been any better or any worse than most of its contemporaries and regularly received its 'Certificate of Efficiency' from the Government Inspector. In 1886, the latter criticised one of the sergeants (the reason not entirely clear), as a consequence of which the sergeant was reduced to the rank of constable and immediately resigned from the force. This resulted in the Watch Committee sending a deputation to the Home Office asking it to 'send down an official to institute an enquiry into the discipline and general efficiency of the Borough Police Force'. There is no record of whether this was done and, if so, what the result was. At all events, Romanis appears to have served without any serious problems until the end of 1888 when he was criticised for being absent from his station without permission for two days in October, prompting him to resign, giving just two weeks' notice.

Although not an incorporated borough, **Ramsgate** possessed an embryo police force from around 1836 and resisted any attempt by the county force to take over the policing of the town after 1856, by which time the force had grown to nine men, plus four night constables. Little is known of the early conditions in the Ramsgate Police although the fact that there was never a shortage of candidates suggests that conditions were not too harsh. Further clues as to the popularity of the force may be gained from the fact that the Watch Committee[34] was able, in 1898, to lay down a minimum height of 5 feet 11 inches – a height considerably above the average for an ordinary citizen in those days. In addition to the usual prohibition on drinking while on duty, members of the Ramsgate force were also forbidden to smoke at any time while in uniform but they were comparatively well paid, getting more than their County colleagues in 1875.

The force was inspected for the first time in April 1857, following which the two longest serving constables were made sergeants and four more constables employed, bringing the strength up to 10 constables plus six night-constables. Night-constables continued to be employed at least until 1874. In 1861, the force appointed Colour-Sergeant Harper of the 2nd Cinque Ports Rifle Volunteers as its drill instructor, to

18 Tenterden Borough police station.

give instruction for an hour a day, three days a week. Later 12 sticks were purchased for the learning of sword drill.

When James Livick retired in 1869, Edward Buss from Sandwich was appointed the new chief of the Ramsgate Police and served for 26 years. Soon after his arrival, in 1874, a 'quaint little red-bricked building in Charlotte Place, just off York Street'[35] was taken into use as the town's police station, with accommodation for the superintendent.

Shortly after the Government Inspector's visit in 1878, and presumably on his recommendation, the head of the Borough Constabulary started to be referred to as the 'head constable'. When Ramsgate finally received its charter in 1884, its police force became an official borough force, in recognition of which the bearded Superintendent Buss took the title of chief constable. In October 1887 the Harbour Police was amalgamated with the town police and the Board of Trade relinquished all control over them. This brought the strength of the Borough police force up to 30 all ranks.

Although few forces considered that any training in law, police procedures or the rules of evidence was necessary, some did consider that a basic knowledge of first aid was desirable. The value of these classes may be gleaned from an item in the Annual Report of the chief constable of Ramsgate who commented that, in 1887/8, 19 persons had been 'seized with fits in the streets when constables have been near and able to render … aid'.

Following the passing of the 1856 County & Borough Police Act, the **Rochester** City police force – much slimmed down in the interests of economy – was inspected for the first time in August 1857 by the Government Inspector of Constabulary, who was not impressed with what he saw. As a result, the force was remodelled in July 1859 with a superintendent, five sergeants[36] and 20 constables. Superintendent Tuff was pensioned off with an annuity of £26 as being 'worn out' and John Henry Radley, a Metropolitan Police officer, took his place. As a consequence of these modifications, the force was certified as efficient in December 1860.

In October 1862, three additional constables were appointed to form a River Patrol, the strength of which remained the same until 1884 when a fourth man was appointed.

In September 1859 an Act of Parliament provided for the setting up of police superannuation funds and Rochester, having consulted some of the other borough councils in the county, agreed to set up such a fund by the deduction of 2½ per cent of each man's pay and the inclusion of certain fines and penalties. However, pensions were only payable after the age of 50, unless the man was certified as medically unfit, and these were a concession rather than a right. One wonders how many men were dismissed from the force on trumped up or trivial charges towards the end of their working life to save a few pounds on the rates?

The headgear was changed to 'caps' from 'hats' in June 1861 (although it is not clear what type of cap this referred to) and leggings were provided early in 1865. In March 1862 the members of the force were issued with a copy of the 'Regulations Made for the Government of the Police Force of the City of Rochester'. These regulations were amended and updated in January 1879 and contained on a single sheet of paper, issued to all members of the force. Constables were required:

(i) To devote the whole of their time to the force
(ii) To obey all lawful orders
(iii) To be paid 6d. a week less if off sick, unless this arises from the execution of his duty
(iv) To be liable for dismissal for drunkenness, unfitness, negligence or misconduct
(v) To give one month's notice to quit
(vi) To refrain from carrying a stick or umbrella while on duty
(vii) All money from fines, etc. to be paid into the Superannuation Fund.

Despite the perception one might have of Rochester in our own times, it is clear that the city was not always a tranquil backwater. In 1873, Sergeant W. Broadbridge, a former Metropolitan policeman, made a brave and persistent attempt to apprehend some armed burglars. While he was pursuing these desperate men, the sergeant was twice shot at, one bullet passing though his helmet. Although they managed to elude him, he got a good look at his intended assassin when he fired the last shot and his description led to the would-be murderer's arrest in a neighbouring county. He rose to the rank of inspector and, when Superintendent Radley died in May 1877, Broadbridge was promoted to superintendent.

As we have seen, **Sandwich** was required to form a police force in 1856 and the first head constable was Sergeant John D. Warren who was in charge of two constables. In 1868 he was replaced by Edward Buss but only two years later Edward Buss was appointed the superintendent at Ramsgate and Sergeant John Brothers, an 'active and nimble officer' from Deal, was appointed head constable of the Sandwich Police. John Cuthbertson arrived on the scene in 1875 and, two years later, was replaced by William Page who was still in charge when the force was compulsorily amalgamated with the Kent County Constabulary in 1889.

Like Sandwich, **Tenterden** was another very small force, consisting of only four men. In 1856 James Barns was appointed the superintendent, albeit on a part-time basis, Mr. Barns continuing to exercise his profession of shopkeeper. In 1881 Benjamin T. Goldsmith was made the town's superintendent but, as the population was under 5,000, the town did not receive any grant from the government towards the cost of the force and it was disbanded in 1889. Only towards the end did the Tenterden Borough police have a police station as such. There was an existing lock-up at the Tollgate House on the corner of Church Road and the police presumably worked from their homes. In 1879, with the abolition of local road tolls, the council decided to rebuild the Gate House and the lower part of the building opened as a police station in 1884.

In June and July 1857, when the new Kent County Constabulary was being formed, there was a very real danger that **Tunbridge Wells**, not being subject to the Municipal Corporations Act, would lose its police to the new county force. The Police

19   Tunbridge Wells Police, 1874.

Committee sent a number of 'memorials' to the Courts of Quarter Sessions in Kent and Sussex setting out why it should retain control of its own police, and the justices, no doubt with an eye to economies, readily agreed. Cyril Winnington Onslow, who had been appointed to head the Tunbridge Wells police with the title of 'inspector' in 1853, continued to lead the force, the post being renamed 'superintendent' four years later. Although he held the job for some nine years, Onslow eventually fell foul of the Police Committee and was required to resign as it was felt that he was not doing the job properly. The next chief superintendent seems to have been more of a success than many of his predecessors. John Joseph Embury, a sergeant in the City of London Police, was appointed in August 1862 and held on to the job until he retired in 1891.

The Tunbridge Wells Police Committee issued a set of rules for the police similar to those issued in other towns but adding that a Constable was '... to walk along the outside or kerbstone of the pavement, always giving the wall to persons passing him'.

This injunction was adopted by most forces and continued, albeit in a less formal manner, well into the 20th century.

Duties and Disorders

In the borough and city forces, where the police were the executive arm of the local council, much emphasis was placed on the reporting of defective street lamps, sanitary matters and the enforcement of local bye-laws covering annoying but hardly criminal activities. A constable's work was very much concerned with nuisances of one sort or another – smoke (from chimneys and locomotives), hawkers, street cries, costermongers, noisy and unruly children, stray dogs, etc., all of which aroused the ire of the worthy citizens of the town who expected the police to take firm action. The enforcement of the liquor licensing laws also occupied much police time and was followed over the years by such legislation as the Petroleum and Explosives Acts, the Pedlars' Act,[37] the Chimney Sweeps' Act, Food and Drugs Regulations, Weights and Measures and so on. There is the happy tale of a superintendent who instructed his new driver to go into a certain public house and obtain a sample of whisky. The driver returned shortly afterwards, licking his lips and pronouncing the whisky as very good!

The police also quickly became the recognised repositories for found property and had to take charge of a wide and curious range of errant items. In July 1874, the Ramsgate superintendent reported that the sum of 10s. had been given to the police to hand to the finder of a set of false teeth which had been lost(!) in the town. The finder declined to accept this reward and so it was paid into the Police Superannuation Fund.

In an agricultural county like Kent animals always took up a lot of police time, especially the infectious diseases which afflicted them such as the serious outbreak of 'Cattle Plague' which occurred in 1865/6. Another serious disease was rabies (hydrophobia); a number of cases having occurred in the county, the police were given Home Office authority to destroy any dog reasonably suspected of being mad. Stray dogs became a police matter in 1871.

Another aspect of rural life is the presence of travellers/tinkers/gypsies/pikies/didicois or persons following such a lifestyle, by whatever name they are known.

Relations between the rural police and these people have always been somewhat confrontational and, as early as 1880, a memorandum was issued to the Kent County Constabulary regarding:

> Pikey Encampments: Complaints having been received of the number of encampments made by these people upon the Waste Lands in the County, particularly on the borders of the Metropolitan Police District, Superintendents will direct their Constables to report all cases within their knowledge with the view of proving the case on the prosecution of the Lord of the Manor or other owner of property to whom Superintendents will make the necessary application to prosecute.

Every September Kent had to cope with the invasion of Londoners, travellers and gypsies for the hop-picking. For around a month many quiet villages were swamped by these 'foreigners' who set up home in tents or crude hopper huts. They worked hard all day and drank hard every evening. The public houses frequented by these visitors, such as the *Blue Bell* at Beltring, were unable to pump beer fast enough and would save time by filling tin baths with ale from which they filled their customers' glasses. An early county policeman, Constable William Kelway, recalls in his journal that, in the 1860s, he '... helped to arrest several Irish hop-pickers for assaulting Sergeant Mayes ...' and later he describes how he was called to a 'riot' at Golden Green, near Tonbridge where hop-pickers were rampaging, armed with 'hooks' (bill-hooks?). He '... went into them alone. Got their hooks away from them and stopped the fight and never got a scratch. I was praised for that.'[38] This phenomenon continued up until the Second World War and, to a decreasing extent, until the 1960s when mechanisation finally took over from these hand-pickers.

Another misdemeanour that occupied the Kent County Constabulary was illegal gaming such as prize fights. To avoid interference by the police, these events were conducted with a great degree of secrecy in remote places. In one early case, the chief constable commended Constable George Baker 'for single-handedly stopping the fight on Oakham Marshes between Sullivan and Tyler for £25 a side'. The constable waded up to his middle through a creek and forced his way onto the ring, pulling up some of the stakes with his own hands.

In March 1860, the chief constable issued a lengthy memorandum to the force on the following lines:

> The Chief Constable, with a strong determination to prevent the prize fight between Sayers and the American taking [place] within his jurisdiction, directs Superintendents forthwith to place one Constable on duty at each Railway Station within their respective divisions ... for the purpose of Telegraphing informations until after the fight comes off. The Chief Constable is of the opinion that it is also practicable, by stationing a single constable upon different railway bridges ... to keep up a chain of communication through adjoining Divisions ... each constable being provided with a small white and red signal flag, the white, upon which the word 'Up' should be written to prevent mistakes, intimating that the fight is up, the red down the line.

In 1860 the superintendent in charge of Canterbury City Police was appointed an assistant relieving officer and, similarly, in response to requests from the Poor Law Board, the chief constable of Kent agreed that certain of his officers should be appointed assistant relieving officers, to examine the claims of vagrants for admission to the various workhouses in the county. This step was based on the view that:

> ... the habitual vagrant has generally made himself amenable to the law by criminal acts, and dreads being confronted with the police; and the effect of this arrangement, where it has been

adopted, is said to have produced the speedy disappearance of the greater proportion of the usual applicants ... and the presence of an authority capable of enforcing order has checked their usual insolence and turbulence.[39]

This duty was not relished by the policemen concerned and the Kent County Constabulary surrendered it as early as 1871, although some Boroughs continued the practice much longer.

Being small units, the borough and city forces in Kent had great difficulty when faced with a large event, disaster or disorder. Sometimes the force had to call upon the military for assistance but the practice soon arose whereby each force agreed to assist the others if required. When the County force was established, this provided a very useful and substantial source of aid. For example, County policemen were quite often sent to assist the Borough police in Maidstone to help them keep order at public hangings, and to Gravesend where it was common for Royalty and other notables to disembark from ships. In August 1858, two superintendents, eight sergeants and 89 constables were sent to Gravesend to assist with 'the transit and embarkation of Her Majesty' (Queen Victoria) and, in May 1859, two superintendents, six sergeants and 52 constables attended the arrival of Prince Frederick William of Prussia. Similarly, a total of 114 men and their senior officers were detached to Gravesend on 7 March 1863 in connection with visitors for the wedding of the Prince of Wales (later Edward VII) to Alexandra. These early examples of 'mutual aid' were regarded as a 'special service' and paid for by the borough concerned.

The Canterbury City force had to call for assistance in respect of processions, fairs, hop-picking, circuses, horse races (on Barham Downs) and cricket weeks, especially as this sort of event attracted a large contingent of pick-pockets and other felons. On civic occasions the military were called upon to line the route through the city while the police took part in the procession but, after 1857, the Kent County Constabulary was able to assist. In 1860 the city called for 50 county men to assist at the Royal Agricultural Society's annual show, together with a number of detectives from London.

Nineteenth-century elections had a nasty habit of developing into disorders. In Tonbridge in 1880 there was a full-scale riot during which eggs, stones and brickbats were thrown at the unprotected police. Twelve constables, including the chief constable, were severely injured but not one constable's staff was drawn during the 24 hours before order was restored. The annual Bonfire Night celebrations were also inclined to develop into serious disorder in some places. Dartford suffered considerably from this and so, in 1863, the chief constable of Kent attended in person with a body of 100 men. Perhaps overawed by this show of strength there was no trouble but the next night, when the reinforcements had withdrawn, a riot erupted and the local policemen were violently attacked. Many of the rioters came from London which prompted the chief constable to suggest that the establishment for the town was inadequate and that perhaps it should form a separate police district, like the autonomous boroughs. An application was made to the Secretary of State but the project was violently opposed by the owners and occupiers of property in the town. The arguments went on for two years, the chief constable reporting to the General Sessions in October 1864 that

I apprehend that s.19 ... (Additional Constables) and s.27 ... (Formation of Districts) would never have been embodied as part of the Police Acts had it been the opinion of the legislature that the organisation of a Rural Constabulary by Petty Sessional Divisions would in all cases prove applicable and sufficient for the watching and protecting of large towns not being corporate bodies but coming within the jurisdiction of the Chief Constable ... I shall have no difficulty in proving that no reason has or can be urged why the town of Dartford with a population of 6,597 and an acreage of 4,286 should not maintain an efficient police force in the same manner as a town of less population 5,853 and an acreage 2,036 (Faversham) which maintains a force of seven constables and is more free from crime than the town of Dartford (Crime in Faversham 71, Dartford 81).

I would also mention the Borough of Folkestone 10 constables as being of less area and only a little above the population of Dartford. Dartford already has more County officers than justified by the three-fold base of area, assessment and population (calculation would only give three constables to Dartford) to the detriment of the rest of the county ... Either this injustice must be continued or the inhabitants must provide the additional constables under the Act quoted or be formed into a separate police district. (This would give the right to five additional constables or eight as a separate district.)

The proposal was not accepted in view of the strong objections by the locals.

These Bonfire Night disorders affected many other Kent towns such as Gravesend and Folkestone. In 1865 the Folkestone Corporation was informed that '... a grand sacrifice to Ultra-Protestantism was to be perpetrated on 6 November (the 5th falling on a Sunday) by the destruction of the wooden church of St Michael and All Angels by fire, to be accompanied with a serious riot.'

The County Constabulary was asked to supply 20 men and the directors of the South Eastern Railway 10 constables (to be near the railway arches) to supplement the town's meagre police force. In addition, the military authorities were asked to keep a squadron of cavalry, ready booted and spurred. The fire brigade was in attendance and the Borough Surveyor and his men stood by. In the end, the only result was the capture and overnight imprisonment of six small boys.

The *Folkestone Chronicle* waxed most indignantly against this 'extravagant folly' which would cost the ratepayers £40 or £50 for '... a breach of the peace which we believe was never for once meditated'.[40] No doubt this champion of the residents' rights would have been even more indignant, had a riot occurred and the authorities been unprepared!

Conflict with soldiers and sailors was a not uncommon occurrence in the early years and the garrison towns of Canterbury, Chatham, Sheerness, Gravesend and Shorncliffe were always busy ones for the police. The troops did not always behave in an exemplary manner and in July 1857 there was a large-scale fight between soldiers and the new County policemen at Sheerness, prompting the chief constable to issue a General Order to the effect that '... [constables] are never to interfere with soldiers quarrelling or fighting amongst themselves but to ... give information at the nearest guard house or to the adjutant of the regiment ... it is only when soldiers are fighting with civilians that the constable should interfere ...'.

There was further trouble in May 1858 when a number of soldiers stormed Sheerness police station in an endeavour to release one of their number who had been arrested. In doing so they caused considerable damage for which the company commander was ordered to pay! A mere month later there was a further determined assault on the lock-up at Chatham. In October of that same year there occurred a major affray at Blue Town, Sheerness, between sailors and marines from the dockyard and men of the North Cork Rifles, in which a number of locals joined. The naval, military and dockyard authorities called for additional police and the appointment of a stipendiary magistrate, a motion that was supported by the police. The chief constable drew attention to the fact that, between April and September 1858, there had been 254 arrests in Chatham and 33 in Sheerness but the petition was rejected by the Government.

During the Victorian era the railways were being extended to all parts, the construction of which involved the influx of large armies of 'navigators'. In February 1859, in reply to a complaint from the Dartford area, Captain Ruxton wrote of '… the great increase of poaching and depredations committed by the Navigators employed upon the works of the East Kent Railway …'.

But this problem was widespread, wherever the railway was being laid, and for this reason an extra constable was posted to Cobham and another to Luddesdown, paid for by the railway company. In April 1866 Messrs. Waring Bros. applied to the chief constable for two extra constables at Hever and one extra man at Cowden to keep order amongst the labourers on the Surrey and Sussex Junction Railway. This was agreed to, provided the company paid for them. Hard-working and hard-drinking men, the 'navvies' spent much of their free time, when not actually drinking, in fighting each other and anyone else who got in the way. On one occasion some 400 English navvies stormed the camp of the Irish workers and tried to drive them away and the chief constable was compelled to appeal to the military for assistance. In August 1866 a body of police, including the chief constable, went to Edenbridge where English and Belgian navvies were fighting. In all 150 policemen attended (over half the whole police force) for about a week during which time they never had the chance to undress.[41]

However, after the mid-19th century the earlier disorders which had marred the first part of that century had largely disappeared from Kent. There were some signs of discontent in 1869 when an instruction was issued to divisions that:

> superintendents will report … their confidential opinion as to whether … any dissatisfaction exists among the working class of their respective divisions. Also their opinions as to what protection is at the present time afforded or could be afforded to the different volunteer armouries for the safe custody of the arms and ammunition therein in the event of any sudden outbreak.

Possibly connected with this instruction, a further order was issued four days later (27 February 1869) to the effect that '… notices to be posted without delay regarding the ordering of militia regiments to assemble for training'.

The volunteer regiments of yeomanry and militia were still quite a significant force at this time and each year a grand 'Easter Review' of these regiments was held in Dover. To assist with them, men were supplied from Rochester, Margate, Brighton and Maidstone as well as the Kent County Constabulary. On 22 April 1868, the 'Volunteer Review' was attended by a large contingent of Kent County Constabulary personnel including Superintendents Buckley, Ovenden and Walker on horseback and Superintendents Everist and Green in plain clothes '… independent of orders as detectives'. Constables were advised to provide themselves with 'a good substantial meat turnover or something of that kind that could be carried small in the pocket for dinner on the ground'. These Easter Reviews continued for many years and into the 20th century.

Many borough police forces were also responsible for fire-fighting. In most cases, a select few were trained in the rudiments of fire fighting and then performed ordinary police duty until such time as they were called out to a fire. So that they might be available if required, these police firemen performed duties in or around the police station, often to the chagrin of their ordinary colleagues. A letter to the *Police Review and Parade Gossip* complained that, although all the police were trained in fire duties, only a favoured few attended fires, whom he described as 'glass-case police firemen'.

> Why should we have to walk eight miles more than these selected few who are resting at ease and smile with sarcasm at us who pad the hoof in blind country lanes and walk about manfully wearing more shoe leather off our boots than they, and they skulk about outside the Police and Fire Station and shake their well-filled purse in our faces after a fire in a country village, where they spend hours in duty time, and we doing double beat duty for them.

There is no doubt that feeling ran high in some forces!

The Canterbury force was one that had fire brigade duties to perform and the police were still responsible for fire brigade duties in 1918. Initially they were simply required to raise the alarm but, from 1850, they had to man the City engine them-selves and call the other four brigades in the area. During the period from 1862 to 1881, the role of the City police at fires varied considerably. On 3 September 1872, a fire occurred in the Cathedral and arrangements were made for two steam engines and 25 men to attend from south London by train because of the importance of the building and the inadequacy of the local arrangements. This was at a time when the City Police were required to raise the alarm, haul the local engine and also keep order at the scene, with the superintendent in overall charge of the volunteers. These willing amateurs were severely criticised for their inexpert knowledge and the decrepit state of the engine, all of which could have resulted in the destruction of the Cathedral. This, and other incidents, led to the superintendent being authorised in July 1877 to apply to the military for assistance in the event of another serious fire. The police were still hauling the engine in 1881 and, on one occasion, they were so drunk that they took a wrong turning. As a result there was an unfortunate fatality for which the superintendent was severely criticised. Brought before the Watch Committee, Super-intendent Davies had no alternative but to resign.

By 1873 the Ramsgate police had relinquished responsibility for the town's fire brigade and a separate superintendent of Fire Brigade had been appointed, but in December 1886 a dispute over the tardy arrival of the brigade at a fire prompted a root and branch re-organisation. The head constable (as he was then styled) was to be the Captain of the Fire Brigade with overall responsibility for it but an experienced fireman (Assistant Officer West from Paddington Fire Station) was employed as the full-time engineer. All the existing firemen were dismissed but given the opportunity to re-apply for the 11 posts which had been created.

When the alarm was sounded it was not just the fire brigade which turned out; all off-duty policemen and a lot of local citizens joined in the excitement and, if actually involved in fighting the fire or saving life, stood to benefit from the reward paid by the insurance company. In November 1886 the considerable sum of £108 12s. 3d. was distributed among 20 policemen who assisted in saving life at a fire. One of them, Constable Williams, had apparently played a significant role in saving lives and got £80 to himself – a huge sum representing around a year's pay! A mortar and maroons were obtained for the purpose of calling out the members of the fire brigade, but in 1889 a defective maroon fell on a nearby house, causing a little damage and a great deal of consternation.

Crime and Punishment

When the Kent County Constabulary was formed in 1857, the chief constable's first instruction to the force reminded the members of the '… great aim and object of the County Constabulary … the prevention of crime and the maintenance of good order'.[42]

It was very soon appreciated that the ordinary policeman on the beat, whilst a palpable deterrent, was only really effective in catching criminals when he stumbled upon them in *flagrante delicto* – a somewhat rare occurrence, although certainly not unknown. A journal kept by Constable William Kelway of the Tonbridge Division tells how around 1865 he stopped a man one night and found him to be in possession of a candle, matches and a skeleton key which '… would unlock every granary and barn in the district'. Later, while attending a fire, he arrested a man for stealing a sheet which he had wrapped around his body under his coat.[43]

The same officer later describes how he and his superintendent made use of a disguise to catch a thief they were pursuing; '… we got through the wood and heard of him two miles ahead. We called at a beerhouse and borrowed two long farmers' smocks and took the lamps off the cart to disguise it. We soon overtook him and I jumped out of the cart and handcuffed him.' The same constable describes how he was called to investigate the theft of soap from the *Bull Hotel* in Tonbridge in 1866 and how, on searching the washerwoman's house, '… we found a lot of bed bugs and afterwards the soap – up a chimney'.

It was quickly realised that some policemen needed to work in plain clothes and also that some had a flair for detecting criminals and were regarded as good 'thief takers'. The smaller forces, lacking experience and expertise as well as resources, usually called in Scotland Yard when they had a difficult or serious case to solve but this could prove expensive so they began to appoint their own men as detectives. In Maidstone in 1840 the Watch Committee approved the purchase of four caps and gabardines for disguises and in Dover, in 1841, the superintendent was given authority to direct any of his officers to dress in plain clothes 'for the better performance of their duty'. From 1875 officers of the Canterbury City Police were frequently employed in plain clothes although this was often more for the detection of offences against the liquor licensing and betting and gaming laws than crime as such.

Kent, especially the Romney Marsh, has long been famous for its sheep and it is not surprising that sheep-stealing was a major problem for the new county force. In June 1861, Captain Ruxton wrote to a complainant describing how the thefts of these ovine creatures were effected: 'Sheep robberies are done this way – drovers are driving a flock to market, passing a field with sheep in they drive some of the best out, mix them with their drove and sell them at market on their own account, where all trace is lost'. Five years later the chief constable had to issue an instruction to the force that '… constables are to stop all droves they may meet and obtain the name of the drover, from and where to and number of sheep and check this number'.

Poaching is usually seen as a relatively harmless country pursuit, carried on by poor agricultural workers to augment their meagre diet but, in fact, there were serious, armed poaching gangs around who were not above killing or injuring anyone who got in their way. The chief constable of Kent felt that the powers conferred by law were inadequate and, in a letter in January 1861, referred to the '… Murder or Murderous attacks on the Servants legally appointed to carry out the Game Laws'.[44]

The background to this concern was a battle which took place in East Peckham between a gang of armed poachers and the keepers and watchers employed by William Cook of Roydon Hall. During the conflict the head keeper received a gunshot wound from which he later died. The police arrested five suspects but they were later discharged for lack of evidence.

Not all poaching and thefts of animals were accompanied by violence. Constable William Kelway writes in his journal of a case of theft of 30 game fowls in Tonbridge in the mid-1860s:

> I put on my thinking cap and from very tender enquiries I got on the scent and found that there had been a large quantity of bloody water running from the sink at the back part of a house occupied by a man named Giles. The Superintendent [Dance] got wind from one of our men what I had found out and anxious to get the case, went by himself to Giles' house, but Giles had bolted and has never been apprehended. The Superintendent should have taken me with him. We should have been able to apprehend Giles and got the £10 reward. I think it serves the Supt. right.[45]

The use of official rewards in serious cases was quite a widespread practice in the mid-Victorian period and Superintendent Hulse, in charge of the Malling Division, did not hesitate to claim a £50 reward from the Home Office for the arrest of a wanted criminal so it was quite likely that Superintendent Dance wanted to get involved in the fowl stealing case to be able to claim at least part of the £10 reward for himself.

On 24 August 1873, Constable Israel May of the Kent County Constabulary, stationed at Snodland, was viciously assaulted and killed with his own truncheon. Near the scene were found a bloodstained cap and a broken pair of braces that were identified as belonging to one Thomas Atkins who was apprehended six days later. He confessed to the killing but claimed to have acted in self-defence. At the trial, witnesses stated that the constable had tried to awaken Atkins from a drunken stupor and had been threatened with violence for his pains. In his defence it was revealed that Atkins' father had earlier been convicted of the murder of his wife, Atkins' mother, and had been declared insane. The jury apparently took pity on the prisoner and convicted him of the lesser crime of manslaughter. He was sentenced to 20 years' imprisonment and served 15 before emigrating to America. Constable May had been a policeman for 14 years and was described as being of excellent character. Nevertheless, his widow, left with three young children, was merely awarded a gratuity of under £64 'an amount not exceeding one year's pay … the said constable having contributed to the superannuation fund for a period of not less than three years'. These were indeed harsh times and there was little room for sentiment.[46]

It cannot be denied, however, that ever since the days of Jonathan Wild, the 'Thief-taker General' in the 18th century, some of those employed to catch criminals displayed unfortunate criminal tendencies themselves and various Kent forces found that those entrusted with law enforcement, were, in modern parlance, 'bent'.

Perhaps the greatest scandal affecting the County Constabulary occurred in 1870. On 1 January that year, Superintendent English took charge of the Ashford Division and, on 12 September, he was dismissed the force, having absented himself without leave on and from 5 September. Behind this rather bland statement lies an intriguing story: early in 1870 a Mary James was arrested for petty theft and, when her house was searched, some £350 and a bank book were discovered by the two officers carrying out the search who handed them over to the superintendent. When Mrs James was released from prison later the same year she went to Ashford to reclaim her possessions only to find that they and the superintendent had gone. She quickly reported the matter and it was found that Superintendent English had sailed for Australia with a lady friend. The Kent police ascertained that he would dock at Brisbane and Constable Robert Breeze of the Kent County Constabulary was sent after him, using the Suez route, which meant he arrived in Brisbane before the felonious superintendent, who was sailing via the Cape and was arrested on his arrival. Further investigation of the superintendent's affairs revealed that this was not his first departure from the straight and narrow. Some eight years previously he had converted to his own use some stolen jewellery that had been recovered. He had also taken two gold watches on approval from a watchmaker in Folkestone and failed to pay for or return them. In 1867 he sold a boat that had been stolen from a ship and then recovered.[47] At his trial in April 1871 he was sentenced to seven years' penal servitude[48] but only served two years,[49] after which he again left this country for Australia, this time legitimately. The two other officers involved, Sergeant Marsh and Constable Holland, were dismissed for having failed in their duty by handing over to the superintendent a large sum of money without having this counted in their presence and without entering the fact of their find in any book or return. The chief constable was concerned that, although it was clear that the superintendent's crime was known to at least some of his subordinates, no one 'blew the whistle' on him. Captain Ruxton therefore emphasised to his men that they had a duty not to '… allow a dishonest man, no matter what his rank may be, to continue to serve by his side and without having the tact or acumen to discover and expose him'.

Mary James never recovered her property.

Communications

From the very earliest days of policing, when a solitary representative of law and order sallied forth into inhospitable slums, remote rural districts and other dangerous places, the need to be able to communicate was strongly felt. This need was originally addressed by issuing the parish constable and his urban counterpart, the watchman, with a wooden rattle. Not much of a defence but its sound carried surprisingly far, especially in those far off days when it did not have to compete with the noise of modern times. When the first Borough Police forces were formed in Kent in the 1830s and, when the Kent County Constabulary was formed some 20 years later, this remained the primary means of attracting attention. It was later replaced by the ubiquitous police whistle – in the County force in February 1885, but as early as 1862 in Ramsgate – one of the first police forces to issue them.

But the principal means of communication in all forces, borough and county, from their inception until the 1960s, was the system of conference points. All forces worked a system of beats, either following a prescribed route or else 'discretionary'. In both cases the constable was given a series of conference points at which he was expected to be at a given time and where he could be visited by a supervisor to check that all was well. In the case of the discretionary system, the officer was free to go anywhere on his beat provided he was at each conference point at the prescribed time. The fact that the officer had made the point was carefully recorded in his pocket book and, if the sergeant or inspector made a visit, the latter would sign the entry, after the constable had reported 'All correct, Sergeant', or informed him of any anomaly. Woe betide any constable who reported 'All correct' when there was an insecure shop or other property on his 'patch'. Should a constable not make his point without obvious reason, a search would be made of places where he was likely to have been detained and, if he failed to make the next point, a full-scale search would be initiated, working on the basis that some harm may have befallen him.

The issue of whistles added another facet to the system of conference points. A General Order issued to the Kent County Constabulary in 1885 instructed that, where a visiting officer found the constable was not at a conference point, he was to blow his whistle twice on arrival and twice five minutes before leaving. The constable concerned, who may have been delayed, was to blow his whistle once in response. Since most of the area covered by the force was extremely rural, it was unlikely that all this whistle blowing disturbed the locals, other than a few sheep or cows!

Other early communications consisted of handwritten letters and reports. The typewriter was invented in 1870 but it was many more years before this contraption found its way into police offices. In the borough forces the dissemination of information and orders from the chief constable to his men was relatively easy and could be effected verbally or in (hand)writing; in the County force, however, the distances involved created considerable difficulties. A copy of every general order and memorandum had to be sent by hand, post or telegraph to each of the 12 Divisions where it was laboriously copied into specially provided leather-bound registers.

But policing was now about to enter another significant stage ...

THREE

TOWARDS A GREATER PROFESSIONALISM
1888-1943

The Local Government Act, 1888

1888 saw the passing of the Local Government Act which introduced county councils and had far-reaching effects on the police. No longer would the county forces be controlled solely by the justices sitting in quarter sessions but by a standing joint committee of equal numbers of county councillors and magistrates. In Kent, the successive chairmen were:

S.P. Groves	1889-1899
F.S.W. Cornwallis	1899-1910
R.G.E. Locke	1910-1920
Kenneth McAlpine	1920-1923
Lt. Col. R.G.E. Locke	1923-1940
Lord Cornwallis	1940-1945

In addition, small borough police forces were compulsorily amalgamated with the surrounding county force and so the Deal, Faversham, Hythe, Sandwich and Tenterden forces were merged into the Kent County Constabulary. The 'superintendents' in these forces were compensated for the loss of their jobs and discharged while the constables transferred to the county force. Initially, the absorption of these boroughs into the county force made no difference to the manner in which the force was divided into 12 territorial divisions, the relevant County divisions simply incorporating these districts and using any facilities which existed there. In the case of Hythe, the County force did

20   Kent County Constabulary, *c.*1890.

21 Kent County Constabulary, Tonbridge Division, *c.*1890.

22 Major H.H.E. Edwards, Chief Constable of Kent, 1894-1895.

23 Kent County Constabulary, *c.*1895.

not use the town gaol, but held any prisoners at its Seabrook police station, conveying them to the Hythe court as required. The gaol became the town mortuary and then a private house, known as 'Mortuary Cottage'. When repairs were carried out to this cottage in 1922, a number of old warrants, proclamations, etc., dating back some 90 years, were revealed, plastered to the walls.[1]

In August 1894 Captain Ruxton, by then the only surviving serving member of the original Kent County Constabulary, lost his wife and this, coupled with advancing years (he was now nearly 77 years of age), prompted his resignation. His retirement after so many years caused quite a stir in police circles, or rather military circles, for it was still the military man who was the likely replacement. This

24 Lt. Col. Henry Warde, Chief Constable of Kent, 1895-1921.

is confirmed by the fact that, out of 70 applications for the post, the short-list consisted of one captain, seven majors and two colonels. Captain Ruxton's deputy, Superintendent Johnson, a career policeman, does not appear to have had a look in.

Ultimately, it was Major Henry Herbert Edwards, a deputy governor of Pentonville Prison and formerly of the Royal Welsh Fusiliers, who, in September 1894, was named as the new chief constable of Kent. His appointment was a controversial one,

25 Kent County Constabulary, *c.*1895.

26   Kent County Constabulary Wingham Division cricket team, 1927.

given his lack of police experience and the fact that he was the son-in-law of the chairman of the County Council. However, in the event Major Edwards did not hold the post for long as in April the following year he suddenly died and so was unable to leave his mark on the force.

The Standing Joint Committee drew up a short list of applicants which comprised four from the previous short list,[2] plus Lieutenant-Colonel Henry Warde and one other. The appointment of Warde to the job was also widely criticised, the periodical *Truth* commenting:

> The new Chief Constable ... has had a distinguished career as a cavalry officer, but he cannot know anything whatsoever of police work, and soldiers, as a rule, do not make good policemen. Such an appointment when some of the most experienced and highly qualified police officers could have been found for the place, is obviously a piece of unscrupulous jobbery ...[3]

One of Warde's first actions was to issue an instruction in 1896 requiring men to pay their own medical fees except in cases where they had been hurt in the course of their duty, had suffered an accident which required surgery or a serious illness resulting in incapacity for more than two weeks. Health continued to concern him and he felt too little attention was being paid to the men's feet by 'regularly paring corns, cutting nails, daily baths, etc.'. Sergeants were made responsible for ensuring that the men met the required conditions.[4] Just how they were to do this was not specified and one assumes they were expected to hold regular foot inspections – an unenviable task! If any neglect was found the constable was to be medically treated at Headquarters at his own expense and that of his section sergeant.

To foster an interest in fitness and health, involvement in suitable sports was encouraged. The Kent County Constabulary formed a Sports Committee in 1897, consisting of two superintendents, two sergeants and four constables, whose task was to organise annual athletic sports meetings, the first of which was held on 22 June 1898.

27 Gillingham police station.

In May 1911, the members of the force were somewhat patronisingly advised by the chief clerk (Superintendent Jessup) that 'the Chief Constable and Mrs. Warde have again expressed a wish to provide tea for the wives of members of the force and their children at our Sports. This again exemplifies the good feeling they have towards members of the force and their families.'

The County Police sports were held alternately at Tonbridge and at Folkestone. The Divisions trained vigorously and, on the day, the superintendents were out on

28 Gillingham police station.

the field, cheering their men on, hoping to win the Divisional Shield. Cricket was also encouraged, the Shield nearly always going to the Reserve Division (i.e. Force Headquarters) as most of the best players somehow found themselves posted there! Football was not regarded as a suitable game for gentlemen and was not encouraged until the 1940s.

The turn of the century saw the completion of the original police station building programme, the last ones being:

1889: New Brompton (Gillingham)
1892: Lydd
1895: Herne Bay, Knockholt
1898: Broadstairs
1900: Southborough (Swanley was added in 1902 and Faversham in 1904).

29   Faversham police station.

When the deputy chief constable, Superintendent Johnson, retired in 1899 there appears to have been a change of policy and, instead of appointing existing members of the force to the job, external appointments were made, usually of men considered to be of chief constable stature. Consequently Superintendent Charles de Courcey Parry briefly became the deputy in 1899, leaving the next year to take up the chief constableship of Bath. Superintendent Harvey Philip Lane was then appointed DCC and placed in charge of the Bearsted and Headquarters Divisions. He resigned in 1902 to take up an appointment in the Liverpool City Police and subsequently became the chief constable of Lancashire where he was knighted. Captain Hall Dalwood came next but he too resigned in 1907 on his appointment as head constable of the County Borough of Leicester.

Another of Colonel Warde's initiatives was to form an official Detective Branch, consisting of one sergeant and three constables, the sergeant (Edwin Fowle) being promoted to detective inspector in 1906. In 1904 every County Division was issued with a fingerprint outfit and photographs of prisoners were taken from 1911. Also in 1911 it was ordered that the plainclothes sergeants and constables should be regarded as belonging to the Detective Branch[5] and, although under the direct orders of the divisional superintendent, they were to report to the detective inspector all cases of crime which they were investigating for collation and co-ordination.

30 Kent County Constabulary, Faversham Division, 1899.

Warde was a strict churchgoer and expected his men to be the same. In 1900 he instructed all ranks to enter in their journals whether or not they attended divine service on Sundays and, if not, why not. Superintendents and inspectors were later reminded that services were held both in the morning and in the evening and, if unable to attend one, they should be able to attend the other. Warde strictly enforced the Sunday Closing Act and shopkeepers were told to keep their shops closed on Sundays. He was quickly taken to task by the London newspapers as this meant Kent newsagents were unable to sell Sunday papers. Through these and similar instructions, Colonel Warde gained a reputation as something of a martinet but went on to earn considerable respect for his control of the County during the First World War.

Although it would to be a long time before police dogs were introduced, the County force began experimenting with tracker dogs and, in October 1908, the chief constable was authorised to hire bloodhounds from London for the detection of 'crimes of a grave nature'. It is not recorded whether these were ever used and, if so, whether they were successful. Some men, especially those on lonely country beats, were in the habit of taking their pet dogs with them on duty, as company and possibly as protection. The new chief constable was having none of this and, in May 1898, ordered that the practice must cease. Most borough forces had prohibited their men from carrying sticks and umbrellas around the middle of the 19th century but the Kent County men who worked a rural beat were permitted to carry a stick until the practice was definitively forbidden in 1913.[6]

31 Kent County Constabulary, Rochester Division, 1903.

32 Kent County Constabulary, Rochester Division, 1907.

33 Kent County Constabulary, Rochester Division, 1909.

34   Kent County Constabulary, *c.*1910.

All applicants to join the Kent County Constabulary had to undergo a medical examination, the main causes of rejection being ruptures, flat feet, varicose veins, tumours, skin disease, stiffness of joints, cough, narrow chest, weak sight and facial deformities. In 1906 it was decreed that, in future, married men would not be entertained unless specially recommended. Furthermore, no man would be allowed to marry until he had at least three years' exemplary service. For many years, the physical attributes of recruits were more prized than intellectual ability and, even up to and beyond the middle of the 20th century, height, chest measurement and eyesight were important criteria. When ex-Sergeant Ron Cockram first applied to join the County Constabulary in 1938, he was turned down because he could not expand his chest measurement from 36 inches to 38 inches. However, with the Second World War imminent, requirements were relaxed and he was accepted in March 1939.[7]

The Constabulary rank and file were housed in cottages, rented by the Standing Joint Committee and, to make the members of the force more readily available to the public, brass plates with the words 'Kent Constabulary' were issued in 1896 for display on all places where police officers lived, including single men's lodgings. County men were required to serve wherever in the County they were sent and, by the beginning of the 20th century, the Standing Joint Committee was becoming concerned and expressed its 'fervent hope' that removals would be kept to a minimum on the grounds of cost and also making the men restless and disturbing the continuity of education.

In November 1897 Colonel Warde abolished the rank of instructing constable and restyled the existing holders 'corporals'. The Home Office subsequently pointed out that this appellation was 'without statutory authority' and, in 1902, the chief constable recommended that 30 of the corporals be immediately promoted to the rank of sergeant and the remainder absorbed into the sergeant ranks as vacancies occurred. Improved training arrangements had made the employment of instructing constables (or corporals) unnecessary and there were few who mourned the passing of the intermediate 'rank'.

35 Kent County Constabulary, *c*.1910.

In 1901 Colonel Warde decided to split the Faversham Division into two to match a similar division of the courts. Previously, the divisional headquarters had been at Sittingbourne, with an inspector at Faversham but, under the new system, there was a superintendent at both stations. In November 1912 the Rochester Division was renamed the Chatham Division but otherwise remained the same as it had always been.

Further evidence of the chief constable's military background and thinking may be found in the order issued towards the end of 1903 to the effect that '... when more than two men are proceeding on duty from one place to another, the senior officer present (or senior constable) will assume command, parade and march his men there

36 Kent County Constabulary, *c*.1910.

37 Kent County Constabulary, *c*.1912.

and back and will be responsible in every respect for the proper conduct of the party.'
He also introduced an unofficial qualification for promotion:[8]

> Members of the force who desire promotion should, if possible, make them selves acquainted
> with this most useful subject [shorthand]. Although not absolutely obligatory, the Chief
> Constable will take [this] qualification, with others, in consideration when promoting candidates
> to the higher ranks. No constables will in future be appointed clerks unless they show a fair
> knowledge of the subject.

Recruits still received no professional training but, in spring 1903, Chief Constable
Warde introduced voluntary classes in basic police law and procedure. These consisted of two hours instruction per week given at the force headquarters at Wren's
Cross and appear to have been well-supported since, from the next year, the annual
sum of two guineas was paid to the churchwardens of the parish church for the
provision of pews for men attending annual training. Foot drill was still regarded as
important and the Kent County Constabulary held regular drill parades at the county
headquarters. In July 1907, Chief Constable Warde complained that, at the last
inspection by H.M. Inspector of Constabulary, the superintendents did not appear to
have taken any interest or trouble respecting their knowledge of drill. He instructed
that, in future, whenever the chief constable arrived to inspect a division, the superintendent would be required to demonstrate his ability to drill the men.

38 Kent County Constabulary, Sittingbourne Division, *c.*1913.

In that same year the chief constable of Kent instructed that any sergeant seeking promotion to inspector would be required to pass an examination in dictation, essay writing, arithmetic and police duties. This sensible and basic requirement was not always followed in the borough forces where no doubt the chief constables felt they had an intimate knowledge of the strengths and weaknesses of the (few) men under their command and did not consider formal examination necessary.

Also in 1907 a Major Lafone was appointed deputy chief constable of Kent but left in 1910 to become a chief constable in the Metropolitan Police. Major Lafone was succeeded by Captain H.E. Chapman who was appointed superintendent of the Reserve Division and deputy to the chief constable in April 1910.

In November 1912 with the war clouds gathering, county superintendents were instructed to submit the names of any reliable horse dealers or large livery stables from whom cavalry or artillery horses could be purchased in time of war. Given the slaughter of horses that was shortly to take place in France, this was a prudent step to take.

Evidence of a changing attitude to the welfare of the members of the force may be gleaned from the Memorandum of 5 October 1912 which instructed that, where constables in the towns were working the eight-hour system of night duty, superintendents must try to arrange for them to have hot tea or coffee about half way through the night. Where there was a constable on Reserve (station officer) duty, he prepared this for collection by one of the beat men for distribution to the others. Where there was no Reserve officer, one of the beat men was detailed to prepare the beverage and take it out to the others in their tea cans. The cost of this was to be borne by the men themselves.[9] It will be noted that there was no question of the men coming into the station for a warm and a hot drink – it had to be consumed on the streets, together with their supper.

In 1913 work began on a plot of ground at the junction of Sun Lane and Prospect Road, Hythe and, by the end of that year, a new County police station and police house was in place.

39 Kent County Constabulary, *c.*1914.

The First World War

The police were generally unaffected by overseas hostilities until the South African Wars began in 1899 and serving policemen on the Reserve list were recalled to the Colours to fight the Boers. However, the next conflict, the First World War, had a much greater effect on the police and, indeed, on the population as a whole, since the German Zeppelins could, and did, attack mainland Britain. This appears to have been anticipated since, in 1909, Kent officers were instructed to report any sightings of airships and, as early as June 1906, members of the force were instructed to report '… any persons of foreign nationality seen making sketches'. It was not specified how the police would identify such persons, nor is it clear whether a sketch of the Kentish countryside qualified or whether the sketch had to be of something of possible military importance.

Anticipating the outbreak of war, a Home Office circular in 1911 stressed the need for each police district to keep a register of suitable persons who would be available to assist the police in a serious emergency: '… It would be especially useful if at any time [there was] a national mobilisation of the Reserves, for it would then enable the Chief Constable promptly to replace those Army Reservists serving in the Police Force who are called to join the Colours …'.[10]

These reserve policemen would be of two categories, the **First Police Reserve** (see later) and the **Second Police Reserve**, the latter consisting of persons sworn under the 1831 Special Constables Act, divided into those who would serve regular tours of duty for payment, and those who were ready to assist at times of danger. The chief constable of Kent's return to the Home Office showed that 163 men were willing to perform regular duties, with a further 42 in reserve. As a result, the Kent County Constabulary enrolled special constables for the first time.[11] They were issued

40   Kent Special Constabulary, Sheerness Division, 1917.

with an armlet in 1915, bearing the county badge, together with a buttonhole badge and a cap as well as a truncheon, handbolts and a whistle. Head officers were supplied with a tunic at their own expense but repeated requests from the other ranks for a uniform were rejected since, as there were 8,000 of them serving with the County force by the end of 1916, the cost would have been prohibitive.

The Home Office circular of 15 September 1911 set a pattern which remained largely unchanged for 30 years, even though there were doubts as to the legality of appointing a large number of special constables in the absence of the conditions outlined in the 1831 Act.[12] Because of this uncertainty, a further special constables Act was passed in August 1914 which allowed Special Constables to be appointed for the duration of the war.

The regular force was not uniformly hospitable towards these new colleagues and, in a letter to the *Police Review*, one Kent officer complained that their daily rate of 5s. was more than a regular with 10 years' service received. Furthermore,

> Among our Special Constables there are a number who have previously tried for our force and been rejected, when the pay was three shillings and threepence a day and now it is five shillings a day they are taken on …. Should anything serious turn up, I suppose it will be the permanent men who will be sent to attend to it, and the Specials will take our places at home.[13]

That there was some justification for this criticism may be gleaned from a letter which the Vice-Lieutenant of Kent wrote to the chief constable in which he stated:

> In connection with the recent raid by aircraft [Zeppelins] on the night of 17 August 1915, the Vice-Lieutenant came across two cases of Special Constables who were not offering to be of any assistance in the neighbourhood … . On being interrogated, they gave as their reason that they must stay by the womenfolk. Such people are obviously useless in an emergency and he ventured to suggest to the Chief Constable that, in all probability, a weeding out of the Special Constabulary would eliminate some of these shirkers to the advantage of the whole force.

The chief constable promptly sent a memorandum to the heads of Special Constabulary stating 'If this sort of thing is likely to recur, men of this description will be better out of the Force than in it and [he] hopes that Heads will make their Special Constables acquainted with the Vice-Lieutenant's remarks'.

As mentioned above, the concept of a First Police Reserve was first mooted by the Home Office in 1911 and introduced under Rules made under the County Police Act of 1839. Unlike the Second Police Reserve, i.e. the Special Constabulary, it was suggested that FPRs should be issued with uniform where possible, paid a yearly retainer and receive payment whenever they performed duty. They were sworn in to serve as constables on a limited engagement and had full police powers. Despite the fact that members of the First Police Reserve were almost invariably former policemen, the chief constable of Kent felt constrained in August 1914 to inform the superintendents and other supervisory officers that he had noticed that many FPRs '… seem to think they can do as they like, both as regards their behaviour and their appearance …'. He had seen some who were dirty, unshaven and smoking clay pipes on duty. They were to be reminded that they would be treated exactly the same as the regular officers and could face disciplinary charges.

Once the war started, the main task of the County Police was to ensure that telephone and telegraph wires remained intact and that they were not tapped or cut by enemy agents or sympathisers. The roads along which these lines passed were patrolled at night by cyclists, each covering a three-mile stretch and avoiding using any lights. To begin with daylight patrols were carried out by boy scouts but these were soon replaced by special constables who also assumed responsibility for day-to-day police duties so as to enable the regulars to be released for wire-watching. The advantages of using motorised transport to carry out this task were quickly appreciated and superintendents were instructed to enquire whether any vehicle owners in their Division would be willing for the police to use them for this (and any other) purpose. The owner was required to drive the vehicle and also to act as 'Patrol Supervisor'. In November 1914 these main road patrols were replaced by static checks, one set up at a different place each night.

All police leave was cancelled from August 1914 and, in October, orders were issued to 'arrest all Germans and Austrian subjects between the ages of 18 and 45. The whole of the south coast and east coast is to be made a prohibited area for Germans and Austrians'. This resulted in 31 enemy aliens being detained in Folkestone, 12 in Ramsgate and 30 in Tunbridge Wells and probably others elsewhere.[14]

Policemen with a reserve commitment were quickly called up – 86 members of the Kent County Constabulary in August 1914 who were replaced by a similar number of First Police Reserves. In January 1915 Captain Chapman reported that he had been considering applying for the post of chief constable of Essex but had decided to sink all personal considerations at this critical time and remain as DCC and not to apply for the post. In fact he was recalled to the Colours in September of that year, being replaced on a temporary basis by Captain F.L. Stanley Clarke. Chapman served with his regiment until 1917, returning with the rank of major.

War does not bring about a reduction in crime and this is reflected in the fact that, in 1916, the chief constable of Kent was authorised to increase the Detective Branch to include a superintendent (Det. Supt. Ambrose) with a detective inspector at Chatham and sergeants at Sittingbourne and Force Headquarters.

This Certificate is Presented with the thanks of the County of Kent to Special Constable. **David Day** by the Standing Joint Committee in recognition of Valuable Services rendered during the Great War. 1914 — 1918.

CHAIRMAN

GOD·SAVE·THE·KING

41 Certificate presented to Specials after the Great War.

In this same year (1916) the chief constable of Kent encouraged single men of military age to sign on as he felt that '... many of them would be only too glad of an opportunity of joining those members of the force who have already proved their worth in the field ...'.[15]

One wonders whether Lt. Col. Warde, the chief constable of Kent, fully appreciated what he was asking of his men; by the end of 1917, 11 members of the force had been killed in action or died as a result of their wounds. Despite this, in April 1918, he notified the force: '... the Authorities having called for an extra 40 men to be supplied from the force at once, the Chief Constable has decided that all single men are to go and all under 33 who have joined the Regular Force and the First Police Reserves since the commencement of the War to go first'.

The continual haemorrhaging of men from the Kent County Constabulary prompted the making of arrangements in May 1917 for special constables to take on increased duties to replace the regulars who were serving under the Colours. These included (a) their employment in towns rather than rural areas; (b) the work of one regular to be covered by four special constables working in pairs; (c) special constables to share the pay of one police constable, i.e. around 7s. 6d. a week for each special to cover wear and tear; (d) specials to provide their own dark suit, black ties and dark overcoat but would be issued with a cap and cap badge at a cost of 2s. 6d. and a Metropolitan Police armlet (1s.) to be paid for out of his first week's pay, the button-hole badge to be worn at all times; and (e) special constables to serve at least nine months – preferably for the duration of the war.

Despite the criticism occasionally levelled against them and the antipathy shown by some members of the regular force, there is little doubt that, as a general rule, the special constables performed their duties conscientiously and well. One group of countrymen in the Faversham area even formed a mounted section, referred to as the East Kent Mounted Constabulary. They rode their own steeds, wearing a grey uniform and an armlet with 'EKMC' in white letters. With the ending of the war, the First Police Reserves were advised to seek other employment as they would be discharged with just one week's notice as and when the regular officers returned from the Services. Divisional superintendents were instructed to draw up fresh lists of trained men willing to serve as First Police Reserves should an emergency arise at any time in the future.

The question of what should be done with the specials (who had been sworn in for the duration of the war only) was solved by a Home Office circular in 1919 which recommended the maintenance and expansion of the 'Second Police Reserves'. Existing special constables and men returning from the Army were encouraged to register as part of an emergency reserve. In July 1919, the chief constable of Kent issued the following order: 'Peace having been declared and ratified, the Chief Constable notifies the Force of Special Constables for the County of Kent that their services are no longer required and they are therefore disbanded.' He thanked them and hoped 'as many as possible will now re-enrol in the Reserve[16] as requested by the Home Office'.

In all, the Kent County Constabulary sent 217 men to fight for King and Country, of whom 18 never returned and another seven were incapacitated. As if that were not enough, the great flu epidemic of 1918/19 took another six men.

The Inter-war Years

The improvement in conditions by the beginning of the 20th century did little to alleviate the general dissatisfaction that ran through the whole of the police service prior to and during the First World War. Pay had dropped to poverty level and, in 1913, a National Union of Police and Prison Officers was formed. Many protest meetings were organised, including a large one in Chatham near the Town Hall and one in King Street, Gillingham.[17] The union's demands were rejected and, in August 1918, 6,000 London officers came out on strike. Although greatly sympathetic, policemen in provincial forces such as Kent were not involved in the strike which was confined to the capital and was virtually total. A hurried government meeting granted two of the union's demands but deferred a decision on recognition until after the war.

A committee was set up in 1919 under Lord Desborough to consider the grievances and its findings formed the basis of a Bill presented to Parliament. This including a substantial pay rise but prohibited police officers from joining any union and set up

42 Police Outing by char-a-banc, *c.*1920.

an alternative consultative machinery. This provoked the Police Union to call a further strike in August 1919, which was more widespread than the previous one but was poorly supported and was a disaster for those involved. All the strikers were dismissed regardless of their character and length of service.

The 1920 Police Regulations[18] implemented most of the committee's recommendations, standardising the pay in all forces and resulting in a rise from 30s. a week to £3 10s. 0d. – more than 100 per cent! The Regulations included a definitive description of the various ranks and titles to be used (including that of assistant chief constable) and defined what a 'beat' was as well as a 'division'.[19] Police officers were denied the right to strike and membership of a trade union continued to be banned, the Police Federation being formed instead.

The post-war period saw a number of other improvements in conditions including a standard eight-hour day. A County Constabulary memorandum of 1 January 1920 laid down that where 'Guards' were worked, these should be as follows:

No 1 Guard   3 p.m. to 11 p.m. (20 to 30 minute break allowed)
No 2 Guard   8 a.m. to 11 a.m. and 9 p.m. to 2 a.m.
No 3 Guard   11 a.m. to 2 p.m. and 11p.m. to 4 a.m.
No 4 Guard   2 p.m. to 6 p.m. and 4 a.m. to 8 a.m.

There is little doubt that the modern police officer would find these split duties extremely unsociable and arduous; in fact, the following year they were amended to provide that night duty would be performed in one tour of eight hours with a 20-minute break.

By now, the old Wrens Cross building was proving inadequate and the search was on for suitable new premises for the headquarters of the County Constabulary. A site at Sheals Court had been purchased in 1913, the existing house being used to

43 Kent County Constabulary Great War veterans, *c.*1920.

44 County Police Headquarters, Sutton Road, Maidstone.

45 Ch. Supt. P. Ambrose, Chief Clerk and first Chief Superintendent.

46 Major H.E. Chapman, Chief Constable of Kent, 1921–1940.

47 Kent County Constabulary, *c.*1920.

48 Kent County Constabulary, Wingham Division, *c.*1921.

49 Kent County Constabulary, Dartford Division, *c*.1925.

accommodate the assistant chief constable until the early 1920s but the project was abandoned in 1923 and the site sold off. An extensive new site on the Sutton Road was acquired in 1935 and the new headquarters of the Kent County Constabulary was completed in 1939 and taken into use the following year. The old headquarters at Wrens Cross was abandoned and gradually became derelict. Two new ranks were introduced into the County force in 1920 when Superintendent P.F. Ambrose, the chief clerk, became the force's first (and, for a number of years, only) chief superintendent in March.[20] Shortly afterwards, in November 1920, Major Chapman was made an assistant chief constable, it being decided that, in future, the deputy to the chief constable would hold that new rank.

After some 26 years in the post, Lieutenant Colonel Warde stepped down as chief constable of Kent in 1921, to be succeeded by his deputy, Major Harry Ernest Chapman. The new ACC/DCC was Major Robert Lambton Surtees OBE who took up his duties in June 1921. Chapman ruled the force through a triumvirate consisting of himself, his deputy (Major Surtees) and his chief clerk (Chief Superintendent Ambrose), known respectively (if not always respectfully!) as 'Harry', 'Old Bob' and 'Father'. Major Surtees retired in March 1943, immediately prior to the amalgamation with the borough forces.

Major Chapman made a number of changes and, in 1929, reunited the Sittingbourne and Faversham Divisions and called it Swale Division, with its headquarters at Sittingbourne. A further change took place in 1931 when the Bearsted Division, which covered the general area around Maidstone, was divided between the new Swale Division and the Malling Division. Still further changes took place in April 1934 when the Cranbrook Division also ceased to exist, the area being absorbed by the neighbouring divisions. Similarly, in January 1939 the Elham Division was broken up and its area covered by the Wingham, St Augustine and Ashford divisions, so that by the end of Major Chapman's reign there were just nine Divisions.

50 Kent County Constabulary, *c.*1930.

51 Kent County Constabulary, Tonbridge Division, 1926.

52 Kent County Constabulary senior officers, 1926.

In May 1926 a General Strike was declared and, although in Kent this widespread dispute was generally good-natured and peaceful, some ugly scenes developed at Dover Marine Station where the Cross-Channel service was being run by volunteers. The Special Constabulary was mobilised to relieve regulars for strike duty and unmarried officers were posted to vulnerable towns. Men from the Royal Navy ran the local electricity generators and one Gravesend borough constable was sent to man the gate at the electricity generating station where he was forgotten for two days! Using the improvisation skills for which policemen are famed, the constable agreed to let one of the ratings out of the station to the pub across the road on the understanding that he returned with something for the hungry and tired policeman to eat. The sailor readily agreed to this and, as word went round, the constable received a constant supply of victuals as the matelots slaked their thirst.

By 1931 the training given to the Kent County officers was sufficiently highly regarded for Gravesend to arrange to send its own recruits to Maidstone. These were not alone as the county force also trained men from Folkestone, East Sussex and, later on, West Sussex and Tunbridge Wells. A thorough training in law and police duties was given but conditions at the training school left much to be desired by modern standards. Self-catering was the order of the day and each day the recruits had to light and clean an old black stove on which joints of meat were placed prior to starting the morning's lessons. Few if any of the recruits had any idea of cooking and, as a consequence, the joint was usually either very rare or burnt to a cinder by lunchtime. The story is told of one recruit who, being told that a boiled egg needed four minutes to cook, calculated that 20 eggs would need 80

53 Kent County Constabulary, Bearsted & Reserve Divisions, *c*.1929.

54 Kent County Constabulary, Chatham Division, 1932.

55 Kent County Constabulary, Cranbrook Division, 1934.

56 Kent County Constabulary, Sevenoaks Division, 1935.

minutes, with dire results! Students ate, slept and had their lessons all in one bar-rack room, the wooden floor of which had to be scrubbed to the satisfaction of the inspector before any student could leave for a short weekend break, wearing the civilian hat which he was required to buy and wear whenever he left the barracks.

Pursuing the quest for physical fitness, training in the 1930s involved a weekly 'Dolly-brook' in which ten or a dozen students were given boxing gloves and required to join in a general free-for-all on a large mat spread on the floor. Bleeding was staunched with a wet sponge by the 'trainer' and the unfortunate student pushed back into the fray. Ron Cockram, who was mentioned earlier, claims that, although he served in both the army and the RAF during the war, he never encountered anything approaching 'the appalling conditions of service at Wrens Cross'.[21]

57 Kent County Constabulary, Sevenoaks Division, 1939.

In the earliest days, all the tasks connected with the police service were carried out by constables, including cooking, cleaning and occasionally even painting and decorating. Clerks and secretaries were policemen and such jobs were highly prized. When Superintendent Jessup retired as chief clerk to the Kent County Constabulary in April 1914 there was a proposal to replace him with a civilian but this was vetoed by the Home Office. In August 1934, however, 11 young men were appointed to work in the County and Divisional Headquarters of the Kent County Constabulary. These were the first of a number of 'junior clerks', the last of whom were appointed police constables in February 1941 – the last recruits until after the war. Apart from these, and the occasional highly-controversial employment of a lady shorthand-typist as a chief constable's personal private secretary, there were no non-police personnel to be found in any of the police stations in the County by the time the Second World War broke out.

Mention has already been made of the restrictions imposed on a policeman in the period prior to the Second World War and it should be remembered that similar restrictions were placed on his wife. Before she could marry she had to produce references and her family history was carefully scrutinised. Any type of employment was generally frowned upon – a woman's place was in the home, providing meals and comfort for her spouse! This did not prevent forces expecting wives to carry out certain chores in support of their husbands, especially in rural areas, where they were expected to act as an unpaid cleaner, receptionist, telephonist, counsellor and friend as well as to provide meals for any prisoners her husband might bring in. They were expected to answer the telephone within 20 seconds or questions were asked. Much like the country parson's wife, a policeman's spouse was very much part of the community in a village or small town and, up until well after the Second World War, every village in the County had its local constable (and his wife). In November 1940, listeners to the one o'clock news heard Constable Ayers of the Kent force describe his experiences which included the following tribute to his wife:

> My busiest but happiest day was when four planes were shot down within the boundaries of my four parishes … My motorcycle careered from plane to plane at a very undignified speed and it was not long before my wife had four German prisoners in the parlour. By her triumphant attitude I knew that they were more scared than she was and their sullen behaviour did not affect her a bit. … My wife is invaluable to me, telephoning reports to my headquarters and generally conducting my station whilst I am away. I should be lost without her.[22]

Uniforms and Equipment

At the commencement of the period covered by this chapter (1888) the Kent County Constabulary was still wearing the comparatively unusual shako cap and a general order issued by the new chief constable in July 1895 instructed that the chin straps should be worn on the tip of the chin and not underneath as previously. Colonel Warde also made something of a name for himself by publicly expressing his dislike of 'mutton-chop' whiskers or 'door-knocker' appendages on his men's chins and decreeing that they should be clean-shaven or wear only 'military moustaches or full, well-trimmed beards'. The *London Evening News* of the time reported that barbers' shops in Kent were overflowing with policemen anxious to comply with the chief constable's wishes.

A major change occurred in 1897/8 when the force replaced its shako caps with helmets. The original helmet plate consisted of the County badge (a rampant horse) surrounded by a laurel wreath. In the 1930s the more usual type of helmet plate, based on the Berwick Star, was introduced and continues in use until the present time, the only variation being the type of crown which surmounts the plate which alters with every change of monarch.

When officers were working in plain clothes they were to carry their staff, handcuffs and whistle. A special pocket was to be fitted to a pair of civilian trousers to carry the staff and uniform trousers were not to be worn when on plain clothes duty as '… anything 'uniform' might lead to the identity of a policeman'.[23] This adaptation was probably aided by the fact that the force employed a sergeant at county headquarters who was paid an allowance for providing plain clothes to the detective branch in lieu of uniform.

In 1901 the whole force was ordered to wear an armband from 25 January to 5 March following the death of Queen Victoria and superintendents and inspectors were ordered to wear these armbands for six months in 1936 following the death of King George V. This was probably the last time these symbols of mourning were worn.

58   Constable Trimnell, Kent County Constabulary in 1920s uniform.

59   Kent County Constabulary uniforms, *c.*1910.

60   Superintendent Thomas Fowle KPM (served 1862-1915).

At the end of the Great War superintendents and inspectors were issued with a normal, military style cap, instead of the 'pill box' type worn previously.[24] Around the same time, members of the force were issued with electric torches in place of the oil lamps previously supplied. These provided a much better and safer light but were useless as a hand-warmer on cold winter nights.

Police uniforms were the subject of Home Office scrutiny and in 1924 it suggested that there should be some standardisation in the materials used – the first step towards greater uniformity – and in 1929 a new type of tunic was approved for inspectors and above, based on the army officers' tunic. In 1930, lower ranks were supplied with a new pattern jacket, known as the 'Tweed' jacket, which was to continue in use for the next 20 years. This had just two breast pockets and was worn without a belt.

No picture of Captain Ruxton in his dress uniform has been traced but his successors were furnished with an ornate uniform of the type worn by diplomats and senior army officers, complete with plumed fore-and-aft hat. This practice seems to have died out with the retirement of Major Chapman in 1940, possibly as an austerity measure.

61   Kent County Constabulary senior officers, 1934.

Traffic and Transport

Throughout the latter part of the 19th century agriculture was increasingly using traction engines for harvesting and these had to travel from farm to farm. Their movements were strictly controlled by the Locomotive Acts which laid down that these 'steam locomotives' must not use certain specified roads, except at night, and must keep to a 2 m.p.h. speed limit in built-up areas and 4 m.p.h. elsewhere. The County police were kept busy enforcing these statutes and were constantly encouraged to do more by the justices. In addition, Kent County Council byelaws made on 6 March 1897 and 10 January 1901 required all vehicles to carry lights at night. This was held to include perambulators but no proceedings were to be taken unless the offender had been cautioned previously.

New dog carts were supplied to County superintendents in 1890, this time of the four-wheel variety, whilst in 1901 they were reminded to ensure that the divisional horse was ridden for one hour early each morning for exercise, unless it was to be used for a long journey in harness. Stress was placed on the need to *ride* the horse to ensure the horses' backs were up to riding condition should they be so required. The police carts were regularly used to convey prisoners to Maidstone or Canterbury

62   Constable in uniform as worn in 1930s.

63   Kent County Constabulary senior officers, 1938.

64   Kent County Constabulary Superintendent with dog-cart, *c.*1897.

65   Mounted officer, *c.*1920s.

66   Kent County Constabulary
Mounted Branch, 1912.

67   Kent County Constabulary
Mounted Branch, *c.*1915.

prisons and the death of a certain Samuel Wilson in 1892 prompted the issue of an instruction that a covered vehicle was to be used for this purpose in inclement weather and prisoners should never be conveyed in an open vehicle 'without a sufficiency of clothing'.

The Kent County Constabulary had long had a groom on each Division, whose task it was to feed, care for and ride the divisional horse when it was not being used to draw the superintendent's dog-cart. These dozen, scattered men formed the force's Mounted Section which could be mobilised as required. Groom constables were issued with 'pantaloons' and jackboots instead of booted overalls around 1900 and a mounted constables' 'Marching Order' was also prescribed, consisting of the helmet, tunic, sword and belt. By the latter part of the 19th century, the County Constabulary was using mounted constables on an increasing scale and a General Order of 25 June 1897 instructed mounted constables, if they were going to be away from their station for more than four hours, to take with them a nose-bag of feed, their own meal of bread and cheese, a horse brush, clothes brush and rubber. On arrival at their destination they were to dismount, brush the horse, rub up the appointments and brush their own clothes. The Kent County Constabulary continued to use horses long after the old dog carts had been replaced by motorcars and the last horse was not disposed of until 1940.

By the turn of the century, the railways had become a common form of transport. The Royal Train had largely supplanted the need for ships to travel as far as Gravesend to deposit their aristocratic passengers and, when it passed through the County, the police had to man all the bridges on its route. An order was issued to the Kent County Constabulary in September 1903 to the effect that, when watching bridges on the occasion of the passing of the Royal Train, they were to stand to attention. This instruction was supplemented two years later by a reminder that no one was to be allowed on the bridge or the line and a senior officer was dismissed for allowing a person to stray along the track. When King Edward VII died in 1910 the Royal Train provided a shuttle service for dignitaries arriving for the funeral. The King's Private Secretary later wrote to the chief constable of Kent, thanking the force for the very efficient manner in which it '… performed its duties regarding the exceptionally large number of sovereigns and representatives who have travelled over the lines by London and Dover.'

Around this time, bicycles were becoming much more common and, in 1896, one or two bicycles were issued to each division in the County force for use by patrolling officers but only with the superintendent's permission and provided the superintendent was satisfied that the constable was capable of riding it.[25] Returns were required of all men capable of riding a bicycle and also any who had their own machine. The chief constable of Kent felt it necessary to issue an instruction to his men in October 1903 to the effect that '… members when cycling or driving are to salute by smartly dropping the hand nearest the officer and turning the head in his direction, not by the normal salute which very rarely looks smart or is a success'.

This move towards mechanisation was obviously a success, prompting the chief constable of Kent to issue a further memorandum in November 1904 that it was '… most essential in order that a section in the County can be successfully commanded […] all Sergeants [who do not know how to ride a bicycle] should take early steps to

68   Kent County Constabulary cyclists, *c.*1905.

learn. In future this qualification will be taken seriously into consideration [...] when appointments are made to this rank'.

In May 1904, cyclists were issued with a pair of knickers and puttees, together with a forage cap. A new cyclists' cap, with a peak and chinstrap, was issued in March 1915. The ability to ride a bicycle was a skill not possessed by all and, in October 1911, constables were reminded that, if they were desirous of promotion, they must own a bicycle and be able to ride it.[26]

The motorcar or horseless carriage did not make its appearance until the very end of the century and was even then very much a novelty – a rich man's toy rather than a serious means of transport. To begin with these vehicles had to be preceded by a man with a red flag to warn other road users of its approach, but this requirement was lifted in 1896 and the speed limit raised from four miles an hour to twenty. Many non-motorists regarded this as far too high and, by 1902, complaints were regularly arriving at police stations concerning the speed of cars, and so two stopwatches and a tape were purchased to enable constables in the Cranbrook Division to time the speed of motorcars in accordance with the Motor Act of 1902. The motorists in Kent claimed that the police tests were wildly inaccurate and appealed to the Automobile Association which was formed in 1905 to protect motorists. In an endeavour to ward off complaints, the chief constable of Kent instructed in 1908 that all speed controls were to be carried out in uniform and should be clearly visible.

It soon became apparent that the police themselves could no longer ignore this phenomenon and would have to join this galloping mechanisation. In 1905 Colonel Warde applied for permission to hire a motor car in connection with the visit to Benenden of the Princess Christian and by 1914 he was in receipt of a car allowance. County superintendents began to hire motorcycle combinations just prior to the First World War but these were quickly replaced by cars. An instruction issued in July 1916 laid down that superintendents who had a County cart and horse at their disposal were to borrow a motorcar only where absolutely necessary.

In October 1914, a Mr Aveling supplied a car to Superintendent Rhodes of the Rochester Division and he duly applied for an allowance. At the same time, Deputy Chief Constable Chapman was granted £150 a year car allowance. An addition to the County fleet was obtained in 1916 when the chief constable was authorised to obtain a licence for a car detained by the police and now used for police purposes. It is not

69 Model T Ford police car, c.1926 (PC Reginald Brooker at the wheel).

recorded on what grounds this vehicle was 'detained'. In 1916 Mr Barrett of Canterbury supplied a 1914 Ford Model T for use in the Elham Division[27] and the vehicle was proudly taken into use by Superintendent Castle. In 1919 cars were obtained for the Sittingbourne, Ashford, Chatham and Wingham Divisions. By this time six of the 12 County Divisions had been equipped with a motorcar, presumably Ford Model Ts, and both the chief constable and his deputy had a car. Cars were obtained for the Bearsted, Ashford, Dartford and Sevenoaks Divisions in 1921, as well as a Triumph motorcycle for Headquarters. In 1922 cars were bought for the Cranbrook, Malling, Home and Faversham Divisions.

On 19 May 1922, shortly after Major Chapman had assumed command of the County Constabulary, the *Daily Mail* ran an article on 'Mad Motorists', asking

> What can be done to stop reckless motorists driving to the danger of the public on the narrow, crowded roads of England this summer? Last year the Kent County Constabulary sent out additional constables on cycles and, although most of them were on pedal bicycles, the result was such as to justify their employment again this year.

Chief Constable Chapman obviously took this advice to heart and, in summer 1925, he instructed that constables, working in pairs for corroboration purposes, were to do duty on all dangerous bends on main roads, especially at weekends, and report all cases of driving to the danger of the public, i.e. '... motorists who travel at a very fast speed and pass other vehicles on dangerous bends'.

Up until 1924 most if not all the cars obtained for use by the County Constabulary appear to have been second-hand but in that year a new Ford car was purchased for the superintendent at Tonbridge. The following year, the Standing Joint Committee's policy of only buying Fords was discontinued and the chairman was authorised to

70 Examples of pre-Second World War vehicles.

purchase any other make, preferably English. As a result, between 1925 and 1927, 11 Bean cars were purchased and Faversham got an Austin 12 in 1928. Motorcycles came back in favour in 1930 with the purchase of machines for eight of the County's rural sergeants, the others being given an allowance to run their own motorcycle on police business.

The cost of controlling the ever-increasing road traffic caused forces to petition the Home Office, which had some effect since it agreed to pay a grant towards the provision of motor patrols. The Kent County Constabulary immediately set up a Mobile Branch early in 1931 and 19 BSA motor cycles were issued to Divisions for Traffic Patrol duties, plus a Rover car at Force Headquarters. In July 1934 these motorcycles were replaced by 17 new ones plus two light cars and two MG sports cars. The original Rover car was replaced by a Hillman 'Hawk' in 1936. The Mobile Section now consisted of a sergeant and 31 constables and the fleet was augmented the following year by six Austin 12s. In 1937 the motorcycles and two MGs were sold and replaced by 12 MGs and seven Singer 9s. By 1939, the traffic patrol fleet consisted almost entirely of MG sports cars with just one Wolseley 18. Divisional superintendents were issued with Wolseley 14/60s or Hillman 10s in 1939 and two new 18 h.p. MG sports cars were bought in 1941.

The first Road Traffic Act in 1930 removed the 20 m.p.h. speed limit but this led to an alarming increase in accidents; in 1930 there were 170 fatalities in the County area, which was a significant increase on previous years.[28] Consequently the 1934 Road Traffic Act set a general 30 m.p.h. speed limit in built-up areas. Accidents continued to be a serious problem in the 1930s and also during the black-out in the

early years of the Second World War.
Nationally, it was not until D Day that
deaths through combat exceeded those
on the roads.[29]

Speed was regarded as the main cause
of the many accidents. As motor vehicles
became more sophisticated and faster, so
enforcement of speed limits became a
major preoccupation for the police. The
use of stopwatches and measured distances was abandoned and police forces
began to use cars to follow and time
speeding vehicles. The 15 fatal casualties
which occurred in 1935 on Wrotham Hill
(A20) alone gave considerable cause for
concern and so special attention was paid
to the area the following year and the
fatalities dropped to ten. Another problem
area was the newly-built A299 Thanet
Way which embodied all the latest safety
ideas as regards junctions, gradients, lack
of bends, etc., all designed for safe travel.
Unfortunately this simply resulted in
vehicles travelling much faster and

71 Capt. J.A. Davison, Chief Constable of Kent,
1940-1942.

certainly not more safely. This road remained an accident black spot until towards the
end of the 20th century when major improvements were made, making the road a
dual carriageway and removing many of the black spots.

The Second World War

Major Chapman retired in 1940 through ill-health and was replaced by Captain J .A.
Davison MC who had been an assistant commissioner in the City of London Police.
He came to Kent at the time of the 'phoney war' and quickly set about getting the
force on a war footing. He is described as being completely tireless and utterly fearless
and managed to infect the whole force with something of his restless energy and
zeal.[30] However, in 1942 he was suspended as a result of certain, unspecified irregularities in his handling of the force's assets and was asked by the Standing Joint
Committee to resign as an alternative to dismissal. Sadly this energetic but possibly
flawed young man committed suicide the same year. By this time the amalgamation
of the various remaining borough forces with the county constabulary was very much
on the cards and no replacement was appointed, the force being led by the deputy
chief constable, Major Surtees, until 1943.

The prudent steps taken in earlier years meant that, by 1931, there were 5,356
special constables in the County force, controlled by 18 supervisors and 334 head
special constables. Consequently, when the Second World War broke out
on 3 September 1939 there was a sound nucleus of specials ready to serve their
country. By 1941 nearly all Kent County specials had been fitted with uniform and

72 Gravesend Special Constabulary, *c.*1940.

a chief supervisor was appointed to assist the chief constable with special constabulary matters. Some special constables were taken on for full-time duties and paid for their services on a regular basis.[31] The right of the regulars to a weekly rest day was temporarily suspended, as was the right to retire, but a 12½ per cent allowance became payable in lieu after 26 years' service.[32]

In April 1939, the Government approved the formation of a new body: the Police War Reserve. The County force took on 149 PWRs in 1939 and similar arrangements, albeit on a smaller scale, were made in the Borough forces. Some PWRs were volunteers, others were conscripted for the duration. Employed full-time and wearing normal police uniform, they only performed war duties at first but gradually became absorbed into everyday policing.

Despite the efforts of the Home Office and various social organisations, by the time the Second World War began, fewer than a quarter of the British police forces employed women police and many of these were unsworn. But the war caused a radical rethink on the employment of women in all sorts of jobs hitherto regarded as the preserve of the male. Women were not eligible to join the Special Constabulary or the Police War Reserves and there was a clamour for women to be permitted to take an active role. As a result, in August 1939, the Home Office announced the formation of a Women's Auxiliary Police Corps (WAPC) to replace men in certain clerical, driving and catering jobs. Some were appointed full-time, others on a part-time basis. Two years later they were issued with a uniform similar to that worn by the Women Police. More than 70 WAPCs were taken on by the Kent County Constabulary while the Borough of Rochester employed nine (three ambulance drivers, four telephonists and two canteen staff).

In 1941 the Home Secretary stated that he wanted to see more women enrolled in the police, either as regulars or as aides in the Women's Auxiliary Police Corps: 'It is true that police duty is, for the most part, a man's job but such work as driving cars, typewriting and attending the telephone can be done by carefully selected women. There is no reason why canteen duties should not be taken over entirely by women'.

73 Tunbridge Wells War Reserves and WAPCs.

Sir Percy Sillitoe, at this time still the chief constable of Glasgow (he did not move to Kent until 1943), was an ardent supporter of the scheme. He wasted no time in recruiting WAPCs, including his own wife and daughter, the former being instantly raised to the (unofficial) rank of Assistant Commandant, described by his biographer as '... a flagrant example of the nepotism of which Sillitoe was guilty on more than one occasion ...'.[33]

In July 1940, the Home Office directed that:

> The police are not part of the Armed Forces of the Crown and therefore, in the event of a landing and effective occupation of an area by the enemy ... should not use arms or carry arms in the occupied area. In the event of a landing by isolated parties who do not form part of an occupying force, ... the police ... are [not] debarred from resisting and, if possible, destroying the enemy ...

In 1940 a Special Investigation Unit was formed to deal with national security matters, forming the basis of the post-war Special Branch and, with invasion imminent, County superintendents were instructed to make preparations for means of 'frustrating enemy movements'. Their potential involvement was summed up in the instructions issued to the Kent County Special Constabulary in an un-numbered memorandum in 1940:

> Your first duty is to stay where you are, keep calm and obey orders ... You must also endeavour to induce others to stay. Crowds of refugees are what the Germans like ... (1) The main roads must be kept clear at all costs for military traffic (2) refugees should be directed on to side roads in a generally Southerly and Westerly direction. Beware of false orders ... If the orders come from a stranger ... and you are at all doubtful ... get in touch with your superior officer or a [Regular] ... Do not try and interfere with enemy troops [!]. Car owners have instructions to make their cars immobile ... by (1) removing the distributor arm ... As a last resort, cars which are likely to fall into enemy hands must be put out of action [by] injecting ... water, paint, varnish, etc. through the sparking plug holes, smashing the distributor ..., or even cracking the cylinder block with a sledge hammer.

Kent's role as a military and naval centre was enhanced by the war. Chatham continued to be the base for the Royal Engineers and, of course, the Royal Navy. On the whole, 'Jolly Jack' did not cause too many difficulties for the police, the main problem being the number of prostitutes who plied their trade in the streets of the

74 Canterbury Special Constabulary, *c.*1945.

town. During the war these 'ladies of the night' (who were not averse to working in the daytime as well!) were busy enticing seamen into the back alleys to provide 'comfort' for them. Not all put their heart and soul into their work and one constable recalls seeing a sailor with a 'lady' up against the wall behind Chatham Town Hall, slap her face and tell her to take more interest in her work as she persisted in eating her fish and chips whilst on the job.

An early success for the Kent Police came in 1940 with the arrest of probably the only spies to land in Kent. Four agents landed on 2 September 1940 from a fishing boat, two on the beach near Hythe, who were quickly challenged and detained by Army sentries, and the other pair near Dungeness. Shortly afterward, one of these was brought to the police office by a civilian and a soldier. A search was made for the remaining spy who was found the next morning, walking along the beach and was duly arrested by Sergeant Tye.[34] Three of these unsuccessful and unwelcome visitors were subsequently hanged as spies.

Discipline

It had long been a requirement that police officers should, for obvious reasons, be free from debt. The borrowing of money, especially from members of the public and particularly from licensees, was strictly forbidden. In 1896 the chief constable of Kent made it clear that debts incurred in respect of any publican would lead to instant dismissal and that any other debt would render the debtor liable to the same punishment. To back this up, in August 1901 he issued a further order requiring all sergeants and corporals to submit monthly reports, certifying that the constables in their sub-division or section were free from debt. These supervisory officers were required to show that they had made personal enquiries to substantiate their report. Cases of officers dismissed for incurring debt and borrowing from licensees persisted and, as late as 1939, an inspector at Malling was reduced to the rank of constable for borrowing from a publican.

Nor was supervision an entirely one-way process; when Sergeant Wall of the Faversham Division was reduced to the rank of constable in November 1901 for being drunk on duty, two constables were disciplined for failing to report him to their superiors.

The peccadilloes of the more senior ranks did not diminish and, in January 1908, Superintendent Kemp, in charge of the Dartford Division, was severely reprimanded, fined one week's pay and reduced to the rank of inspector for (a) being absent without leave from 20 December to 3 January whilst suspended from duty, (b) failing to be at Quarter Sessions on 2 January and (c) being incapacitated owing to illness brought on by excess alcohol. In view of this punishment Superintendent Kemp retired from the force. In 1909, Superintendent Henry Mount, in charge of the Bearsted Division of the Kent County Constabulary, was reduced to the rank of sergeant for (i) being under the influence of drink, (ii) failing personally to take the charge against two prisoners brought to Wren's Cross police station and (iii) generally neglecting the office work of his Division. His successor, Superintendent Blackwell, was similarly demoted for neglect of duty in 1915.

It is not often appreciated that, even into the 20th century, it was an offence to leave one's employment without leave to do so. When Constable Judd of the Cranbrook Division absconded in November 1910 he was instantly dismissed. When he was later discovered in Woolwich he was arrested and brought back to Cranbrook where the magistrates fined him 'for having withdrawn from his duty without giving the requisite notice'. However, when Sergeant Walter Tubb (Tonbridge) went absent without leave in 1900 he was dismissed from the force but does not appear to have been prosecuted.

As one might expect, any senior man who used his position improperly could expect short shrift. Inspector Reader (Sheerness) was reduced to the rank of sergeant in September 1900 for (a) having frequently returned to his station under the influence of drink, (b) having allowed two 'favoured' constables to work only until midnight, and (c) his general irregular conduct at Sheerness. In December 1912, Sergeant-Major Hook was required to resign for having accepted bribes and gratuities from probationers under his instruction at Headquarters and taking money for the granting of leave to constables.[35]

Although policemen were prohibited from writing to the press without the chief constable's permission, quite a number have done so over the years, usually employing a pseudonym. In January 1915, whilst the Great War was in full swing, the chief constable of Kent felt constrained to issue a reminder, stating that those members who wrote

> ... grumbling and discontented letters to the *Police Review*, airing their particular supposed grievances, are doing the other members of the force a serious injury ... If any member of the force has a complaint or grievance, real or imaginary, let him adopt the manly, straightforward course of laying his complaint before the Chief Constable in the proper manner.

Other men were disciplined for marrying without permission and in one case a constable was dismissed for '... taking a woman down the side passage of a house whilst on duty in the uniform of the force ...'. In January 1900 Constable Harry Adams of the Malling Division was required to resign forthwith for 'having behaved in a scandalous manner by corresponding with a single woman and visiting her in

75 Canterbury City Police, *c*.1913.

Kemsing, he being a married man', while in July 1912, Constable David Parsons was dismissed for failing to marry Miss Slingsby after so promising and obtaining the chief constable's permission and for 'being responsible for the condition of Miss Slingsby's pregnancy'.

The Borough Forces

Around 1909/10, the Home Office was promoting desirability of each Borough force having a small mounted unit for dealing with rioters and dispersing crowds and unlawful gatherings.[36] The HMI suggested that places like Rochester, Maidstone, Folkestone and Dover should equip two men with saddlery, etc. for mounted duty 'in case of necessity' and should exercise on horseback at least 12 times a year. Many borough forces thought this an unnecessary expense and it is not known how many forces actually complied. Folkestone pointed out that it already had an arrangement with the County Constabulary for any mounted men it might require but Rochester complied with the recommendation and, in 1911, two constables were trained in their mounted duties by Major Thorpe of the East Kent Yeomanry, the horses being obtained from the army barracks as required. Dover also acceded to this demand and, in 1911, purchased five sets of saddlery, four pairs of riding boots and mounted police truncheons for use on ceremonial occasions. The equipment was last used in July 1914 for the installation of the Warden of the Cinque Ports and then gathered dust for nearly two decades. In October 1931 it was finally agreed that this equipment should be disposed of.

1888 saw the retirement of Chief Constable McBean of the **Canterbury** City force. He was replaced by the ambitious 30-year-old Inspector Robert Peacock who had ten years' experience with the Bacup Borough Police. He did not remain long in the city but went on to be the chief constable, first of Oldham and then of Manchester, where he was knighted. In 1892 John W. Farmery took over, followed in 1907 by L.T. Dunk.

76   Canterbury City Police, *c.*1914.

John H. Dain was in charge from 1913 and for most of the First World War, handing over to Benjamin Carlton in 1917 when he moved to Norwich. Mr Carlton served until 1922 when he was reduced to the rank of sergeant for reasons that have not been disclosed. Captain J.A. McDonnell was given the task of sorting matters out between 1923 and 1930 when he handed the baton over to George T. Hall, who was to be the last chief constable of the city.

The military presence in the city continued to cause problems and Constable Jesse Manuel had his nose broken and his head cut open twice in fracas with soldiers. On another occasion, however, the military hailed him as something of a hero when he bravely separated two soldiers, one of whom had bitten off his opponent's finger, the gallant constable being carried shoulder high to the strains of 'For he's a jolly good fellow'.[37] Interestingly enough, in 1918 the chief constable of Canterbury was able to report to the Watch Committee that 'the behaviour of the troops has been exemplary over the past years', even though a war was raging and the life expectancy of a soldier was very short.[38]

In January 1915, the War Office called for police volunteers for appointment as lance-corporals in the Military Mounted Police and many men responded to the call. One of these, Constable Bert Webb of the Canterbury City force, having been on traffic duty in Canterbury one weekend, found himself the next weekend directing traffic in Ypres Square 'with plenty of heavy "ironmongery" falling about to make the job interesting'. Not to be outdone, Sergeant John Ives, who had 32 years' service with the Canterbury City force and was therefore no youngster, was permitted to

77   Canterbury City police uniforms, *c.*1920.

78   Canterbury   City Police, *c.*1925.

79   Canterbury City Police, *c.*1930.

80 Dover Borough Police, *c.*1912.

retire in 1916 'to join His Majesty's Forces' and served as a sergeant-major instructor in the Buffs.

Around this time, the chief constable was wearing a very ornate, military-type of uniform with elaborate silver braiding, topped off with an equally elaborate helmet with an imposing Prussian-style spike. But, by the 1930s, this had been replaced by an ordinary, army officer's-style uniform, with Sam Browne belt.

The provision of cars for the Borough forces was evidently a low priority and it was 1932 before Canterbury Police had one at their disposal. A Ford 22 h.p. car was introduced in 1939 and used by a motor patrol officer who supervised traffic on the city outskirts.

The City Special Constabulary was very active and, in 1939, there were 119 special constables available for duty, about half of whom had been issued with a uniform. Such was their enthusiasm that they formed a Motor Section, using their own cars to patrol the city and surrounding area, the idea no doubt being based on the Faversham Mounted Section during the First World War.

A busy port and garrison town, **Dover** had more than its fair share of problems of immorality. The police regularly arrested prostitutes and closed small houses of ill-repute. Complaints were frequently received about the goings-on in the various parks and gardens in the town, as well as on the quays. In May 1900 the force was grateful for the presence of the military when the Relief of Mafeking celebrations got out of hand and a great deal of damage was caused. The military promptly responded to an appeal for help and the disturbances were quickly quelled.

Superintendent Sanders retired from the Dover force in 1901, and the next four incumbents were promoted from within. The first of these was the force's only inspector, H.N. Knox Knott whose post was named 'chief constable' in 1905 and

81 Dover Borough Police, 1920.

who retired in May 1908 after serving in the Dover Force for some 30 years. By this time the force had a chief inspector and the current holder, Chief Inspector David Henry Fox, who had joined the force in 1881, was the next to be appointed chief constable, serving until 1920. In 1920 Chief Inspector Charles Green was appointed chief constable and carried on until 1924. His successor, the penultimate chief constable of Dover, was Inspector Alexander M. Bond but, although still a comparatively young man, his health was failing and he had to step down in 1935, by which time he had served 35 years in the police, all of them at Dover.

Despite being independent, from time to time Dover had to call on the other Kent forces for assistance with events, such as the visit of the Prince of Wales in July 1893. The Kent County Constabulary sent 78 men and four mounted officers to assist and Folkestone and Canterbury each sent 12 men. There were even four detectives sent from the City of London. Three years later Dover had to call for 75 County officers and two City of London detectives in connection with the installation of the Warden of the Cinque Ports. For the visit of the French President, Emile Loubet, in May 1908, 150 men were supplied from the county force alone.

Up until this time arrangements for mutual aid were *ad hoc* but, in 1909, the Home Office reminded forces that the Police Act of 1890 set out the need to make formal agreements for the provision of aid as and when required. Acting on this advice, the chief constable of Dover approached the chief constable of Kent to see if he would be willing to enter into such an agreement. The deputy chief constable, Major Lafone, sent a brief response to the effect that the Act was designed to allow borough forces

82 Visit of President Loubet to Dover, 1908.

to help each other and did not concern the County force. The town clerk of Dover promptly responded with a clarification of the law on this point, showing perhaps that the DCC may have been a good soldier but he was no lawyer. The formal arrangement was duly signed in 1909.

The use of policemen in 1930 to paint Dover police station brought strong protests from local painters and decorators, who complained that there were skilled men on the dole. In fact, it had been the practice for at least thirty years for the station officer and one other to don overalls and whitewash the cells and the corridor each year in the winter months, a job which took them about two weeks. The chief constable was of the opinion that it was inadvisable to have outsiders wandering around the police station and pointed out that, if professionals were going to be used, then they would be the Borough Surveyor's direct labour force, not outside workers. Submissions to the Home Office received an equally dusty reply, stating that this was not an improper use of police labour.

The Dover Borough force bought its first car, a Triumph 'Scorpion' for £200 in March 1931. This was later replaced by a Hillman which was in turn replaced by a Wolseley 18/80 saloon—the type of police car so often seen in old films.

In 1935 the Watch Committee went outside the force for its new chief constable and Marshall Hayton Bolt was appointed. He had joined the Huddersfield Police in 1920 and served through the ranks in that force before moving to Newark as chief constable in 1933.

Around this time, in the run up to the war, the question of the police manning the fire engine was reviewed. It was decided that, because the chief constable was being swamped with Air Raid Precautions, he should no longer be the chief execu-

83 Chief Constable Reeve, Folkestone
Borough, *c*.1910.

84 Folkestone Borough Police, *c*.1899.

85 Women Police during the Great War.

tive officer of the fire brigade although he would still be its chief administrative officer. In 1940, one of the police firemen, T/Sergeant Brown, was awarded the George Medal for bravery during a fire on board a ship in the harbour and, the following year, Mr Bolt was seconded to the new National Fire Service as the chief regional fire officer. By this time, amalgamation with the Kent County Constabulary was imminent and so the Chief Inspector, Herbert A. Saddleton, was placed temporarily in charge.

In 1940 a brand new police station was built in Ladywell, incorporating a flat for the chief constable. Just two months after the official opening, the police station was severely damaged in an air raid and was in fact damaged a total of 18 times during the war. When the force amalgamated with the County Constabulary the station was taken over by the County force and remained in use for the rest of the century.

The air raids on the county, the long-range shelling from France and, ultimately, the flying bombs, took their toll of military personnel and civilians – including the police – alike.[39] In August 1940 an RAF plane crashed in Dover, killing PC William Maycock and his wife Mary and, a month later, one of his colleagues, PC Saville, lost an arm through shrapnel wounds. The Chief Commandant of the Dover Special Constabulary, Charles Beaufoy, was injured and blinded by a shell burst around the same time.

John Taylor remained in charge of the **Folkestone** Police until he retired in 1899 and, in May 1900, the 34-year-old moustachioed Inspector Harry Reeve was appointed to lead the force; he served Folkestone as its chief constable until the end of 1922. His uniform around this time was a fairly sombre affair, relieved only by quite a lot of braid and frogging in the same colour as the uniform. A rather more fancy version of the constables' helmet was worn by the chief constable around the 1920s.

So far as the men were concerned, in April 1889 it was decided that a new style of cap, similar to that worn by the Royal Irish Constabulary, would be issued and in July 1901 lightweight helmets were purchased from a local supplier for summer wear, the force later being issued with 'Hygienic' straw caps. Leggings were supplied the following summer.

By the beginning of the 20th century, the Folkestone town council and, by extension, the police force, were rapidly outgrowing their accommodation in the Town Hall. The Council had some temporary offices in Church Street and, in 1901, the editor of the *Folkestone, Hythe and District Herald* was urging that these would be ideal for a new police station in place of the 'wretched holes of Calcutta' which the police currently had to use. In the event, the council moved fully into the Church Street offices in 1924, leaving the police at the Town Hall, and it was not until after the amalgamation with the Kent County Constabulary in 1943 that steps were taken to improve their lot.

The dangers presented by motor vehicles were clearly demonstrated in December 1908 when two constables were injured by being crushed under a horse-drawn cab which was knocked over by a motor cab in Grimston Avenue. Both were knocked unconscious and one, Constable Frederick Nash, died at the end of the month. The driver of the motor cab was convicted of furious driving.

In response to the Home Office circular on the Special Constabulary (mentioned previously), the chief constable of Folkestone reported in December 1911 that

For several years past it has been the custom for the justices of this Borough ... to swear in, under the Municipal Corporations Act, about 30 men to act as Special Constables for twelve months, should they be required during that period to assist the Borough Police Force. For at least 17 or 18 years, it has not been necessary to call on them for assistance.

He went on to suggest that 50 men be sworn in annually and that there would then be no need for a First Police Reserve.

With the outbreak of the First World War in 1914 two women were appointed in Sandgate 'to keep a look out for suspicious persons and lights on the beach'.[40] It was about this time that a Women's Police Volunteers organisation was formed in London by Nina Boyle and Mrs Margaret Damer Dawson and the Metropolitan Commissioner of Police agreed that they could train women and patrol in London on a purely voluntary and unofficial basis. In 1915 the organisation was renamed the Women's Police Service and in December of that year Mrs Damer Dawson attended a meeting of the Folkestone Watch Committee to explain its work. It was resolved that two women police be appointed, one constable on 30s. a week and an inspector on 42s. a week, subject to two weeks' notice, the object being to deal with the prostitutes and 'enthusiastic amateurs' attracted to the area by the concentration of troops. In the event, Sergeant Stella Fife of the WPS was appointed, together with Constable Gertrude Cooke.[41]

In February 1916 the Watch Committee considered a report on the activities of the women police to date and informed the Borough Council that it did not consider the employment of women officers to be necessary. This recommendation was over-ruled. The situation was reconsidered in November 1916 in the light of the resignation of Miss Kirby (who it is assumed replaced Miss Cooke). The continued employment of women police was strongly supported by the Joint Conference of Clergy and Ministers which expressed a hope that Miss Kirby would be replaced. The Watch Committee disagreed and went so far as to recommend the dismissal of Sergeant Fife, but this was not supported by the Borough Council. Eventually, the situation was resolved by the resignation of Sergeant Fife in February 1917 leaving the force without any policewomen. The chief constable then recommended that a woman be appointed as a 'female enquiry officer' to make enquiries and deal with cases where women and children were involved. This proposal was approved but no further action appears to have been taken until May 1919 when a Miss Stephens was appointed but not sworn until September 1923.

Throughout the First World War Harry Reeve had his hands full with the flood of refugees from France and Belgium, a task which he obviously performed well since he and one of his inspectors were decorated by the King of the Belgians. In January 1915, the Commissioner of the Metropolitan Police wrote to Chief Constable Reeve, thanking him for '... the great assistance rendered to Metropolitan Officers at Folkestone Harbour, in all weathers, accompanying suspected persons arriving by boat to the Examination Room on the Pier'.

Unfortunately, as Reeve's health had begun to fail, he reluctantly retired at the end of 1922 and, in January 1923, Detective Sergeant Alfred S. Beesley from Scotland Yard became the chief constable of the Folkestone Borough Police. Upon his appointment, the Watch Committee agreed that Beesley should be issued with an extensive set of uniforms which, in future, would be purchased by the chief constable

86 Folkestone Borough Police, *c*.1925.

himself. Whether because he did not want to have to spend too much on such items, or whether his previous role as a Scotland Yard detective had accustomed him to working in plain clothes, it appears that Mr Beesley did not wear uniform very often. A little over a year after his appointment it was suggested to him that he should wear uniform more often, to which he replied that he had complete discretion in this matter. The Watch Committee then formally notified him that it wished him to wear uniform when attending court or any function at which the Mayor and Corporation were present and did *not* agree that he had complete discretion in this matter.

Folkestone's police first demonstrated an interest in the internal combustion engine in December 1930 when the force bought a motorcycle combination but two years later this was no longer serviceable and was replaced by two solo machines. In 1936 the force bought a Norton 'International' and also a second-hand car for training police officers as drivers.

Folkestone continued to be a pioneer in the employment of Women Police and, anticipating Miss Stephens' retirement in July 1936, Sybil Browning was appointed in April but she quickly left, to be replaced by Vera Restorick in September 1936. WPC Restorick remained in post until shortly after the outbreak of the Second World War and was replaced by two other women in fairly quick succession.

Although chosen from a total of 75 well-qualified candidates, Alfred Beesley does not appear to have been a particularly good choice as chief constable. He was not a popular man or easy to get on with and there was considerable rancour between him and some of the men under him. This came to a head in May 1941 when Sergeant Floydd[42] sent a statement to the Watch Committee alleging certain irregularities in the conduct of the force. The chief constable was accordingly charged with:

(i) allowing a police car to be used for unofficial purposes and issuing petrol coupons to persons not entitled to them, and

(ii) allowing Inspector Butcher to use a police car to take Mrs Beesley to Tunbridge Wells and to continue on leave, during which time the police car was involved in an accident, together with various infringements of the Petrol Control Regulations, and

(iii) using official petrol for personal purposes.

After hearing various witnesses, the Watch Committee found that none of the allegations had been proved but the chief constable was obviously not content to let matters lie and promptly put the sergeant on a charge for allowing himself to be taken home in a police car and for making false entries in a car's log book. Once again the Watch Committee heard the evidence and, once again, found that the allegations had not been proven.

A month later the chief constable was charged with being drunk on his way to the police station. Again the charge was dismissed and Sergeant Floydd was charged with insubordination and dismissed by the chief constable. However, the Watch Committee refused to ratify the decision and substituted a reprimand instead.

Around this time the force was devastated by a scandal involving a number of police officers. In October 1942, Eric Morgan, a haulage contractor and former Folkestone Borough policeman, was sentenced to nine months' hard labour for 32 cases of shop- and house-breaking. At his trial, Morgan's wife asked loudly, 'What about the others?' and alleged that 13 other Folkestone policemen had been breaking into shops and other property and had in fact been committing thefts since 1935. This was the last straw; Beesley's position had become untenable and, after discussions with officials from the Home Office, he decided to resign forthwith. A firm hand was called for and R.C.M. Jenkins, formerly of the Canterbury City force, was brought up from Penzance, where he had been appointed chief constable four years previously, to take command of this deeply troubled force.

Jenkins set up a full enquiry, assisted by two Scotland Yard detectives. It was decided that, in view of the delay in discovering these offences, it was unlikely that sufficient evidence to justify criminal proceedings would be forthcoming, and that the aim should be to rid the force of those concerned; if criminal proceedings were taken and failed it might be difficult to take disciplinary action. Eventually, five constables made statements admitting their involvement and were dismissed. A sergeant denied involvement but the chief constable found him unfit to remain in the force and called for his resignation. Although other officers were said to have been involved, the chief constable found no evidence against them.

With a force utterly demoralised by the scandals that had tainted even the most innocent of its members, occurring at a time when the town was subjected to heavy shelling and air raids and when morale was at an all-time low, Jenkins had an uphill task but the amalgamation with the County Constabulary shortly thereafter made it possible to bring in some outside men and so raise the morale and reputation of the police in Folkestone.

George Berry was still the chief constable of **Gravesend** in 1888 and remained in office until 1892 when Walter Thornton was appointed. Thornton was another long-serving chief constable and occupied the chair for a further 20 years, not retiring until 1912 when Harry Thurley took over. Mr Thurley lasted a mere 11 years(!) and in 1923 Arthur G. Martin was appointed.

One reason for men applying to join the force at this time was the disappearance of their craft or trade. Bud Friar joined the Gravesend Police in February 1925 because he could see his trade as a wheelwright becoming redundant. The man he replaced was previously a sailmaker, so possibly the same circumstances had prompted his change of career. Constable Friar was issued with a mountain of uniform and

87   Gravesend Borough police uniforms, 1930s.

equipment on his arrival and was advised by the sergeant to hire a handcart to transport it to his lodgings. His first day in uniform was not spent learning the law and police procedure but in cleaning and polishing the brasswork and windows at the fire station (for which the police were responsible). For the next three months he was on night duty and had to pick up the job as he went along. His only access to the law was an old copy of *Stone's Justices Manual* which the local Justices' Clerk gave him out of compassion. Not until some

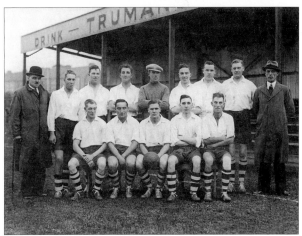

88   Gravesend Borough Police soccer team, 1935.

three years after Constable Friar joined were recruits sent to the Birmingham Police Training School, an advantage he never enjoyed. In 1931 the force arranged for its recruits to be trained by the Kent County Constabulary in Maidstone rather than in Birmingham, which was much more convenient for all concerned.

In 1929, the Gravesend Police installed a number of police boxes and the men now started and terminated their tour of duty from these, rather than parading at the police station. Based on a system used in Newcastle, this is believed to be the first use of police boxes in the South of England. Gravesend also got its first police ambulance in 1929.

Chief Constable Martin was followed in 1930 by the well-known (at least in police circles) Frank L. Bunn. Frank Bunn was a knowledgeable man who was keen to pass on his knowledge to others and consequently wrote a series of handbooks for the police. During his time at Gravesend he published his *Constable's Pocket Guide* which sold well throughout the country. His expertise and experience received due recognition in August 1934 when he was appointed chief constable of Grimsby, later moving on to head the Stoke-on-Trent Police. Finally, from 1934 until the

89 Gravesend Borough Police, *c.*1932.

amalgamation of the force with the County Constabulary, Gravesend was in the capable hands of Keith Webster who retired in 1943.

Unlike several other boroughs, **Maidstone**'s force was always certified as efficient. Henry Dalton was the superintendent in charge from 1882 to 1895 when Angus Mackintosh was appointed to lead the force and was the first to be described as chief constable. A stern man, not noted for his sense of humour, he nevertheless took part in a 'Beating the Bounds' ceremony in 1908, in company with the mayor and various civic dignitaries, plus a number of schoolboys. This was the first time the ceremony had taken place since 1872 and the chief constable was one of many who were 'bumped' on a boundary stone during the two-day event.

In 1908 a new police station and mortuary was built in Palace Avenue, supplemented in 1936 by a series of police boxes. The police station was completely renovated in 1984 and has continued to serve the town ever since.

The penalties imposed by the Maidstone justices in the early 20th century were still fairly draconian and Mackintosh's Annual Reports for 1904-7 reveal that the following sentences were handed down:

90 Gravesend Borough Police, *c.*1939.

91 Maidstone Borough Police tug-of-war team, 1902.

Elizabeth Vinten, 46, for stealing an umbrella – three months' hard labour
William Bourne, 28, for stealing flowers – two months' hard labour
Harry Williams, 29, for housebreaking – nine months' hard labour
George Bridge, 37, for stealing bricklayer's tools – six weeks' hard labour
William Dingle, 35, for stealing rabbits – nine months' hard labour (in 1905)
William Dingle, 37, for stealing clocks – eight months' hard labour (in 1907)
William Bourne, 35, for stealing a box of biscuits – one months' hard labour (in January 1907)
William Bourne, 35, for burglary – six month's hard labour (in April 1907)

proving that the previous sentences had not deterred Dingle or Bourne from a life of crime.

One duty which fell on several Borough chief constables was the function of billeting master. Often this was not very demanding but from time to time the billeting

92 Maidstone Borough police station, Palace Avenue.

93 Maidstone Borough Police, *c.*1920.

master was called upon to prove his efficiency. For example, in October 1908 the chief constable of Maidstone had to find accommodation for eight officers, 163 other ranks and 177 horses of the 21st Lancers who were spending three days in the town en route from Aldershot to Canterbury. In the event the operation went off successfully, thanks to Chief Constable Mackintosh's forward planning.

When, in November 1921, Angus Mackintosh retired after 26 years as chief constable of Maidstone, the town clerk wrote to the clerk of the Standing Joint Committee to propose a merger of the borough force with the county. However, there was a proviso

94 Maidstone Borough Police, *c.*1938.

that either side should be able to 'revert to the old order of things' after three years. The SJC was unwilling to accept the proviso and decided '… to await legislation giving effect to the recommendations of the Desborough Committee with regard to the merger of County and Borough police forces'.

Angus Mackintosh was therefore replaced by Charles Butler who resigned to go to Grimsby in 1936. Butler was in turn was replaced by Henry J. Vann, the chief constable of Lancaster, who left in 1942 to become the chief constable of Birkenhead and, in view of the impending amalgamation, was not replaced, Ch Insp. Beslee being the acting chief constable until 1943.

When Chief Constable Romanis of the **Margate** Borough Police left suddenly in October 1888, his replacement was Detective Inspector Charles Buck of the Stockport Borough Police who took over in March 1889. Buck did not stay long, however, resigning in June 1893 to return to the North on his appointment as chief constable of Rochdale. By this time the Watch Committee was getting concerned at the brief periods its chief constables were serving in the town and, on appointing another Northerner, Detective Inspector Joseph Farndale from Halifax, to the post, it required him to give an undertaking not to seek any other appointment for six years. Despite this undertaking, Farndale left Margate after some four years to take up a position in York and subsequently in Bradford. James H. Clegg arrived to lead the force in 1897 and he and five constables were issued with 'riding accoutrements' and authorised to hire horses as required. About the same time the force entered the modern era of communications when the chief constable was authorised to purchase a typewriter for the police office!

Clegg's tenure was also rather short, but perhaps with good reason, he having fallen foul of petty jealousies between the justices and the town fathers. In June 1902 the mayor and former mayor, both acting as ex officio magistrates, granted an urgent request from several publicans for an extension of permitted hours to celebrate the end of the Boer War. Because of the sudden ending of hostilities, the publicans had not been able to apply in Court in the usual way and their application to the mayor was their only hope. The local Bench considered that this had usurped their authority and maintained that only they could grant extensions and then only in open court. They instructed Chief Constable Clegg to take proceedings against any licensee who kept open beyond the normal permitted hours. The Watch Committee (presided over by the mayor) refused to allow the summonses to be issued and the Bench suspended the chief constable and summoned him to appear before them for neglect of duty. The Watch Committee engaged counsel to represent him and the matter was finally settled by the withdrawal of the suspension and a decision not to prosecute the publicans. The chief constable was not required to resign but he nevertheless expressed his disgust at this petty rivalry and resigned that December.

The Watch Committee once more manifested their preference for Northerners and appointed yet another detective inspector, this time from the West Riding, A.R. Ellerington, who took up his duties in early 1903. Ellerington too proved to be a 'butterfly', using the appointment as a stepping stone to greater things, in his case, the Chief Constableship of St Helens which he took up in January 1905. This time the Watch Committee moved nearer home and found a replacement in the Oxford City Police. Inspector Alfred Appleyard arrived early in 1905 and was the first chief constable to stay in Margate for nearly twenty years. One of his first acts was to obtain a bicycle for selected policemen to use on patrol.

The importance of the Kent Coast towns as tourist centres and the considerable influx of foreign visitors prompted the Margate force to introduce lessons in conversational French for its men in 1908. Each received 60 one-hour lessons, for which the teacher was paid 5s. a lesson. It was probably around this time (1909) that the Margate Police took on the task of giving early morning calls to 'mechanics and others', a practice which was discontinued in 1919, much to the concern of the Gas Board who unsuccessfully appealed for it to continue.

Around 1909, the Home Office started encouraging forces to form a small mounted section to deal with any disorders but Margate had anticipated this by a dozen years and four policemen had already been selected, using the horses normally employed to pull the fire engine.

In August 1914, with the outbreak of the Great War, Margate answered the call to arms by providing five constables as drill instructors for the Army. It appears that they were merely seconded rather than enlisted into the Army.

In May 1919 a previous instruction forbidding the men to smoke while in uniform was amended to provide that 'no member of the force shall smoke in uniform in the streets except when off duty and then only between the hours of 9.30 pm. and 6.30 am.' In November the same year the constable drill instructor asked to be relieved of that duty and a Lieutenant Cornelius was employed to drill the force. He resigned this post in 1932, it being recorded that he had served as a drill instructor to the police for 35 years so he presumably provided this service to some other forces. Once more, one of the constables took on the role.

Inspector Haycock was the force's first chief inspector. He was due to retire in April 1923, the same time as Chief Constable Appleyard but, on being offered the latter's post, Haycock agreed to stay on. It would seem that Mr Haycock failed to satisfy the Watch Committee, probably through age and infirmity and he 'agreed to resign on the grounds of ill-health' in May 1930. He was given three months' leave of absence, to expire on the date of his retirement. Accordingly, in August 1930, Inspector William Palmer moved into the hot seat and remained there until the force was amalgamated with the County force in 1943.

Mr Palmer obviously felt the force should have better transport than the solitary bicycle and so purchased one or two motorcycle combinations in 1931. Later the force also had a Wolseley 'Hornet' and two solo motorcycles.

By the time Chief Constable Buss retired in May 1895, the **Ramsgate** force had an inspector, one Roderick Ross who had joined the force from Canterbury, and he was immediately appointed the new chief constable on a salary of £200 plus free accommodation. The inspector vacancy thus created was not filled for another ten years. Crime was not a great problem in Ramsgate and the first record of a detective officer appears to have been the appointment of Sergeant Rodman as a detective sergeant in April 1891.[43]

In 1898 Ross moved on to command the Bradford City Police before returning to his native Scotland to become chief constable of Edinburgh.[44] During his period in command of the Ramsgate Police, Mr Ross introduced the wearing of a blue and white armlet by sergeants and constables when they were on duty. The blue stripes

95 Ramsgate Borough Police, 1920.

on the constables' armlet ran horizontally while those of the sergeant ran in the more usual vertical direction. In 1898, William Benjamin Jones, the chief constable of Grantham, arrived to take charge in Ramsgate.

In view of the lack of free time and other onerous restrictions, one of the few *divertissements* afforded the Victorian policeman was the Police Summer Outing which was a popular concession offered by many Borough forces. The outings (usually by char-a-banc) continued for many years, those provided in Ramsgate continuing at least until 1899, but with improving conditions they gradually died out. Another example of Ramsgate's fairly generous attitude to welfare may be found in the case of Constable Mortley who committed suicide at Christmas 1900 'during a fit of temporary insanity'. The sum of £50 was allocated to each of his two children, to be held in trust by the chief constable and the senior sergeant and deposited in the Post Office Savings Bank.

In 1909, following an earlier recommendation made by the HMI, a royal crown was placed on the collars of the tunics. The same applied to most other Borough Police forces and appears to have been part of a general campaign to show that the police were the servants of the crown, rather than of the local authority. In July 1911 the Ramsgate force introduced straw helmets like those worn in Margate and some other forces.

With the commencement of the First World War, the losses from mobilisation were offset by the appointment of a further 10 constables, 26 First Police Reserves and a number of special constables. Public reaction to the 1914 Special Constables Act was not universally enthusiastic and the Watch Committee invited 'public spirited citizens to enter their names on the suggested register'. However, the shortage of volunteers led the authorities to use their powers under the Municipal Corporations Act to compel 500 householders to serve or face a fine of £5.

William Jones retired in 1916, his resignation being accepted by the Watch Committee 'with regret', and his deputy, Samuel Flowers Butler, was appointed chief constable. For the first time, the chief constable was not required to live over the police station and occupied a rented house in the town.

During 1920/21 there was violent opposition to the loading of coke onto two German ships in Ramsgate harbour which developed into a series of full-scale riots. Totally overwhelmed, the town had to call for 50 men from the Metropolitan Police and other reinforcements from the Kent County Constabulary, Margate, Gravesend, Dover, Maidstone, Rochester and Tunbridge Wells. Canterbury sent 10 constables who remained at the seaside town for five days. The members of the town's Mounted Police were very much involved, one of whom was dragged off his mount by the mob and seriously manhandled but another officer quickly mounted the steed and continued the fray. The riots were put down only after several baton charges.

Like Folkestone, Ramsgate was quick to consider using women officers and in June 1919 the Watch Committee agreed to the appointment of a Miss Whitelegg. However, she resigned in October 1921 through ill-health and was not replaced. In 1925/6 there were numerous demands from various women's organisations for the appointment of another police woman but they were all told that the Watch Committee did not consider the present time 'opportune'. Nevertheless, in the light of renewed pressure from the Home Office, a Mrs Baldwin was appointed in 1927 'to assist the police' at £30 p.a.[45] Mrs Baldwin served for some six years before resigning and was replaced by Annie Robinson. It is not clear what happened to Miss Robinson as there is no further mention of her in the records. Despite the force's experience with police women, the chief constable of Ramsgate is on record as saying in February 1941 that he considered that none were necessary at that time. Given the fact that the country was at war and there were large numbers of troops around, this seems a rather strange decision.

In 1929 Cavendish House in Cavendish Road, Ramsgate was purchased for conversion to a police and ambulance station and mortuary complex and remained in use as the police station for the rest of the century. In 1930 Ramsgate considered setting up a police/fire box system 'like that in Liverpool' and by the end of 1935 there were boxes at various places in the Borough. In the same year Ramsgate got its first light motor car, a Hillman ('for a price not exceeding £150') as well as an Austin 10. The Hillman was later replaced by a Hillman 'Hawk'.

Having taken over command of the force in the middle of a world war, Samuel Butler remained in charge until the middle of the next one. In the early part of the Second World War, he was injured in an air raid and was given a month's sick leave to help him recover. William Palmer, the chief constable of nearby Margate, agreed to keep an eye on the force during this period but refused any payment for the extra work involved. Samuel Butler resumed his duties after convalescence but never fully recovered and, when the force was amalgamated with the Kent County Constabulary in 1943, he was happy to retire on a well-earned pension.

In 1889 the **Rochester** Watch Committee received a letter from the Home Department regarding Sergeant John Ealden, '… who is 60 years of age, suffers from rheumatism, worn out and unfit for further service'.[46] Sergeant Ealden was retired on two-thirds pay. In the same year, 57-year-old Sergeant Charles Cockerell was also superannuated on two-thirds pay, being '… permanently unfit through heart disease, varicose veins and a rupture'. Perhaps concerned by this manifestation of ill-health,

96   Rochester City Police, civic parade (javelin duty), 1920s.

an order was issued that any Rochester constable on the sick list was to report daily to the Police Office unless the police surgeon certified he was unable to leave his home.

After July 1892 silver piping was sewn to the left arm of Rochester men in the 'Merit' class (i.e., ten years' unblemished service). For the first time in that same year, warrant cards were issued for use when on plain clothes duty but there was a wait until 1903 before official pocket books were issued. Also in 1903 a new type of police belt was issued with a 'snake' fastening instead of the large plate buckle.

Changes also occurred in the hierarchy of the force and, from 1 January 1897, Superintendent Broadbridge was re-titled chief constable. A year later, Sergeants Brooks and Dowsett were made inspectors to assist him in his supervisory functions. In October 1902, Chief Constable Broadbridge died in office having been in the force for more than 43 years, 25 of them as the officer in charge. The loss of his skills and experience was sorely felt and there were many tributes to his sterling service to the City. The vacancy was ultimately offered to 42-year-old Sub-Divisional Inspector Alfred Arnold who had served 24 years in the Metropolitan Police and who took up his post on 20 January 1903 when the whole force was paraded at the Corn Exchange to be introduced by the mayor to its new chief constable.

The River Police was supplied with a new boat in 1894 but, two years later, it was smashed whilst it was moored at the head of Strood pier. A new 14-foot oak craft was delivered in January 1897. Applications were made at the beginning of 1904 for another new boat for the River Section but it is not clear whether this was ever provided. An offer of a steam launch for police use was declined because of the high cost of maintenance and so the river constables had still to rely on their strong arms and a good pair of oars. With the dawn of the new century, the River Section was augmented by promoting one of the constables to sergeant and appointing two more constables, making a total strength of one sergeant and five constables. Since there were only 29 constables to patrol the town itself, this represented a considerable proportion of the force's strength.

It was widely believed around this time that the river sergeant had somehow upset Chief Constable Arnold who declared that there would never be another such appointment. This tale may be purely apocryphal but it is true that, in January 1911, PC Hill was promoted to chief boatman with the pay of a sergeant, and the sergeant's post appears to have been dropped. The chief boatman did not wear sergeant's stripes but wore a badge in the form of a circle of rope tied in a reef knot, crossed by a pair of oars. The rank of sergeant was not re-introduced until 1937.

During the 19th century a police station had been provided in the area of Rochester where Corporation Street now runs but it had ceased to be used as such by 1907 when the new road was built. Even the new police station suffered problems, the chief constable reporting in 1903 that, in view of the class of prisoner housed in the cells, it was impossible to keep the bedding free from vermin. The straw bedding was discontinued and prisoners had to be content with just a pillow, covered with painted canvas.

Rochester City employed constables on plainclothes patrols towards the end of the 19th century and the situation was formalised in 1903 when two constables were officially appointed to patrol in *mufti* on either side of the Medway bridge. They had considerable success – so much so that the same year one of them, Constable Moon, was promoted to detective sergeant, the first time the word 'detective' was used in the force, this innovation presumably imported from London by the new chief constable.

Perhaps as compensation for not being considered for the post of chief constable, Inspector Brooks was made a chief inspector in 1903. With the retirement of the other inspector, it was decided to abolish the rank and appoint instead two sub-inspectors, one for day duty and one for nights. This provided an establishment under the chief constable of one chief inspector, two sub-inspectors, four sergeants, 35 constables, one chief boatman (sergeant) and six river constables. Chief Inspector Brooks remained in post until he died in July 1920, having served the force for 45 years. He was not replaced, no doubt partly as an economy measure as, by this time, the nation was in dire financial straits.

When the Inspector of Constabulary suggested in 1910 that men in all forces should be trained as mounted police, there was considerable opposition and the Guildford Watch Committee launched a petition against the proposal. Many of the forces in Kent supported this petition, including Rochester, but, despite this, later that same year two constables and two police reservists in the City force were being trained in equestrian skills by a sergeant-major of the East Kent Yeomanry.[47] Some forces soon dropped the idea of a Mounted Section but others continued with it for many years. Francis Horlock remembered that, when he joined the Rochester force in 1923, it had an *ad hoc* Mounted Section under the command of Sergeant Eddie Pattenden, known as 'The Galloping Major'. Cab horses were hired as required from local livery stables and were quite untrained, usually disconcerting their riders. However, in July 1934 all the saddlery and tack was disposed of as the force no longer had any mounted constables.

97 Mounted patrol, *c.*1920.

Towards the end of 1915, the Home Office instructed that men of military age (i.e., up to 41) could be attested for military service with the Army Reserve.[48] Both regulars and First Police Reserves were included but it was agreed that they would not be called up without the chief constable's consent. Although optional, virtually every eligible man applied; even in the small Rochester City force this amounted to 31 men. In 1917 the Home Office called for a further supply of men for Army service and Rochester was obliged to provide four single, fit young men, followed shortly by another three. All returned safely home at the end of the War except one, Constable Eve, who was killed in action.

Some respite for the river boatmen came in September 1914 when a 20-foot motorboat, the *Curlew*, was purchased for £100. For the first time the crew had a small cabin in which to escape the worst of the weather. The decision to buy this craft was largely due to the onset of the war and the difficulty in effectively patrolling the river with just rowing boats. The *Curlew* lasted until the early 1920s when it was found that spares for the engine were unobtainable and, in 1923, a new 20-foot launch, the *Alfred*, was supplied by Short Brothers, the local boat and flying-boat manufacturers. This was supplemented by two rowing boats and a stores boat. The *Alfred*, which had been built for and rejected by the Hastings fishermen, proved equally unsuitable for police work but it could not be replaced until 1932 for financial reasons.

The Home Secretary sent a letter to all police authorities in November 1924, suggesting that consideration should be given to appointing women officers to deal with cases involving women and children. The reaction of the chief constable of Rochester was perhaps typical of the way in which this idea was received by most of the intensely conservative police forces. Chief Constable Arnold declared firmly that, in view of the few cases that arose in which women police could be of assistance, he did not consider it necessary to employ any in the city. Arrangements had already been made for Sister Jones of the Church Army to take statements or obtain evidence

98 Rochester City Police, 1924.

where sexual offences had been committed. The subject refused to go away, however, and in 1927 the Rochester Diocesan Board of Women's Work urged '… the great need for Women Police in the Diocese'. The chief constable remained unmoved.

Rochester City's first foray into the world of motor vehicles came in 1927 with the acquisition of a new Morris ambulance. By now the number of vehicles on the roads of Britain had increased to 1,900,000 and a resolution by the Rochester Watch Committee in December 1928 drew attention to the drain on manpower that this represented. It recommended that the cost of traffic control should be borne by Central Government as it was '… becoming increasingly necessary, in the interests of public safety, especially in the Summer, to detail officers for traffic control work, which meant that the force was inadequate to perform its ordinary duties'.[49]

The installation of traffic lights at the Old Prince of Orange crossing in Gravesend in 1929 and the Angel Corner in Rochester in 1931 helped to ease the problems somewhat in those towns, although there was some doubt as to the legality of the former.

In 1931 Rochester bought a Sunbeam combination which was part-exchanged for a Morris 'Major' saloon in 1933. A patrol car of unspecified make[50] was bought in 1935 to replace the Morris 'Major', plus a Sunbeam Talbot two-seater sports car in

99 Rochester City Police Ambulance, *c*.1928.

100   Rochester City Police, 1937.

1936. Rochester bought six bicycles in 1937 to replace two purchased in 1911 and a further ten in 1941 in case of a breakdown in communications due to enemy action.

In June of that year a 35-foot RAF launch was purchased from Chatham Dock-yard and became the *Roffen*. This was replaced in 1939 by a smaller (and slower) 20-foot launch, which confusingly also took the name of *Roffen*. A second vessel, the *Pamela*, was acquired towards the end of the same year from the Port Health Authority. This 20-footer was comparatively comfortable and two men could sleep on board. When the force was amalgamated with the County Constabulary in 1943, the motor launch *Pamela* continued to be used by the new joint force for some time and the members of the River Section became part of the County's Marine Section.

In February 1931 Chief Constable Arnold retired due to ill health. He had then been in the police service for a total of 52 years – 24 with the Metropolitan Police and 28 in Rochester – which must be something of a record. Fifty applications were received for the vacancy, including Inspector R.C.M. Jenkins from Canterbury City (who later became chief constable of Folkestone and ultimately deputy chief constable of Kent) and Inspector Herbert Allen from Gravesend Borough. The latter was duly appointed and obviously brought some new ideas with him as one of his first actions was to seek authority to buy a typewriter for £5! However, his stay was to be a short one, as in November 1933 he was appointed chief constable of Huddersfield.

Fifty-eight applications were received for the vacancy created by Allen's resignation and the short list included Inspector Jenkins again, together with the acting chief constable of Newark, Marshall Bolt (later to be chief constable of Maidstone) and Rochester's own Inspector Horwood. Despite the strong competition from local forces, the Watch Committee decided in 1934 to appoint Inspector H.P. Hind from Nottingham.

Mr Hind too was to have a short stay, being appointed chief constable of Bath in September 1937 at which point the Watch Committee took a rather surprising deci-sion. The vacancy was again advertised and 11 applicants were shortlisted, including Detective Inspector Horwood (the local candidate) and Mr Jenkins, who was by now the chief constable of Penzance. However, despite the competition from experienced policemen, the Watch Committee settled on Lt. Cdr. W.J.A. Willis, MVO, OBE,

101 Tunbridge Wells Police, *c.*1888.

CGM, RN from Gillingham, who took up his post in December 1937. Just why they chose a man with apparently no police experience is not known, although it is true that he went on to become chief constable of Bedfordshire and ended up as one of His Majesty's Inspectors of Constabulary.

Perhaps as a consolation prize, Inspector Horwood was made chief inspector and deputy chief constable in 1939 by which time Chief Constable Willis' tenure was drawing to a close. In April 1940 at long last Kenneth Horwood was made chief constable and was still in post in April 1943 when the Force amalgamated with the Kent County Constabulary.

In 1889 **Tunbridge Wells** was incorporated and became a borough for the first time. The Police Committee became a statutory Watch Committee and the already-existing police force became a true borough force, remaining under the control of Superintendent Embery until his retirement the following year. In May 1891 Sub-inspector John Cuthbert Allison of the Liverpool City Police took over as chief constable but he too proved something of a disappointment. In July 1893 the district auditor reported to the Watch Committee that '… he had required the Chief Constable to furnish him with particulars regarding the accounts of the Police contingent expenses and that the Chief Constable had failed to keep the appointment'.

The town clerk reported that he had been unable to obtain any explanation of the chief constable's absence but the reason soon became clear, since an audit of the chief constable's accounts revealed that he had appropriated money belonging to the Corporation. His appointment was therefore terminated and the £150 security bond taken out by him was forfeited. The total sum missing from official funds was not disclosed.

102   Tunbridge Wells vehicle fleet, 1942.

The short list for the post consisted of six inspectors, plus the chief constable of Cambridge.[51] The final choice fell on Inspector Charles Prior from Reigate who served from 1893 until 1921 when he retired. The vacancy again proved attractive and the short-list included the chief constable of Canterbury (B.H.A. Carlton), a superintendent, three inspectors and one lieutenant-colonel. In the end Captain S.A. Hector, the clerk inspector in the Lancaster Borough Police, was selected and stayed at Tunbridge Wells from 1921 until 1927 when he was appointed chief constable of Coventry.

It was around this time that the Tunbridge Wells force became motorised and it had a motorcycle in the 1920s which was exchanged in 1929 for a car and a police ambulance. A BSA combination was purchased in 1927 and a BSA 'Birmingham' in 1934. By 1939 Tunbridge Wells had a Mobile Squad commanded by a sergeant and possessed a fleet of vehicles consisting of an ambulance, a utility van, a car, a general purpose van, two patrol cars[52] and four motorcycles.

A number of police boxes was erected in the late 1930s, linked to the police station adjoining the town hall with its entrance onto Calverley Street. In 1939 the modern town hall, library/museum and police station complex on the junction of Crescent Road and Mount Pleasant Road was opened and continues in use to the present day.

On the departure of Captain Hector the Watch Committee did not bother to advertise and appointed Inspector Guy Carlton as the new chief constable. Guy Carlton had joined the Tunbridge Wells Police as a constable in 1902 and so had 25 years' service in the borough at the time of his appointment as chief constable. When the force was merged with the Kent County Constabulary in 1943, Guy Carlton retired from the service. On the whole, Tunbridge Wells seems to have been somewhat unfortunate in its choice of chief officer. Of the 10 men appointed in a period of just over a century, one died, two moved on to better jobs, one was inefficient, one disappeared, two ran off with the money and only three served to collect their pension.

Four

A United Force
1943-2000

An order was made on 1 April 1943 for the temporary but compulsory amalgamation of the remaining nine borough and city forces in the county with the Kent County Constabulary. Although applied as an emergency wartime measure, these forces never regained their previous autonomy and the scope of the Kent County Constabulary was to remain more or less the same until the present day. The county divisional boundaries were temporarily unchanged (with the exception of the St Augustine's Division which merged with the City of Canterbury to form a new combined division), the former boroughs and cities forming new divisions.

Sir Percy Sillitoe, the chief constable of Glasgow, was appointed to take command of this new combined force, the post of chief constable being vacant following the death of Captain Davison the previous year. On the day before the amalgamation Major R.L. Surtees retired and was briefly replaced as senior ACC and deputy chief constable by Chief Superintendent Shepherd who had been the chief clerk since 1934. The chief constables of the nine borough forces were given the option of taking assistant chief constable posts within the county or retiring.

Marshall H. Bolt, the chief constable of Dover, accepted the post of ACC No.1 District, based at Tunbridge Wells; Kenneth A. Horwood, the chief constable of Rochester City, accepted the post of ACC No.2 District, based at Rochester; R.C.M. Jenkins, the recently appointed chief constable of Folkestone, accepted the post of ACC No.3 District, based at Folkestone; William Palmer from Margate accepted the post of ACC No.4 District. All the other borough chief constables retired or took other posts outside the county.

The new Divisional structure was as follows :

No. 1 District:
Malling Division (Supt. Jordan MM)
Sevenoaks Division (Supt. Molineux)
Tonbridge Division (Supt. Cook)
Maidstone Division (C/Insp. Beslee)
Tunbridge Wells Division (C/Insp. Sly)

No. 2 District:
Chatham Division (Supt. Webb MM)
Dartford Division (Supt. Baker)
Swale Division (Supt. Cash)
Rochester Division (C/Insp. Large)
Gravesend Division (Supt. Greatorex)

No. 3 District:
Ashford Division (T/Supt. Broughton)
Canterbury Division (Supt. Hall)
Folkestone Division (C/Insp. Hollands)
Margate Division (C/Insp. Fleet)

No. 4 District:
Wingham Division (Supt. Wheatley)
Ramsgate Division (C/Insp. Butcher)
Dover Division (T/Supt. Saddleton)

Headquarters:
Admin. Supt. Woolgar;
CID Det. Supt. F.H. Smeed;
Traffic: Supt. Deacon

103 Radio masts at Police Headquarters.

In February 1944 Dartford (former County Division) and Gravesend (former Borough force) were merged to form a new 'Thames' Division with its headquarters at Gravesend. At the same time Chatham (County) and Rochester (City) Divisions were merged into the 'Medway' Division with headquarters at Chatham. The Chief Inspectors who had been in charge of the former borough divisions remained in post in charge of the newly created sub-division and as second-in-command of the new division.

In May 1944 ACC Jenkins was transferred to force headquarters in Maidstone as the chief constable's executive officer. Consequently, Nos. 3 and 4 Districts (East Kent) were merged under the command of the deputy chief constable, William Palmer. A further change occurred in September the same year when ACC Marshall Bolt was selected for Special Duties at the Home Office. He was not replaced and his district (No.1) was merged with

104 Sir Percy Sillitoe, Chief Constable of Kent, 1943-6.

No.2 to form a West Kent District under ACC Kenneth Horwood. This meant that the force now had one deputy chief constable and two assistant chief constables and was divided into two Districts, a situation which was to continue for some 30 years.

It is a remarkable fact that the amalgamation of 10 disparate forces of varying sizes and levels of efficiency went off comparatively smoothly with no serious problems. This was largely due to the skills of the new chief constable who had no particular

105 Police boat *Marina*.

106 Original *Marina* police boat.

107 New police boat *Marina*.

108 Rural officer on LE Velocette.

allegiance to any of the 10 forces and was seen as a 'clean pair of hands'. Sir Percy also had an extraordinarily wide experience of police work in Africa and in Great Britain. Around this time the opportunity was taken to reorganise the force's numbering system and every member, including the former Borough men, was given a number 'for life', originally based on rank and seniority. This system continues to the present day with recruits being allocated the next available number.

The amalgamation meant that there was a wide variety of uniforms and badges being worn which wartime restrictions did not allow to be immediately harmonised. It was ordered that, with the exception of the former borough chief constables who were taking up appointments as assistant chief constables within the County force, all men would continue to wear their existing uniforms. It was not until the end of 1946 that an order was issued that all were now to wear the county helmet and plate. Caps were only to be worn by inspectors and above, rural sergeants and constables, motorcyclists,[1] Traffic Department personnel and policewomen. Six months later a further order was issued to the effect that inspectors and above would wear white shirts.

With the Rochester City Police responsible for the River Medway from Sheerness to Snodland, and the Gravesend Police overlooking the Thames Estuary, the County force had no commitment to police the rivers until after the amalgamation. In the first instance, the Rochester boat, the *Pamela*, was taken on the strength, with its crew, and continued to patrol the Medway as before. However, once the war had ended, the force set about replacing the existing craft with two 45-foot RAF launches. The first of these became the *Marina*[2] and the other, originally *Security*, became the *Alexandra*.

The new Chief Constable brought Superintendent William Deacon with him from the Glasgow Police to take charge of a new Traffic Department. This consisted of a Headquarters, a Garage and four operational Districts, based on Tunbridge Wells, Rochester, Folkestone and Margate.

In the first years of the Second World War the Kent County Constabulary had a fleet of 40 motorcycles and also had the use of a huge La Salle American drop-head car, FUW 916, which had been given to the force by an unknown benefactor, who no doubt found himself unable to run this 37 h.p. monster on the virtually non-existent petrol ration. It also obtained two MG saloons, a Wolseley 10, a second-hand Morris 8, four Vauxhall 14s, eight Hillman 10s and 11 reconditioned motorcycles. Numerous other vehicles were obtained during and immediately after the War, too many to list here but including 20 Indian motorcycles on loan from the Fire Service. By the end of the war, the County Constabulary was using a bewildering array of motor vehicles such as 23 Austins, three Fords, nine Hillmans, 30 MGs,[3] three Morris cars, one Standard, nine Vauxhalls, 20 Wolseleys, eight vans and five ambulances. There were also 16 AJS motor cycles, seven Ariels, 13 BSAs, 13 Indians, nine Matchlesses, one New Imperial, four Nortons, one P & M, one Rudge, seven Triumphs and 28 Velocettes. These machines were all in the 350 to 600cc range and many were evidently well past their prime for, within two years, most had been disposed of and the motorcycle fleet then consisted of 90 Ariel 350s, 13 Indian 500cc solos and four Indian 500cc combinations.

The Kent County Constabulary was not a pioneer in the matter of women police and it was not until 1942 that an advertisement in the *Police Review* for a woman inspector indicated a somewhat reluctant decision to conform. In the event, this post was not filled until May 1944, when Sergeant Barbara Denis de Vitre was appointed on transfer from Leicester City and promoted to Inspector. An original 'high-flyer', with previous service in Cairo and Sheffield, Miss de Vitre remained with the force less than a year, before being appointed staff officer to His Majesty's Inspectors of Constabulary and ultimately became the first woman Assistant HMI. Nevertheless, she was instrumental in setting up a new policewomen's department and nine new female recruits were appointed on 8 July 1944. The uniform worn was based on that worn in the ATS and WAAF during the war, a rather severe and unflattering, military style tunic with a belt and four pockets which did nothing for the figure. In July 1945, Woman Constable C. Mackenzie was transferred from the Lanarkshire Police on promotion to w/sergeant. She was further promoted to w/inspector on 13 August 1945 – constable to inspector in just over a month! In February 1946 one of the first of the new women constables, Woman Constable Lewis, was promoted to sergeant with some 18 months' service. The female contingent then consisted of one inspector, one sergeant and 17 constables.

As the war drew to its inevitable close, the policemen who had joined the Armed Forces began to trickle back and so the number of Police War Reserves needed to be reduced; they were given the option of resigning, being discharged or accepting a short-term engagement (if offered). At the end of 1945, 206 PWRs took the opportunity to resign and most of the First Police Reserves, who were mainly retired policemen and were now getting on in years, also took the opportunity finally to hang up their helmets.

It now became apparent that the force would soon have to get back to peace-time policing and so, in June 1944, a series of refresher courses was provided for officers up to the rank of inspector and later extended to those returning from the armed forces. The years following the Second World War saw a great boom in recruiting; men who had left the force to serve in the Armed Forces were beginning to return and other ex-servicemen were looking for a job with security, good pay and a pension. Conse-quently, in April 1946, responsibility for basic training was transferred to a series of District Training Centres, that for the South East being located at the former Star and

Garter Home at Sandgate.[4] Superintendent Webb of the Kent County Constabulary was seconded there as commandant and four Kent sergeants were also seconded as instructors. Training was essentially law-based but physical education and the old faithful, foot drill, were also included. Since virtually all recruits had been in the armed forces, these less academic pursuits did not present any great problems and those leaving the Centre were probably the smartest and fittest the force had ever seen.

But recruitment and training took time and there remained a shortage of police immediately after the war. An obvious solution was to move those officers engaged on duties which did not call for police training back onto the street, replacing them by civilians, who were in any case cheaper! The WAPCs in particular provided a very useful source of recruitment; those who had been employed in offices as typists and telephonists handed in their uniform and became

109   Major (Sir) John Ferguson, Chief Constable of Kent, 1946-1958.

Civilian Employees (CEs) while those who had been employed on driving duties were supplied with a slightly different uniform and became 'Uniformed Employees' (UEs). As time went on, the number of civilian employees grew; they were employed as cleaners, vehicle mechanics, drivers, storekeepers, etc. as well as in the more usual office and driving jobs.

In April 1946 a Driving School was opened at Force Headquarters to provide courses for members of the force who were unable to drive or who failed the force test of competency. Superintendent Deacon and two constables were appointed Ministry of Transport Examiners and could test and pass (or fail!) police officers attending basic driving courses. The first of many advanced driving courses was held in April 1952.

In January 1946, the amalgamation being successfully completed and the war now over, Sir Percy moved on to a new challenge as Director of Security at the War Office. The next incumbent was yet another army officer, albeit one with considerable police experience. Major (later Sir) John Ferguson had had a distinguished military career with the Durham Light Infantry. When he retired in 1932 he joined the Metropolitan Police as a chief constable, rising to deputy assistant commissioner in 1935. In 1938 he became the commandant of the newly-formed Hendon Police College and was appointed chief constable of the Sussex Joint Police Force in 1943.[5] In 1945 he returned to the Metropolitan Police as assistant commissioner before being appointed to Kent in 1946. He was knighted in the Coronation Honours in May 1953.

William Palmer, OBE, the recently-appointed deputy chief constable died in April 1947 whilst still serving and ACC Jenkins was then made the DCC and First ACC.

110 Kent County Constabulary senior officers, 1954.

The war caused extensive damage to the nation's housing stock and Kent was particularly badly affected. Many of the houses in 'Hell-Fire Corner' were destroyed or badly damaged and there was a widespread housing shortage. This presented particular problems for the police, anxious to recruit men leaving the Forces, many of whom were married or about to be married. By 1949, 68 married officers were living in furnished or unfurnished rooms and another 25 were living apart from their wives and families. Demand for any existing police houses was therefore keen and, when a rural police house became vacant, a notice was circulated in General Orders, inviting applications from officers interested in taking over the beat and the associated house. A typical example was the house at Throwley Forstal (Swale Division) which, in 1947, was advertised as consisting of '… four bedrooms and three rooms downstairs. It has no bathroom, lighting is by oil lamp and there is a flush closet with septic tank'.

The police house at The Street, Stockbury was also offered, described as having no bathroom, an outside WC with flush, no gas or electricity. There was no shortage of applicants for these houses.

To overcome the housing problem, the Kent County Constabulary embarked on a courageous and innovative housing programme, building numerous standard police houses and purchasing a number of 'spec.' built properties. In 1950 alone, 101 houses were built and four others purchased and in 1953 another 156 were built, including 18 of the superior type for senior officers.

Despite the disbandment of the First Police Reserve, the Kent County Constabulary still took on FPRs for summer duties as before. In 1947, 40 FPRs were taken on specifically to help out in the various seaside towns in the county between April and September. They were required to be former policemen or otherwise specially qualified for the work, fit and of good character. They were issued with normal police uniform and paid 25s. a week. This practice was repeated in future years and,

111 Standard police houses.

apart from a brief suspension in 1952 for financial reasons, continued well into the 1960s.

Others, like Tom Goodall, holder of the Military Medal and Bar, stayed on for a number of years. Working in the Sittingbourne police station's clerks' office, this stalwart finally handed in his uniform in January 1956, still as smart and as upright as he had been as a young soldier in the Buffs during the Great War and as a sergeant in the Kent County Constabulary years before the latest conflict.

On 1 May 1948 Chief Constable Ferguson took the opportunity to restructure the force once more into 12 divisions, plus a Reserve (Headquarters) Division and, for the first time, a Traffic Division. The structure was now as follows:

'A' (Maidstone) Division (Supt. Woolgar)
'B' (Medway) Division (Supt. Broughton)
'C' (Gravesend) Division (Supt. Baker)
'D' (Sevenoaks) Division (Supt.Beslee)
'E' (Tunbridge Wells) Division (Supt. Sly)
'F' (Canterbury) Division (Supt. Butcher)
'G' (Sittingbourne) Division (Supt. Cash)
Admin (Supt. Saxton)

'H' (Ashford) Division (Supt. Redsell)
'J' (Folkestone) Division (Supt. Large)
'K' (Dover) Division (Supt. Saddleton)
'L' (Ramsgate) Division (Supt. Greatorex)
'M' (Margate) Division (Supt. Fleet)
'T' (Traffic) Division (Supt. Deacon)
'R' (Headquarters) CID (D/Ch.Supt. Smeed)

The Traffic Department thus became a division, with vehicles and men at Maidstone, Tonbridge, Tunbridge Wells, Rochester, Canterbury, and Seabrook. The division's particular role was the prevention of accidents by example, advice and, where necessary, prosecution. All the other divisions consisted of two or more sub-divisions, under a chief inspector or inspector.

In 1949 the County Force introduced the first 'Noddy' bikes – 149cc Velocette LE water- cooled motorcycles – which proved a great success, and the following year 24 Triumph 500cc 'Speed Twins' were supplied to the Traffic Division. Twenty-six more Velocettes arrived in 1951, including the larger-engined (192 cc) version, and a further

112   Rural officer on LE Velocette.

113   Radio-equipped Triumph 'Speed Twin', *c.*1958.

40 in 1952. These extremely quiet machines were invaluable in the rural areas and farmers welcomed their use in combating the theft of fruit and fowls. In 1956 these lightweight machines were augmented by the introduction of the Norman 'Nippy' moped but this proved to be much less of a success. The motor car fleet was also being revised and, in the 1950s, consisted of Austin A70s and A40s, Ford Anglias, Populars and Consuls, Hillman Minxes, Humber Hawks and Super Snipes, Morris Isis and Singer 1500s, plus four new MG TFs.

Although Marconi pioneered the 'wireless' telegraph at the end of the 19th century it was some half-century before the police in Kent took an interest. Early in the Second World War, Dover became the first force in Kent to have a radio car, which was in contact with the newly-built Borough Police Headquarters. The Kent Police was without any radio system until its own VHF scheme was brought into use in 1951, shared with the Kent Fire Brigade, and 70 police vehicles were fitted with radios. This scheme was controlled from a new 'Information Room' in the attic of Police Headquarters, forming part of the Central Registry.

A major uniform change occurred in the early 1950s when open-necked tunics were issued to sergeants and constables, together with blue shirts. These were for wear in the summertime only, the older, closed-neck tunic being retained for winter wear. However, by the mid-1950s, the latter had been withdrawn and the open-neck tunic was worn all the year round.

On 4 June 1951, a masked man carrying a Sten gun was seen by witnesses in the Luton area of Chatham. He fired a burst in their direction and they understandably fled. An hour later they strolled into the police station at Chatham to report the incident and Sergeant William Langford, PC Brown and PC Alan Baxter attended the scene in the rather ancient police van. For some reason, possibly because the report of the incident was treated with some

114   Male and female cadets, 1970s.

scepticism, they were not armed, nor was any armed back up or the force tracker dog asked to attend.

On arrival at the field where the gunman had last been seen in a shed, the sergeant went to investigate, leaving PC Brown at the edge of the field and PC Baxter in the van with the radio. On looking through a broken window, Sergeant Langford saw two girls with a man who fired a few shots in his direction. He quickly withdrew and the trio ran from the shed towards the van. A number of shots were heard and, when the sergeant arrived back at the van, the fugitives had disappeared and PC Baxter was lying in the roadway in a pool of blood. The van's radio was apparently defective and so the sergeant took the wheel to drive the wounded policeman to hospital where he died of his wounds.

By this time the assailant had been identified as Alan Derek Poole, an army deserter, who had been living with the girls in the nearby woods. A major hunt was organised and some two hundred soldiers and policemen searched the area. The two girls, absconders from a remand home, were soon found but there was no sign of Poole. It was later discovered that he had returned to his parents' house in Symons Avenue, Chatham which was quickly surrounded. Poole opened fire on the besieging police who returned the fire and fired tear gas grenades into the house. After two hours had passed without further incident, Chief Constable Ferguson, who had arrived to take charge of the incident in person, ordered a direct assault on the house. Poole was found lying dead in an upstairs room, a police marksman's bullet having punctured both lungs.

But to return to more mundane matters, the roads in the county in the 1950s were woefully inadequate for the modern traffic, being little changed since the days of the horse and cart. This, coupled with the fact that the Kent seaside resorts were still very popular (the rush to the Costa Brava was still a few years away), meant that the main roads in the county were grossly overloaded, especially during summer weekends. A popular Sunday evening entertainment for those living alongside the main roads leading from London to the coast was to sit outside their houses and watch the traffic crawl by (TV had yet to become the accepted evening pastime). They were often rewarded

115 Kent County Constabulary Centenary Parade.

by the sight of huge traffic jams, with both vehicles and drivers rapidly becoming overheated.

The practice of taking on young men as junior clerks had been suspended during the war but was resumed in April 1948 when arrangements were made for up to twenty young men to be taken on. Three years later, in October 1951, the Kent Police Cadet Force was formed; 13 former junior clerks transferred to the new body to form the nucleus of what was to become a significant, albeit short-lived, part of the police service.

In 1951 the force acquired its first police dog, a Doberman Pinscher called 'Mountbrowne Justice' and Constable Lawrie was trained as its handler. 'Justice' became the first of a series of police dogs and PC Lawrie the first handler in what was to become a substantial dog section.

Just after the Second World War a number of English police officers was seconded to the Control Commission in Germany to help re-organise the German policing system. As they began to return, demands arose from other quarters. In 1950/1 two Inspectors went to Greece as part of a British Police Mission and, with the beginning of the Malayan crisis, two or three Kent men volunteered for transfer to the Malaysian Police Service as assistant superintendents. The mid-1950s saw the troubles in Cyprus come to a head and, in 1955, four sergeants and 13 constables from Kent volunteered for secondment, with a chief inspector, three sergeants and eight constables the next year. Service in the Cyprus Police was experienced by a number of men who later served in the County, including Chief Constable Geoffrey White and Chief Constable Frank Jordan. Sadly, Constable Rooney (who had transferred to Kent from the RUC in 1952) was shot and killed by a terrorist in March 1956 while serving as a sergeant on the island. All the seconded officers had returned by 1960.

Crime continued to flourish but in some cases the burglar got more than he bargained for. In November 1952, Noah Eastwood, a professional housebreaker, broke into a house in Chatham where Sidney Taylor, a motor mechanic, lived. Unknown to Eastwood, Taylor was so fed up with being burgled that he had rigged up a booby trap. He had fitted a large metal trunk with a spring gun which would go off if anyone opened the trunk, shooting them in the legs. Unfortunately for Eastwood, he kneeled down in front of the trunk to open it and, when the gun went off, both barrels blasted him in the abdomen and he died within hours.[6] Taylor was convicted of manslaughter but the jury recommended leniency. The judge agreed and gave Taylor an absolute discharge.

The women police branch was steadily growing in importance and in 1952 the post of w/inspector was upgraded to chief inspector and five women sergeants were appointed. Also, after many years during which the CID was the exclusive preserve of the male members of the force, WPC Amy May was appointed the first female detective constable in 1951. Then, in 1964, the head of the Women Police was upgraded to superintendent and two more sergeants were appointed with an additional chief inspector provided from 1967.

Although by the 1950s a great many police cars had been fitted with two-way VHF radio, the motorcycles remained radio-less until the end of the decade when experimental sets were fitted to the Traffic Division's Triumph 'Speed Twin' motor-cycles. These were heavy appliances which adversely affected the handling of the machines. Improvements were gradually made and radios began to be fitted to light-weight rural machines, the introduction of transistors greatly aiding the technology.

In August 1955 a near massacre occurred in Thanet when Napoleon Green, American airman stationed at Manston, forced the armoury sergeant to hand over a carbine and a revolver. A fellow black airman, Nelson Gresham, pleaded with Green to drop the weapons and was shot dead for his pains. Green then walked into the base accounts office and shot dead Master Sergeant Valesquez and wounded a female clerk. RAF Corporal Peter Grayer was the next to die, trying to protect another female assistant. Green then went on the rampage, shooting at and hitting a number of people before hi-jacking a car driven by a sergeant. Later, the sergeant managed to escape and a full-scale manhunt began, involving Kent Police and armed USAF military police. Green drove to Broadstairs where he abandoned the car with the pursuers close behind him. He ran for nearly a mile along the foreshore, exchanging shots with the following police until he suddenly stopped and turned the revolver on himself, ending his life.

In 1957 the Kent County Constabulary celebrated its centenary with a grand parade at the force headquarters in Maidstone. Some 500 regular police officers and a similar number of special constables took part and were inspected by the 20-year-old Princess Alexandra of Kent. Sir John Ferguson retired from the force shortly afterwards (October 1958) and was replaced by another soldier, Lieutenant-Colonel Geoffrey White, who had been the chief constable of Warwickshire. Colonel White had served with distinction during the Second World War and was responsible for reorganising and revitalising the Cyprus Police Force during the troubles there in the mid-1950s. He quickly made his presence felt and was widely regarded as a breath of fresh air after his rather austere predecessor. Colonel White was a comparatively young man and fired the force with his enthusiasm. Unfortunately, this energetic and friendly man was not to live to achieve his full potential and died of a heart attack whilst

attending an official function in London on 16 October 1961.

A letter to *The Times* from Field Marshal Lord Harding on 19 October 1961 helps to sum up this remarkable man:

> … Geoffrey White was dedicated to the service of the public in the maintenance of law and order. His devotion to duty coupled with his experience and wisdom in all branches of police work have seldom been equalled and never surpassed by any among the many police officers I have come across in this country and overseas.
>
> … no words can express the gratitude I owe him for his wise counsel, loyal support and cheerful good comradeship in the final campaign in Italy, the troublous early days in Trieste and throughout two anxious years in Cyprus …

116 Lt. Col. Geoffrey White, Chief Constable of Kent, 1958-1961.

Following the Second World War there was a rather more lenient attitude towards discipline. This, coupled with the fact that many of the men had by now experienced military discipline, tended to reduce the number of disciplinary cases. Those that were brought tended to be of a more serious nature than in the early days, with cases of drunkenness being almost unheard of (other than offences of driving under the influence).[7] Where members of the Constabulary were convicted by the courts they were invariably dismissed. In the fifty-odd years following the end of the war, these included cases of theft, blackmail, possession of housebreaking implements, driving whilst uninsured, indecent exposure, false pretences, attempts to pervert the course of justice, making false insurance claims, gross indecency, conspiracy, driving with excess alcohol, and supplying drugs. More banal but nonetheless embarrassing for the force, Assistant Chief Constable David Kelly was reprimanded after being fined £800 for speeding on the M2 motorway.

During the same five decades, officers were dismissed (or required to resign) for a variety of other transgressions that included:

> liaisons with married women; 'acting in an improper and familiar manner towards a female whilst on duty and in uniform' (February 1957); 'an improper approach to a male person and carrying on an improper association (September 1959);[8] making false entries in official books (August 1961); writing offensive letters to the public (April 1982); assaulting prisoner in the cells (May 1984); absence without leave and untruthfully reporting sick (May 1986); failing to obey orders and neglect of duty (May 1989); assault on wife (January 1991); failing to report presence of stolen vehicle and disposing of it without due enquiries (August 1991); conduct towards other officers while off duty at a social function (December 1991); submitting false statements and exhibits in a Road Traffic case (1992); failing to properly deal with person found in possession of drugs and failing to give a proper account of the drugs seized (April 1993); giving

a 17-year-old girl a lift in a police vehicle and his subsequent behaviour (November 1993); reporting for duty drunk, making indecent/abusive remarks to a female colleague and conduct towards other colleagues and supervisors carrying out the breath test procedure on him (November 1993); assaulting a 10-year-old while off duty (January 1994); consorting with criminals and attempting to affect the outcome of a criminal investigation (June 1994); carrying on a liaison with a vulnerable woman and making bogus telephone calls ((June 1994); using a police car for his personal use while off duty (December 1995); inappropriate physical contact and manhandling female prisoners (April 1996); racist/sexist remarks and conduct towards colleagues and possessing abusive printed material (October 1998).

Lesser penalties imposed on officers included:

> Detective constable reprimanded in May 1948 for unauthorised possession of a .22 rifle and shooting at and injuring an escaped prisoner; inspector reduced to constable for borrowing money from licensees and tradesmen in 1951; constables fined for disorderly conduct in a restaurant (February 1979); superintendent demoted to chief inspector for Road Traffic Act offences (October 1979); inspector demoted to sergeant for interviewing a juvenile prisoner improperly whilst off duty (August 1982); a number of cases of improper use of the Police National Computer for private purposes (1989); detective sergeant demoted for failing to report an accident (November 1993); inspector reduced to sergeant for associating with a known criminal (April 1997).

Over the years, conditions in the police service worsened and pay fell well below levels offered elsewhere. This, coupled with certain scandals and other factors, prompted the setting up of a Royal Commission in 1960 under Sir Henry Willink QC whose final report was embodied in the Police Act of 1964. The Commission's terms of reference included instructions to examine:

> The broad principles which should govern the pay of the constable, having regard to the nature and extent of police duties and responsibilities and the need to attract and retain an adequate number of recruits with the proper qualifications.

The case for pay was put forward vigorously by the Parliamentary Advisor to the Police Federation, James Callaghan (later to become Prime Minister) and the General Secretary of the Federation, Arthur Evans, CBE, a member of the Kent County Constabulary, who called for an increase of 40/45 per cent to bring the pay up to pre-war levels. The Commission agreed that a substantial rise was justified and issued an Interim Report in November 1960 which provided constables with a salary between £600 and £970 per annum.

In the immediate post-war years, sport played a very important role in the life of the Kent County Constabulary. The emphasis on physical fitness gradually declined and other, more social activities were permitted and even encouraged, such as fishing, first aid,[9] horticulture and photography. In the 1960s the list of County Sports Club sections included angling, athletics, badminton, bowls, cricket, first aid, football, golf, hockey, indoor games, life-saving, motoring, rugby, sailing, swimming, shooting, tennis and tug-o'-war.

The uniform did not alter to any great extent, the jacket remaining a two-pocket, unbelted affair until around 1960 when lightweight summer uniforms were issued. These were of the new pattern with four pockets and a cloth belt similar to an officer's tunic. The 1960s also saw the introduction of the NATO pullover, which was at first worn by specialist officers such as dog handlers and the Special Patrol Group, but was later extended for use throughout the force when appropriate. The female uniform was changed in 1961 to a more feminine style with a short, cut-away

117 (Sir) Richard Dawnay Lemon, Chief Constable of Kent, 1962-1974.

118 WPC, post-1961.

tunic and a shaped cap (similar to that worn by the WRAC at the end of the 20th century). Further changes were made in 1970 when a pill-box type cap with a peak was introduced, a chequered band being added in 1972. Later the 'Robin Hood' type hat with a white top was taken into use, eventually followed by the familiar 'bowler'.

On 1 April 1962, following the untimely death of Geoffrey White, 50-year-old Richard Dawnay Lemon became the new chief constable of Kent, moving up from Hampshire where he had been the chief constable since 1942. Born in 1912, educated at Uppingham School and the Royal Military Academy, Sandhurst, he joined the Metropolitan Police in 1934 under the Hendon Police College scheme. In 1939 he transferred to the Leicestershire Constabulary and was appointed chief constable of the East Riding of Yorkshire in 1939 – at the age of 27! Dawnay Lemon has been described as the last of the old-style chief constables: scion of a 'good family' and somewhat autocratic, a keen cricketer and golfer. There is no doubt, however, that he continued the progressive moves initiated by his short-lived predecessor. He was responsible for arranging contact with the French and Belgian police and for a number of organisational changes. He was knighted in the 1970 New Year's Honours List and retired in 1974. Deputy Chief Constable Jenkins retired in May 1963[10] and was replaced temporarily by ACC Kenneth Horwood, the former chief constable of Rochester. In October of that year ACC Norman Fowler took over as DCC when Mr Horwood retired. When Norman Fowler retired in his turn in April 1965,[11] ACC Eric Haslam filled the vacancy.

119 WPCs hats, 1961 to 1980.

With a view to coping with possible nuclear war, civil disorders and major incidents, Police Mobile Columns were introduced in the 1960s. These were completely self-contained units which could go anywhere at any time, carrying their tented accommodation and field kitchens and equipped with radios and field telephones. However, the cost and unwieldiness of these PMCs, coupled with the fact that the Cold War threat was diminishing, led to their abandonment in 1972, to be replaced by small support units organised on a divisional basis. Since these would not be used in a war scenario, the need for them to be completely self-contained no longer existed and these slimmer, more quickly mobilised PSUs were designed solely for disturbances and major incidents.

By the 1960s, the force had a good nucleus of well-educated, physically fit men with an average age of 36 and an average height of 5 feet 10½ inches.[12] The police service was becoming increasingly conscious of the need to recruit men and women of above average intelligence and ability in order to be able eventually to fill even the highest ranks from within the service, rather than looking to the military for its leaders. In January 1967 the Kent Police Authority approved the sending of two suitably qualified constables to the University of Kent at Canterbury, but in fact the first serving officer to obtain a degree was Inspector Bob Brice who gained an external law degree from London University in 1968.[13] The Police College at Bramshill was also willing to offer suitable students on the inspectors' course a three-year scholarship to university. Over the years a number of Kent officers benefited from this scheme, the first being Inspector Mick Eames who embarked on a law course at the University of Birmingham in October 1969. Additionally, the formation of the Open University opened up a further avenue by means of which serving officers could aspire to at least a first degree.

120   Kent County Constabulary senior officers, 1973/74.

On the operational side, the 1960s saw the phenomenon known as the 'Mods and Rockers'. Antipathy between the Mods who rode motor scooters and the Rockers who rode motorcycles was high and frequently erupted into disorder, such as in Margate during the Whitsun weekend in 1964. Police were drafted in from all over Kent under ACC Fowler who described the mob as '... nothing but undisciplined hooligans'. The trouble began at first light when kiosks were broken into, shop windows smashed and beach huts vandalised. Later, some 400 youths and girls were engaged in a pitched battle on the sea front. The police drew their batons and charged in the face of a barrage of stones and bottles. Scuffles and rampaging continued throughout the day with a huge crowd gathering around the Clock Tower, surrounded by the police who were again violently attacked. Around fifty arrests were made and at least two young men suffered knife wounds. Another particularly large gathering in Hastings over the August Bank Holiday in the same year prompted the Sussex police to call for reinforcements from Kent to try to contain the situation.

In 1943 the County Constabulary took over responsibility for the former borough police stations and, apart from a new police station built in Deal in 1930, many of the police buildings were around a hundred years old and had often suffered war damage. Canterbury was in the unique position of having two police stations – the City one in Pound Lane and the Home Division headquarters in Kirby Lane. Upon amalgamation, the East Kent District office and Canterbury Sub-Division were housed

121 Canterbury police station, Old Dover Road.

122 Sheerness police station.

in Pound Lane while the new Divisional Headquarters was at Kirby's Lane. The first new police station to be opened after the war was in Tenterden in 1956. Another new police station was built on Fort Hill, Margate in 1961 and new police stations were also built at The Brook, Chatham[14] and Cross Street, Sheerness and taken into use in 1964. New stations at Northfleet and Canterbury followed the next year and a further year on saw the opening of the new stations in Cazeneuve Street, Rochester and Central Avenue, Sittingbourne. Cranbrook police station was completed in 1968 and Swanley and Ashford in 1969. The signs of manning difficulties were beginning to be

123 Leysdown police office.

124   Margate police station, Fort Hill.

seen by 1966 when it was decided that the police stations in the smaller, quieter towns of Cranbrook, Rainham, Southborough, Broadstairs, Sandwich, Herne Bay, Faversham, Tenterden and Hythe would be closed at night, as would the Maidstone Rural Office on the Sutton Road. Northfleet police station followed suit in 1968.

In January 1965 it was decided to reorganise the force and reduce the number of divisions. Accordingly, the Tunbridge Wells and Sevenoaks Divisions were combined, as were Dover and Folkestone. Later that year the process was extended to Ramsgate and Margate. This was the first of a number of major reorganisations of the force.

In December 1965 the old information room in the attic of Police Headquarters was replaced by a new operations room, located on the ground floor of the main building and the opportunity was taken to centralise all emergency calls on the new centre, from where all radio-equipped cars were controlled. In 1956, under the old system whereby 999 calls were received at and dealt with by Divisions, the force received 7,481 emergency calls. By 1964 this had risen to 17,566 and it was antici-pated that this figure would rise in a few years to some 25,000, thus justifying the new procedure. In fact, in 1966, a total of 31,445 calls were received, greatly exceeding expectations. As if this were not enough, the number of emergency calls continued to rise, reaching 52,150 by 1973 and over 100,000 by 1980.[15]

In the two decades following the Second World War, the police housing pro-gramme had been vigorously pursued but, by 1964, the wheel had turned full circle and more and more police officers were anxious to buy their own property. This presented a problem for the Kent Police whose generous housing policy was now beginning to backfire. How could the force give officers permission to move into their own homes (and be paid a rent allowance as required by Police Regulations) when it owned so many houses itself? In 1967 it was agreed that applications would be granted subject to certain conditions and this concession was increasingly extended over the years.

Until the mid-1960s, apart from a few, cumbersome and obsolete 'walkie-talkie' sets, all radio communication had been between Force Headquarters and radio-equipped cars but in 1966 UHF 'Pocketfone' two-piece (transmitter/receiver) radios were introduced which paved the way for the era of Unit Beat Policing. Pedal and motor cycles had continued to be the basic means of transport, both in towns and in the rural areas, but this scheme, introduced in Kent in 1967, gave virtually every police officer a car or van to use. By the last quarter of the 20th century, the sight of a police officer on a bicycle was as rare as the sight of one on foot! The Unit Beat Policing Scheme, noted for its use of single-manned 'Panda' cars, was dependent on the use of personal radios; for the first time beat officers could contact their station at any time.[16] However, the Unit Beat Policing system had fatal flaws and was ultimately abandoned.

Also in 1967 the first Special Patrol Group was formed, consisting of an inspector, two sergeants, two dog handlers and eight constables. Based in West Kent, its role was to provide a rapid response support and reserve for the territorial divisions and any special operations. The East Kent SPG was formed in 1968. The Police Support Unit concept was revised in January 1974 when each of the seven Divisions had to provide at least one complete PSU, comprising an inspector, three sergeants, 30 constables, plus a motorcyclist and a coach driver. The command structure was reinforced in 1995 by the introduction of 4.2 LSE Range Rovers as Incident Command Vehicles, available for the management of incidents of all kinds. The vehicles were fitted with radio, fax, computers, etc. but were found to be too cramped and were subsequently replaced by Mercedes 'Sprinter' vans.

Sadly, 1965 saw the deaths of two young but experienced traffic officers, PC Beattie and PC Knight (No.3 Traffic Area) who were killed in a road accident on the M2 motorway. Although the most serious, this was far from the only accident involving a police vehicle and, in January 1968, concern was being expressed at the number of such incidents. An order was issued to the effect that speed limits were only to be exceeded when in immediate pursuit and the audible and visible means of warning (later often referred to as 'blues and twos') were to be used only in cases of *exceptional* urgency. The passing of red traffic lights was barred and chases at speed were confined to cases where it was absolutely essential. Two more policemen's lives were lost in October 1973 when PC Boakes and PC Ryan, both of 'F' (Canterbury) Division, were killed in a road accident. There is little doubt that the proliferation of accidents involving police vehicles was directly connected with the introduction of the Unit Beat Policing scheme, under which a large number of mostly untrained officers were driving police cars and getting involved in chases for which their inexperience did not equip them. Previously, virtually the only police cars involved in chases were the high-powered and well-equipped Traffic Patrol vehicles driven by highly-trained Traffic Division officers. There are good grounds for believing that there are still too many inadequately skilled officers driving cars and the effective closing of the Kent Police Driving School, which was held in high repute throughout the country, cannot have helped matters.

A significant management change occurred in 1967 when Mr F. Dewhirst was appointed the force's senior administrative officer. Once he had settled in, the chief clerk (a chief superintendent) stood down, thus ending a practice which had existed for around a century. This was the first step towards what was to become a major shake-up and civilianisation of the senior administrative staff. Up until 1971 the administration of each Division was in the hands of an inspector or chief inspector (Administration) with one or more clerk constables as well as a bevy of civilian clerks and typists. During the year all these posts were civilianised and the police personnel transferred to other police duties.

Around the mid-1960s, there was concern about the number of illegal immigrants, mostly from the Indian sub-continent, landing clandestinely in Kent. It was known that they gathered in the French Channel ports before making their way across the Channel by night in small boats. However, lack of contact with the French police meant that there was no detailed intelligence. To overcome this problem, Chief Constable Dawnay Lemon instructed the commander of the Channel Ports Division to go to France and make contact with his opposite numbers in the French *Police Nationale*. Accordingly, on 22 November 1968, Chief Superintendent Mills, accompanied by a French-speaking chief inspector, had a meeting with the head of police for Boulogne on board the cross-Channel ferry lying in the port; the Kent officers did not set foot in France. This was followed by further visits in which the Kent pair stayed in France to discuss the problems and further fruitful meetings were held. It quickly transpired that the French officers, with their comprehensive intelligence system, had a detailed knowledge of the prospective immigrants. The obvious question, 'Why didn't you tell us?' met with a similarly obvious response, 'You didn't ask'! Once they had been asked, the French Police were extremely co-operative and thus began a long-standing arrangement of mutual co-operation. Similar contact was later made with the Belgian Police which was to prove invaluable when the *Herald of Free Enterprise* sank in 1987.

To take advantage of this increased cross-channel co-operation, in January 1970 the French Police agreed that a cross-channel liaison officer could regularly visit their stations and generally liaise with their officers. For a highly bureaucratic national service like the French Police, this was a major step forward. When Detective Inspector Jack Harmer retired in 1982 he was replaced by Detective Sergeant Frank Gallagher.[17] This initiative was swiftly followed by a number of exchange visits which took place from 1974 with Kent policemen travelling to France and similar groups of members of the *Police Nationale* coming to Kent to study each other's methods.

Work on providing new police stations continued and a new Sevenoaks police station was completed in 1973 whilst Dartford police station in Instone Road was opened in 1974, followed by one in Windmill Street, Gravesend the following year. In 1974 a new police dog compound and house was provided at Stockbury, and a new garage for the No.1 Traffic Area was built at Coldharbour, just outside Maidstone. Although the force still owned 1,565 houses, by 1971 police officers were being actively encouraged to purchase their own houses. There were considerable problems, especially with regard to the large police housing estate adjacent to Force Headquarters (around 100 houses), and rural houses which were combined with a police office. The only answer was to sell off surplus houses and by 1987 the housing stock had dropped to 643 and 2,172 members of the force owned their own homes.

125 Visit of French Police to Dover, 1975.

In 1974 the controversial restructuring of local government in England and Wales by the Heath government occurred. To accord with this, on 1 January 1974 the force was divided into just seven divisions:

A – Maidstone/Malling
B – Medway Towns
C – Gravesend
D – Swanley/Sevenoaks/Southborough/Tunbridge Wells/Tonbridge/Cranbrook
E – Margate/Ramsgate/Deal/Dover
F – Sittingbourne/Sheerness/Faversham/Canterbury/Herne Bay/Whitstable
G – Ashford/Tenterden/Romney Marsh/Folkestone

In addition, the concept of two District Commands (East and West Kent) with an ACC responsible for each was abandoned and a centralised command structure with the three ACCs taking responsibility for particular aspects of the force – Operations

126 Barry Pain, Chief Constable of Kent, 1974–1982.

(ACC Ashley Warman), Administration & Supply (ACC Michael Gibson) and Personnel & Training (T/ACC John Cruttenden) – was substituted. The East and West Kent Support Groups (as the Special Patrol Groups were now known) became Support Groups 1 and 2, each led by a detective superintendent.

The retirement of Sir Dawnay Lemon saw the arrival of the first of the new breed of chief officers – a career policeman who had worked his way up through the ranks. A grammar school boy, Barry Pain joined the Birmingham City Police in 1951 after National Service as a 2nd Lieutenant (A/Captain) in Kenya. He progressed through the ranks until he took command of the Kent County Constabulary in 1974.

Although it had previously been convenient to appoint serving assistant chief constables as the deputy as vacancies arose, the Police Act 1964 made it compulsory for all vacancies for ACC/DCC to be advertised and the appointee to be subject to the Home Secretary's approval. Consequently, Eric Haslam became the last deputy chief constable to have served all his time in Kent. When he retired in September 1974 to take the chief constableship of the British Transport Police, Roger Birch, an ACC from Cambridge, was appointed deputy chief constable. He in turn left after four years to become the chief constable of Warwickshire and, subsequently, Sussex, where he was knighted. His replacement, Frank Jordan, was another career policeman, starting in the Staffordshire Police in 1950 and spending two years in Cyprus (1956-8). He took the job of deputy chief constable under Barry Pain in 1979.

In the latter part of the 20th century enthusiasm for sports declined and support for the annual Sports Days diminished to such an extent that, in August 1974, a 'Families Day' was organised instead. In 1977 a very successful Police Open Day was held to celebrate the Queen's Silver Jubilee and attracted a large crowd. Held on the only sunny and warm day in a period of poor (typical?) summer weather, a good attendance of around 10,000 was expected. In fact some 30,000 people turned up at the force headquarters and enjoyed a well-organised day out. Although entry was free, the various stalls and side-shows raised almost £4,000 for charity. Building on the success of this venture, further Open Days were held in 1980 and 1983.

There had been a resurgence of IRA activity since 1968 and Kent had its first real taste of this in September 1975 when a bomb exploded outside the *Hare and Hounds* public house in Maidstone. This was a popular meeting place for men from the nearby Royal Engineers barracks and was targeted for just this reason but, thanks to

127   WPC, post-1972.

the keen observation of a young sapper, loss of life was avoided. Two young police-men were slightly injured by flying glass and considerable damage was done to the public house.

The force still retained a strong rural and foot patrol presence, Chief Constable Barry Pain, stating in his report for 1975 that:

> It is hoped that as the establishment becomes more realistic, police coverage of rural areas can be augmented. During the latter part of the year, as recruitment improved, considerably more men became available for foot patrol in urban areas – particularly town centres. This is a pleasing trend which it is hoped to continue.

In 1975, the Sex Discrimination Act was passed and so, from January 1976, the Women Police ceased to exist as a separate specialist body and all women were absorbed into the general police system. The woman superintendent was appointed staff officer to the chief constable with special responsibility for women staff.[18] The distinction between males and females in the Force no longer existed.

The traditional checking of unoccupied premises continued until well into the second half of the 20th century with a total of 11,574 properties being checked during 1956 alone. Eventually, however, with the growth of holidays abroad and ever-increasing leisure time, visits to unoccupied houses had to be curtailed and ceased altogether in 1975. One property which received special attention for a number of years was that known as 'Chartwell'. Now the property of the National Trust, it was for many years the home of Sir Winston Churchill. During the time he was Prime Minister there was a constant police presence at the house, whether he was in residence or not. Young single men were drafted in to the Westerham Section for six-month tours of duty where they took it in turns to guard the house, three working eight-hour shifts while a fourth was enjoying his rest day. A similar situation arose in June 1977 when HRH The Prince of Wales took possession of Chevening House and police were needed to patrol the grounds and man the police post there.

By the 1970s, the force had a fair sprinkling of graduate officers who had either attended university prior to joining or who obtained their degree whilst serving, through one avenue or another. This interest in higher education occasionally proved to be a mixed blessing as a number of those who obtained degrees left the force to pursue a career elsewhere, possibly in the academic world where the pay was good and the conditions more congenial. For example, Inspector 'X', BSc, MA, AIL, Barrister-at-Law, who was selected for the Special (Accelerated Promotion) Course as a young constable in 1976, retired on an ill-health pension 10 years later. Similarly, Inspector 'Y', BA, MA, another Special Course officer, completed a Harkness Scholarship in the United States and was awarded the degree of Master of Public Administration by Harvard University in 1986. The same year he was also admitted to the degree of PhD in Applied Mathematics by the University of Kent and was promoted to chief inspector. He would seem to have been set for a glittering career in the police service, but he resigned the following year when he had a mere 10 years' service (much of which had obviously been spent on various courses).

Other officers who had been selected for accelerated promotion and granted university scholarships left the force shortly afterwards. Others advanced rapidly through the ranks, often to the chagrin of the 'street policemen' who had gained considerable practical experience in their chosen profession but were overtaken by these 'flyers' whose 'street cred.' was limited to say the least. Such was the growth of university courses that Chief Constable Pain had to recommend to the Police Authority that no more than four officers a year should be permitted to attend such courses. Of course, this did not prevent officers studying in their own time for Open University degrees or the London University external degrees. By 1986 the force included 109 graduates (3.7 per cent of the force), rising to 130 in 1989.[19] Subsequent levels were not published in the chief constable's annual reports but, in 1994, no fewer than 12 officers, from constable to chief superintendent, were awarded first degrees by the Open University and two obtained master's degrees. In the 1990s, Portsmouth University began to offer special, part-time and distance-learning graduate and post-graduate courses in police studies and, in 1997/98, seven Kent officers were awarded first or second degrees from that university alone. In 1997 arrangements were also made with the Canterbury Christ Church University College to offer a BSc (Hons.) degree for members of the force and, in August 2000, the first 37 graduates, roughly 25 per cent of whom were females, were admitted to the degree.

The two police boats, *Marina* and *Alexandra*, continued to give sterling service for many years and, in 1976, were supplemented by an additional, glass-fibre launch, working from Ramsgate. With a singular lack of imagination, this was named the *Alexandra II*. In early 1981, the Marine Section was reduced to two sergeants and nine constables and the following year both older boats were sold and the *Alexandra II* was moved to Strood.

By the mid-1970s morale in the police service had fallen considerably due to discontent with pay and conditions and the Edmund Davis Tribunal was set up to

128   Patrol boats *Marina* and *Alexandra*.

look into these matters. The substantial increases in police pay resulting from the Tribunal's recommendations resulted in a tidal wave of applications to join the force and, by October 1980, the force was up to its revised established strength.

A Police Brass Band was formed in 1977 which the then chief constable cited as an indication that morale in the force (apart from the question of pay) was at a high level.[20] It is known that a Police Band existed in Margate as long ago as 1899 but little is recorded of its composition or capabilities.

The Operations Centre within the Headquarters building quickly proved much too cramped and so a new building was erected on the tennis courts behind the main Headquarters building and opened by Prince Charles on 25 April 1977. This state-of-the-art complex incorporated the latest in computer, communications and video equipment but became obsolescent within two decades. So, in 1999, work was commenced on a new CC21[21] Force Communications Centre to replace both the existing Force Communications Centre and the Area Communications Centres.

Also in 1977 a Police Advisory Board Working Party on the Special Constabulary was set up and its recommendations were adopted in their entirety by the Kent

129 Francis (Frank) Jordan, Chief Constable of Kent, 1982-1989.

County Constabulary. Accordingly, from 1 January 1978, all special constables adopted the chequered cap band as worn by the regular force and a new rank system was introduced. The Special Constabulary now had an establishment of 955 men and women, comprising seven divisional commandants (three silver bars indicating the rank), 19 sub-divisional officers (two bars), 101 section officers (one bar) and 828 special constables.

By the mid-1970s a wide range of weapons was available to the force, including Smith & Wesson Model 10 four-inch barrel revolvers, Model 36 two-inch barrel revolvers, Walther PPK automatics and Enfield 'Enforcer' rifles. In the course of the next year or two, a total of some 350 officers had been trained in the use of the Smith & Wesson, with tactics being covered as well as officer safety. However, this proliferation of firearms users had its drawbacks, especially the problem of keeping them fully trained and practised. An incident in London in 1984 led to an enquiry which highlighted the need for greater training and fewer authorised firearms officers. In Kent these were reduced to 24 per Division plus some specialist and support officers.

Financial restrictions resulted in the demise of the Cadet Corps and recruitment ceased in 1981. The existing cadets were gradually absorbed into the regular force, the last ones being appointed constables in June 1982. The Cadet Corps had lasted some 30 years – just a brief period in the history of the Kent Police – but the lessons learned by the former members stood them in good stead, many rising to senior ranks in the ensuing years.

In 1982 Chief Constable Pain was appointed commandant of the National Police College at Bramshill, holding the rank of inspector of constabulary, whence he retired in 1987.[22] He was followed by another refugee from the West Midlands – his deputy, Francis Leo (Frank) Jordan. Dennis O'Brien from Greater Manchester became the new deputy chief constable and eventually followed Eric Haslam's example and retired to become the chief constable of the British Transport Police. Edward M. Crew, who had transferred to Kent from the Metropolitan Police as an ACC in 1984, became the new deputy chief constable in June 1985.

An extremely wide range of professional training courses was being provided in the 1980s by the Force Training School in Maidstone, in conjunction with Police College. These included various firearms courses, race relations and multi-cultural communities, police and ethnic minorities, industrial relations, advanced reading techniques, psychology for police officers, HGV drivers, transport of hazardous substances, aircraft accident procedures, crime prevention, fraud investigation, surveillance, fingerprints, potential instructors, security, home defence and war duties, communications, PT and self-defence instructors, tutor constables, Police National Computer supervisors, to list but a few. Many of these courses reflect the fact that the early '80s was a period in which 'effectiveness' was the key word and race (arising from the Scarman Report) and community relations was very much the 'flavour of the month'. But more directly professional matters were not overlooked; the training of probationer constables was constantly being scrutinised and, in 1983, a formal system of 'tutor constables' was instituted. Probationers who had completed their initial training were to spend at least eight weeks on the streets, supervised by a specially trained, experienced tutor.

Contrary to George Orwell's forecast, 1984 did not see England under an oppressive police state with 'Big Brother' and 'Thought Police'. The year was, however, a very significant one for the police in England and Wales in that it saw the passing of the Police and Criminal Evidence Act which introduced a wide range of controls over the police, particularly through the imposition of Codes of Conduct. So far as evidence was concerned, the Judges Rules and the well-known 'caution' that had served the police and the courts for so long were replaced by the provisions of the 1984 Act. The requirements of PACE (as it became known) meant that a considerable number of sergeants and constables had to be trained in custody sergeant duties – a new and complex role introduced by the Act.

In 1984/5 an all-out strike was called by the miners' leader, Arthur Scargill, in opposition to the Thatcher government's plans to close down many of the nation's coal mines, including those in East Kent. The Kent miners, having devised a success-ful strategy during the strikes in 1972 and 1974 which had led to the downfall of the Heath administration, hoped for a similar success this time. However, union support was not 100 per cent since the strike had been called without a ballot of the members and this time public sympathy was lacking. The Kent miners refused to accept what many saw as the inevitable and there were some ugly clashes between the police and pickets at Tilmanstone. But, as the months went by, the country did not come to a standstill as the mines had large stockpiles and the main Kent power stations could all burn oil as easily as coal. The last straw was the arrival of a huge Russian tanker at Kingsnorth power station to unload thousands of gallons of strike-breaking oil. Many of the miners became disheartened and drifted back to work but the Kent branch of the NUM was the last to admit defeat. Despite the miners' efforts, the Snowdown pit never re-opened, Tilmanstone closed shortly afterwards and Betteshanger eventually followed the others.

Apart from policing the local mines, Kent also sent officers to assist at some Northern coalfields and the strike was a severe drain on police resources. Rest days were few and far between, 12-hour days commonplace and the force was stretched to the limit for over a year. It was hard, thankless work for the police officers, trying to keep the peace in the face of violent opposition from the strikers.

The situation during the miners' strike was redolent of the early days when the police were faced with violent demonstrations against them, but the old-time policemen would have been astonished at the array of technology now available to the police. As they became less expensive, more and more computers were brought into use and, during 1985, a computer terminal was installed in every police station. In 1994 an

Operational Information System (OIS) was introduced on which all incidents were recorded, thus replacing the hand-written Occurrence Book which had served the force so well for so long but was now very much 'old technology'. This was swiftly followed by GENESIS – a force-wide IT system, part of which provided crime reporting, intelligence and custody facilities to the force.

The uniform, too, was changing. The belted tunic which had been in use since the 1950s was replaced in the 1980s by a different jacket without epaulettes and with just two breast pockets. The use of divisional numbers having been discontinued, a badge which included the officer's registered number was worn on the left breast. Nevertheless, the uniform now being worn would have been recognisable to the Victorian policeman but he would have been bemused by the bright, fluorescent yellow jackets which became the general work apparel of the male and female police officers at the end of the 20th century. The ever-increasing amount of equipment now required to be carried led to the issue of the 'Christmas Tree' type of belt on which handbolts (new rigid type), side-handle truncheons, CS gas spray, etc. etc. could be hung like festive decorations.

At this time the emphasis nationwide was on 'economy, efficiency and effectiveness' as a result of a Home Office circular on the subject. The need for economy led to stringent measures being imposed, reminiscent of the 1930s. Coming at a time when the force was growing larger and larger and the administration more and more complex, this prompted the devolvement of much financial responsibility onto divisional commanders. No longer would virtually all financial decisions be taken at force head-quarters but local commanders would have a budget and it would be for them to decide how to spend it. In January 1987, day-to-day financial matters were further devolved onto sub-divisions, the policy being generally accepted as a major step forward and prompting the HMI to state in his report for 1990 that 'The Force is to the fore in devolving responsibilities to sub-divisional commanders … it is one of the leaders in England and Wales in the devolution of budgets and the enthusiasm shown by all ranks … was readily apparent.'

January 1985 saw yet another reorganisation of the force with the territorial divisions being further reduced to five:

'A' = Maidstone, Malling, Cranbrook, Tonbridge and Tunbridge Wells (Ch. Supt. Brian Stephenson)
'B' = Medway Towns (no change) (Ch. Supt. Alan Bourlet BA)
'C' = Gravesend, Dartford, Sevenoaks and Edenbridge (Ch. Supt. Brian Kendall)
'D' = Dover, Folkestone and Ashford (Ch. Supt. Alan Parker)
'E' = Canterbury, Herne Bay, Whitstable, Faversham, Margate, Ramsgate (Ch. Supt. Alan Stuart, QPM)

Traffic Division (Ch. Supt. Robert Findlay, BA) was reduced to just three Areas (Coldharbour/Rochester, Sevenoaks/Swanley and Nackington/Ashford).

To quote Chief Constable Frank Jordan's report for 1985: '… the word "change" more than any other exemplified what occurred during the year.'

In the same year, a completely 'Open Housing Policy' was introduced, officers being permitted to live anywhere in Kent, provided they could properly perform all their duties. The traditional local links between police officers living in their area of work and the public in that area were thus severed; in future, even the officer in charge of a division could be living on the opposite side of the county with few personal and social links with his area of responsibility.

130 Norton 'Interpol' motorcycle.

In the late 1980s a serving Kent officer made allegations that certain detectives were boosting their crime returns by getting convicted criminals to admit to offences that they had not in fact committed. As the prisoners were unlikely to be tried and further sentenced for these offences they had nothing to lose and the police succeeded in keeping the apparent number of unsolved crimes down. The allegations were taken up by the national press and a full-scale enquiry was carried out. As a result, one detective sergeant was dismissed and five other detective officers fined for obtaining improper crime write-offs from prison interviews.

1987 was a particularly bad year for Kent. In January it experienced some of the worst weather ever known with temperatures plummeting to -13 degrees C, the coldest since 1867, and a number of villages were cut off by impassable snow-drifts. The M2 and M26 motorways were blocked for a week and the police were fully stretched dealing with traffic problems, rescuing stranded persons and getting food and supplies to cut-off villagers. The following October, the county was devastated by the infamous hurricane which destroyed thousands of trees and caused enormous damage. Electricity pylons toppled over, cars were crushed, cara-vans overturned, roofs ripped off, ships capsized and communications were crip-pled. As usual, the police played a crucial role, with the other emergency services and the military, in trying to alleviate the problems this unexpected natural disaster caused. In one case, police officers were called to assist an ambulance crew who, due to fallen trees, were unable to reach two seriously ill children in a rural resi-dential home near Sevenoaks. A police Land Rover was used to cross fields, hedge-rows and other obstructions and the children were transported on mattresses to the waiting ambulance.

131   Vauxhall 'Senator' patrol car, *c.*1990.

Strangely enough, the most serious incident in which the Kent Police were closely involved that year was one that occurred well outside the county boundaries – in fact in a foreign land. On 6 March 1987, the Townsend-Thorensen cross-Channel ferry, the *Herald of Free Enterprise*, capsized just outside Zeebrugge harbour. Some 200 passengers and crew lost their lives and Kent Police sent a team of liaison officers to Belgium to assist with identification and communications problems. A Casualty Information Bureau was set up at the Force Headquarters in Maidstone and, at the height of the incident, more than 300 Kent officers and civilian staff, together with special constables, were fully involved. The excellent liaison established with the Belgian police was very largely due to the efforts made nearly two decades previously to establish links with the police forces in Europe.

At the end of 1987, a reappraisal of the traffic policing of the county was undertaken. The demands imposed by the development of the motorways and other strategic roads in the county pointed to the need for a dedicated team to service this growing commitment. At the same time, safety on roads throughout the County had to be maintained within the Force policy that sub-divisions should have primacy in providing the policing service. Therefore, from February 1988, responsibility for traffic regulation and law enforcement was shared between the Traffic Division (responsibility for selected strategic roads[23]) and the territorial sub-divisions (responsible for all other roads). As a result of this decision, a number of Traffic Division vehicles and personnel were transferred to the various sub-divisions. The slimmed-down Traffic Division became a Department, commanded by a superintendent, with Traffic Offices at Nackington (Canterbury), Sevenoaks and Coldharbour (Maidstone) each under an inspector. Each of the territorial divisions was allocated a staff officer (Traffic) who was responsible for traffic management matters. A rationalisation of traffic patrol vehicles was also carried out, with the Traffic Department using Vauxhall 3.1i 'Senators' and the sub-divisional traffic units using Ford 2.0 'Sapphires'. Around this time, the traffic motorcyclists began using BMW K100s in place of the R80s used previously. In 1990 the Driving School was decentralised with all driver-training taking place on Divisions with the instructors going to each sub-division or Traffic Area to carry out training. There were three levels of driver-training: Test Plus (mainly probationers); Standard (three weeks); Advanced (two weeks) with a series of specialist modules for 'speed detection', 'incident signing', 'pursuit', 'skid' and 'surveillance driving'.

Although at a fairly high state of alert, nothing could have prepared Kent for the terrorist outrage which took place on the morning of 22 September 1989. Bandsmen at the Royal Marines School of Music in Deal were returning from early morning practice when a Semtex bomb exploded, killing 11 bandsmen and injuring many more. Despite intensive efforts by the Kent Police, the Metropolitan Terrorist Group and the Security Services, no one was charged with this outrage. Fortunately, through political initiatives, the threat of terrorist action by the IRA diminished in the last decade of the 20th century and one can only hope that this state of affairs will continue into the 21st.

Given the proximity of Kent to the continent of Europe, the desirability of officers being able to speak French had been recognised since the latter part of the 19th century and, with the growth in cross-Channel movements, language training again became an important consideration. A number of selected officers, whose work was likely to bring them in contact with foreigners and who already had a good grounding in the language, attended advanced courses in conversational French, provided by the then Maidstone Technical College. In 1989, the imminent opening of the Channel Tunnel provoked further interest in this matter and intensive eight-week residential and other courses in French were organised to assist in forging closer relationships with the French Police.[24]

Few French officers spoke English and, although improved educational standards and the greater number of graduates entering the Kent force meant that, by the latter part of the century, there were several officers with degrees in modern languages or a high level of fluency, these were proportionally very few and a suitable means of intelligent communication was called for. This was provided by an innovative use for computers in the form of the 'PoliceSpeak' (later 'Linguanet') system around 1992. Specifically designed by a mixed team of Kent officers and academics from Cambridge University to facilitate communication between the Kent and French officers policing the Channel Tunnel, an automatic machine translation of certain set words and phrases was provided so that a standard message typed in English on this side of the Channel would be received in France in French and vice-versa. Specific names, places, times, etc. could be added as necessary.

When Chief Constable Jordan retired in 1989 his successor was a man who was going to make a name for himself. Paul Leslie Condon joined the Metropolitan Police in 1967 and was awarded a Bramshill Scholarship to Oxford University from where

132 (Sir) Paul L. Condon, Chief Constable of Kent, 1989-1993.

he graduated as a Master of Arts. He proceeded to move swiftly through the ranks, being appointed an assistant chief constable of Kent in 1984. This was clearly just a stepping stone as, in 1987, he returned to the Met. as a deputy assistant commissioner, being promoted to assistant commissioner in 1988. Following Frank Jordan's retirement, Paul Condon returned to Kent as its new chief constable but this, once again, was but a transient move since, in 1993, he was appointed Commissioner of the Police of the Metropolis and knighted. Early in 1990 Paul Condon set out where he saw the force going in a document entitled 'The Way Ahead' which contained four sections headed: 'Our Duty', 'Values', 'Priorities' and 'Aims'. This was to be the blueprint for the force for the remainder of the century.

The Headquarters organisation (which had now grown considerably from the old 'Reserve' Division as introduced by Buck Ruxton in 1857) was completely restructured. The three assistant chief constables would now have responsibility for (i) Territorial Policing, (ii) Support and (iii) Personnel, while the civilian head of Administration and Finance would henceforth enjoy the status of an ACC, reporting directly to the chief constable. Various minor changes in the sub-divisional organisation ensued but the great upheaval was reserved for January 1992 when the divisional structure was completely overhauled and the force divided into 13 policing districts to be known as Areas. Each Area was to have a management team of a superintendent (in charge), one chief inspector (Operations), one detective chief inspector (Crime Management), an area support manager (civilian), seven inspectors and one or two detective inspectors. Traffic Department was to become a discrete Area under a superintendent and a chief inspector with an inspector in charge of each Traffic Office. The Areas were to be almost completely autonomous and expected to cope with all except the most serious level of incident.

The reader who has been paying close attention will no doubt here experience a feeling of *déja vu*, recalling that the Kent County Constabulary in 1857 consisted of 12 divisions, each commanded by a superintendent. Admittedly, these divisions did not include the autonomous boroughs but, after the amalgamation in 1943, the force was soon again divided into 12 divisions which incorporated these boroughs.

It is not clear just why the tried and tested appellation of 'division' was abandoned in the Kent force by a man who was to go on to command the Metropolitan Police, where the old divisional structure is retained and an 'Area' is a different and larger body. Few other forces have followed the Kent example and the change of title seems merely to confuse matters. Be that as it may, the new arrangement was as follows:

Area 1 - based on Dartford (Superintendent Chatten)
Area 2 - based on Gravesend (Superintendent Humphreys)
Area 3 - based on Chatham/Rochester (Medway) (Superintendent Coltham)
Area 4 - based on Gillingham (Superintendent Starbuck)
Area 5 - based on Sittingbourne/Sheerness/Faversham (Swale) (Superintendent Clapperton)
Area 6 - based on Canterbury (Superintendent Gammon)
Area 7 - based on Margate/Ramsgate (Thanet) (Superintendent Walker)
Area 8 - based on Dover/Deal/Sandwich (Superintendent Wharf)
Area 9 - based on Folkestone/Hythe (Superintendent Shipman)
Area 10 - based on Ashford/Tenterden (Superintendent Hatcher)
Area 11 - based on Tunbridge Wells/Cranbrook (Superintendent Fairbrass)
Area 12 - based on Sevenoaks/Tonbridge/Edenbridge (West Kent) (Superintendent Plummer)
Area 13 - based on Maidstone/Malling (Superintendent Hext)
Area 14 - Traffic (Maidstone, Sevenoaks and Nackington garages) (Superintendent Spearman)

Although considerable misgivings were being expressed in the lower ranks about the way the force was going and a management seemingly obsessed with gimmicky titles and change for change sake, the regime obviously succeeded in attracting the sought-for appreciation in high places and, in September 1992, the force was one of 36 organisations (from 300 applicants) which were awarded a Charter Mark Award by the Prime Minister.

To coincide with these changes, the Special Constabulary nomenclature was again altered and the posts of chief commandant and two commandants were reintroduced at County level. Brenda Butler was appointed to the former post and David Knight and Anthony Ball the latter two. Chief Commandant Butler was awarded the MBE in 1995 and retired in February 1999, to be replaced by Anthony Ball. Another change took place in February 1995 when new categories of special were introduced – the 'Parish Special' and the 'Neighbourhood Special'. The recruitment and training of these was the same as other special constables, the duties of the parish and neighbourhood specials being restricted to the parish or area for which they were appointed. By this time special constables were wearing helmets and were virtually indistinguishable from their regular colleagues.

Incidents involving firearms were increasing everywhere and there were 76 in the County in 1990. Fortunately, the number of occasions on which the Kent police have actually had to open fire remained negligible although in July 1993 a man was shot in the stomach by police near Dover after running amok with a shotgun and firing several times at pursuing policemen. The slimmed-down Traffic Area was given the task of providing the force's initial armed response capacity and a number of firearms officers were transferred to that Department to man Armed Response Vehicles. These carried a locked firearms cabinet in the boot and patrolled the strategic road network 24 hours a day, 365 days a year, with a crew of two firearms officers. Back-up was provided by the Uniform Support Group and a Tactical Firearms Unit which was trained in weapons tactics and methods.

However, the growth in the number of calls for the attendance of the ARVs (around 160 involving firearms in 1993 with a similar number involving shotguns and bladed weapons) led to a Central Tactical Support Unit being formed in May 1994. The ARVs were removed from the Traffic Department and attached to the Support Groups which provided highly-trained specialists, often ex-servicemen, to man them and also to provide VIP protection and weapons training for the rest of the force.

133   (Sir) John David Phillips, Chief Constable
of Kent, 1993 onwards.

Coincidentally, experiments were being carried out, both in Kent and nationally, to find a non-lethal form of restraint. In 1995 trials were carried out in Medway using CS gas canisters as part of a national scheme. These appeared to be successful and, although some forces continued to have reservations concerning this type of control, it was adopted in Kent *faute de mieux*, while experiments continued.

The removal of the ARVs resulted in Traffic losing its Area status in September 1994 when it reverted to a Department under a chief inspector. The garages at Swanley and Nackington were closed and the new Traffic Department consisted of a Motorway Unit and a motorcycle team. It also assumed responsibility for traffic management and intelligence, plus accident investigation and a technological enforcement unit (radar, Gatso, video car, etc.).

As the 20th century was drawing to a close, Kent's last chief constable of the century, John David Phillips, was appointed. David Phillips, as he was more usually known (later Sir David), was born in 1944 in Lancashire and joined the Lancashire Constabulary in 1963. After serving as an assistant chief constable in the Greater Manchester Police and deputy chief constable of the Devon & Cornwall Constabulary, he arrived to take charge of the Kent County Constabulary in March 1993. Sir David established a wide reputation as a leading proponent of intelligence-led policing and quickly made his mark on the force by the introduction of the 'Kent Policing Model', setting out the policing concept which was to carry the force into the 21st century.

Also in 1993, Deputy Chief Constable Crew moved on to become chief constable of Northamptonshire and, subsequently, the West Midlands Police where he too was knighted. His replacement was Dennis O'Connor who in June 1997 moved back to the Metropolitan Police as an assistant commissioner and, later, to Surrey as chief constable. The last deputy chief constable of the century was Robert Ayling; Bob Ayling came to Kent from Hampshire on promotion to superintendent. He was subsequently promoted to chief superintendent and then ACC, becoming deputy chief constable in June 1997.

The opening of the Channel Tunnel in May 1994 meant that, for the first time in history, French policemen were working on English soil within the Tunnel complex, while Kent police officers were employed at the French end. In July 1991 a European Liaison Unit was set up, based in the Port of Dover and, at the same time, an Integrated Frontier Control Unit was formed, the Kent force having taken over full responsibility from the Metropolitan Police for Special Branch work at all

Kent ports in April 1978. A completely new, purpose-built police station was constructed at Longport, within the confines of the Channel Tunnel terminal near Cheriton, to house the officers responsible for policing the terminal area.

Many of the vehicles using the county's roads around this time were heading to or from the Channel Ports and the opening of the Channel Tunnel merely increased this traffic. All the time the ferries and the tunnel were working well the traffic flowed quite smoothly, with only the occasional hiccup but a series of strikes by (mainly) French port workers resulted in cancelled sailings and trains, causing a tremendous backlog of HGVs and other traffic. To reduce the chaos caused by this log-jam, the force initiated Operation Stack for the first time in November 1996. This involved closing the lower end of the M20 motorway and using the carriageways as a kind of lorry park until such time as matters returned more or less to normal. Although this caused numerous complaints, in the absence of a suitable and sufficiently large vehicle park in the vicinity of the Channel Ports, there was really very little option open to the police.

But it must not be thought that France was the only country to see Kent officers in the latter part of the 20th century as, over the years, officers were selected for various secondments and postings overseas. In February 1980, two sergeants and ten constables were sent to Rhodesia (as it then was) at the time of the elections. In February 1987, Detective Chief Inspector Flood was posted to the Hague as drugs liaison officer and, in February 1995, Assistant Chief Constable David Valls-Russell was appointed assistant director (IT) of the newly formed Europol organisation in the Hague. In July 1997, Chief Inspector Michael Peters was seconded to France as counter terrorism liaison officer. In February 1988, Superintendent Wilkinson was seconded to the Royal Oman Police while two officers (inspectors and sergeants) went to Guyana, two to Jamaica and two to Barbados. Between 1992 and 1996, four constables were seconded to the Royal Cayman Islands Police for two years. In response to a plea from the Pitcairn Islands for a community policing officer, Woman Constable Gail Cox spent the autumn of 1997 on that island. The troubles in former Yugoslavia meant that Kent police officers were attached to the UN International Police Task Force in Bosnia, Croatia and Kosovo between 1997 and 1999 and, also in 1999, Chief Superintendent Andrew Felton was seconded to Romania to head the task force set up to help the Romanians demilitarise their police force. Similarly, in 1999, Assistant Chief Constable Mike Bowron paid two short visits to the fledgling Indonesian democracy, followed the next year by a six-month secondment to assist the Indonesian Police to separate from the military.

If the morale of some junior officers was low during the early 1990s, the publication of the infamous Sheehy Report caused morale throughout all ranks of the service to fall through the floor. The Report, commissioned by John Major's government, recommended sweeping changes to police conditions of service. Chief Constable David Phillips described the Report as proposing

> ... changes of such extraordinary complexity that the very fabric of the police seemed threatened. The Service recoiled in dismay. My view is that the proposals – reducing pay, removing allowances, removing opportunities for advancement and totally undermining the pension scheme – threatened to reduce the quality of entrant and suppress the new spirit of professionalism.[25]

Such was the uproar and resistance from the service that only a few of the recommendations were ultimately adopted, the most significant of which was the removal of the right to a rent allowance for officers joining the service after 1994. The fact that existing officers continued to receive a (pegged) allowance thus created a two-tier force and was the basis for a great deal of discontent.

A significant landmark in 1994 was the separation of the Kent Police Authority from the County Council; new legislation imposed changes, the intention being to introduce an independent and directly elected element into the police authority and thus seeing the end of a relationship which had existed for over a century. The new Kent Police Authority consisted of 17 members, including just three magistrates and nine county councillors. The remaining five members were appointed by a complex selection process with a short list being provided by the Home Secretary. They included a company secretary, a former senior fire officer, a retired lawyer and a practising solicitor, plus a Brigadier General. At its first meeting the new Authority elected as its chairman Sir John Grugeon who had chaired the previous authority since 1992 and been a member of it for much longer. Sir John stood down in 1998, being replaced by Mrs Penny Stubbs, one of the magistrate members. The role of the Authority was to produce an annual Policing Plan, set an annual budget and review police performance against set objectives and targets.

It cannot, therefore, be held responsible for the further reorganisation of the force which took place on 1 January 1995, reducing the number of Areas from 13 to nine:

Area 1 - North Kent (Dartford and Gravesend)
Area 2 - West Kent (Tunbridge Wells, Tonbridge and Sevenoaks)
Area 3 - Maidstone
Area 4 - Medway (Chatham, Rochester and Gillingham)
Area 5 - Swale (Sittingbourne, Sheerness and Faversham)
Area 6 - Canterbury
Area 7 - Thanet
Area 8 - South East Kent (Dover and Shepway)
Area 9 - Weald (Ashford).

This was to be the last rehash of the divisional/area organisation, the tenth since the amalgamations of 1943. During the first 100 years of its life, the Kent County Constabulary did not undergo any significant change until the amalgamation with the borough forces during the Second World War. In the last 26 years, however, the force operational structure was completely revised no less than four times (1974, 1985, 1992 and 1995). One can only wonder whether such disturbances were really necessary and the extent to which they diverted the officers on the ground from concentrating on their primary functions of preventing and detecting crime. And it was not only the operational divisions which changed; the originally tiny headquarters staff multiplied out of all recognition and this too did not escape regular changes of name and function. It is perhaps significant that, during the last 25 years, the force saw a vast number of assistant chief constables come and go, most of whom used the force as a springboard to bigger and better posts in the police service. Each of these no doubt felt the need to make his or her mark and what better way than to propose sweeping changes which would 'revitalise' the force? Of course, Kent was merely reflecting contemporary policing practice. As one writer put it,

It isn't just the tools of our trade that have changed with time, we have also managed to modernize various departments such as Complaints and Discipline, now renamed in many forces as 'The Professional Standards Department' or something similar ... Administration titles change with monotonous regularity as do the various specialist departments to the confusion of all.[26]

Town centre constables were introduced in 1995, an innovation described by the HMI in his report as '... a unique and imaginative response to the perceived reduction in uniform patrols'. Certainly this was something the public had long been calling for, popular opinion regarding any kind of foot patrol officer as an endangered species. Judging from letters to the local press it does not seem that this idea lasted very long in practice and the lack of foot patrols continued to be a major subject for editorial discussion for the rest of the century. However, perhaps the last word on this subject should be left to David (now Sir David) Phillips who, in his report for 1999-2000 stated:

> While crime is at the centre of our business, we are also asked to assist the public whenever they have no other service to turn to ... People are asked what kind of policing they would like as if policing could easily be switched to a different set of priorities ... The cost of doing one thing has to be set against the opportunity forgone of not doing another ... I stress that it is not that we would not wish to have more officers on visible patrol duties ... It is simply that within the realm of present resourcing, policing, which is a very expensive commodity, has to be focused to get the best return ... Burglaries committed in rural locations are rarely committed by village residents ... It is small comfort if you have just been burgled to be told that statistically the burglary rate has reduced dramatically ... [but] since we began our intelligence based approach, house burglary has dropped from 19,255 in 1993 to 8,177 in 2000 ... Most of the difficulty with public perception concerns observable anti-social behaviour ... We understand this and are [working] ... with other agencies to develop new strategies ...

There is no room in this volume to describe all the outstanding criminal cases which occurred in the county in the last two centuries but, if there is one case that held the nation's attention in the last decade, it must be the murder of Lin Russell and her daughter Megan on a quiet bridleway at Chillenden, near Canterbury, in July 1996. They had been beaten about the head with a hammer-like weapon, as had their little dog. Much of the attention has centred on the astonishing survival of Lin's other daughter, 10-year-old Josie, who was badly injured and left for dead. Terribly traumatised by the incident, Josie was unable to speak for many months afterwards, although she gradually began to return to a more normal existence. After many months of painstaking enquiries, the Kent Police eventually charged Michael Stone with the murders and attempted murder and he was convicted at Maidstone Crown Court in October 1998.[27]

There was also the Noye case. In January 1985, two policemen from the Metropolitan Police C11 special surveillance squad were keeping watch on Hollywood Cottage, West Kingsdown. This large, luxurious house was the home of Kenneth Noye, suspected of involvement in the £26,000,000 Brinks Mat gold bullion robbery at Heathrow just over a year previously. Hiding in the grounds, the two officers were detected by three guard dogs. One of the officers withdrew, hoping to draw the dogs off but, followed by Noye, they headed for Detective Constable John Fordham. There was a struggle and Fordham fell to the ground, stabbed ten times, two of the wounds piercing his heart. Noye was arrested for murder and also in respect of the gold bullion found in the house. Noye's defence at his trial was that

134 West Malling police office.

he had disturbed a man hiding in the bushes whom he took to be a burglar or worse. He claimed he had attacked in self-defence and the jury accepted this version. He was later tried in connection with the stolen gold and was sentenced to 14 years' imprisonment.

Eleven years later, Noye was a free man again and came to the notice of the police once more. In May 1996, Stephen Cameron, a 21-year-old motorist, was left dying by the M20/M25 interchange near Swanley after being stabbed by a 'road rage' driver. The crime was committed in broad daylight and witnessed by at least 29 people. After extensive enquiries, suspicion fell on Noye and it was found that, within 24 hours of the murder, he had left the country in a private jet. He was finally traced to Spain where he was later identified by Stephen's girl friend and so, in August 1998, Kent officers went there and a confident Noye was arrested for murder. He then made several mistakes that would seal his fate. Firstly, he denied any connection with Stephen Cameron (which did not sit well with his later plea of self-defence); secondly, he refused to return to England voluntarily which meant the police had to begin long drawn-out extradition proceedings, delaying Noye's return for nine months. This gave the police more time to build up their case while he was in custody; had he returned to England the police would have had to release him on bail (with the strong likelihood of him absconding) or charge him before their case was complete. As it was, the prosecution had a strong case to put to the jury when, nearly four years after Stephen Cameron's death, Noye was tried for his murder and convicted. Perhaps Constable Fordham's death had also been avenged.

Around the end of the 20th century, the chief constable also identified a new breed of criminals who were slipping through the net because they were too small to attract the attention of the National Criminal Intelligence Service but were bigger than local, street-level criminals.[28] There were around 150 of these professional and successful criminals in the County at any one time, with about 20 under surveillance or close to arrest. Many were involved in drug dealing, bootlegging, burglary and fraud and so confident in their immunity from arrest that they adopted a very ostentatious life-style with big cars and houses and lots of jewellery. Chief Constable David Phillips said that, although the force had been very successful and crime overall had gone down, criminals were becoming more organised, hierarchical and hardened: 'In fact, what we are seeing is a kind of banditry where [the criminals] are

135   Traffic Warden, 1960s.

careless about their activities. They don't mind taking on the police and are likely to ram a police car.'

To combat this phenomenon, the force's criminal intelligence officers were increased from 20 to over 200 with the top gangs targeted by a further 200 officers based on the local Areas, but the force lacked the resources to follow the intelligence through in all cases. Seven gangs had been identified in Kent; one dealing in drugs, another organising trailer thefts, a third specialising in counterfeiting and yet another in big-house burglaries. But these gangs were so well organised that extensive resources were needed to bring the offenders to justice and these resources were simply not available. It is a sad fact that many modern criminals have access to far greater resources than the forces of law and order and so can avoid arrest and conviction.

Although police stations in Kent had been closing at an alarming rate, the old Tonbridge police station was demolished in 1998 and a completely new building erected on the site and opened by the Duke of Kent. Work on adapting the former Orion Insurance offices in Bouverie Road West, Folkestone as the new police station for the area was commenced in 1999 and it opened for business towards the end of 2000. The force faced an unusual challenge in 1999 with the opening of the Bluewater

136 Supervising sheep dipping, *c.*1960.

shopping centre near Dartford. The size of a small town, the site covers 50 acres of parkland with more than 320 stores, three 'leisure villages' and parking for 13,000 cars. The sheer size of the site and the number of daily visitors and vehicles pose special challenges for the police and security staff and a team of 21 Kent officers was allocated to police the complex. A special arrangement with the developers means that the latter pay for these officers and provide a police station for them.

To return finally to the question of road traffic, traffic policing at the end of the millennium is best summed up by a comment in *Police*, the journal of the Police Federation of England and Wales, which stated:

> The national debate on traffic has raged for several years. The debate was linked to the arrival of the Home Secretary's priorities in the early '90s, which had no mention of roads policing or road safety. This pressured chief constables to redirect their focus away from roads policing issues. Forces have reacted in different ways, but generally resources have been directed towards general policing and crime.

This would certainly seem to sum up the situation in Kent by the year 2000.

Over the years, there have been very few duties for which, at one time or another, the Kent County Constabulary, and the former Borough forces which it now incorporates, were not responsible. They have been used as assistant excise officers, assistant surveyors of highways and bridges, water bailiffs, conservators of rivers, firemen, appointed as inspectors of workshops, common lodging houses, weights and measures, meat markets, hackney carriages, diseases of animals, railway trucks and old metals. They have been Poor Law relieving officers, sea bathing supervisors, social workers, gaolers, pathologist's assistants, mortuary attendants, and a hundred and one other extraneous duties.

Fortunately, 'when constabulary duty's to be done', the police of Kent have been ready to perform that duty, efficiently and uncomplainingly, for nearly two centuries.

Appendix One

Awards and Decorations

Over the years, many Kent officers[1] have been decorated for their courage and devotion to duty, whilst others have been awarded honours for their services to policing and the maintenance of law and order. These are, therefore, listed below according to three categories:

(a) awards for bravery in the course of police duties
(b) awards for bravery in the Armed Forces
(c) honours and decorations for outstanding police service

1. Police Bravery

Kings Police Medal. In July 1909 King Edward VII introduced the King's Police and Fire Services Medal, awarded in two categories – for conspicuous devotion to duty and for exceptional courage. It was later restricted to the police and became the King's (or Queen's) Police Medal. This medal has been awarded to the following members of the Borough Forces and the Kent County Constabulary for exceptional courage:

> (1928) Constable E. Pollington, Dover Borough – saving life from drowning. In Dover, as in several other seaside towns, a number of officers were commended for saving persons from drowning in the sea; (1936) Constable R. Martin – for bravery at fire at Harbledown and saving two elderly persons.

George Medal. The George Medal and George Cross were instituted by King George VI during the Second World War for outstanding courage or heroism in cases where a purely military honour was not applicable.

> (1940) Constable W. Spain, Folkestone Borough – for bravery during air raid on town. Constable Spain joined the force in 1913 and served in the Army in the First World War and was therefore one of the older men in the force. The blast from the landmine seriously affected his eyes and he later lost his sight; (1940) T/Sergeant C. Brown (Dover Borough) – for bravery attending a fire on board ship in Dover harbour; (1941) Constable C. 'Taffy' Williams, Folkestone Borough – for rescuing a severely injured building worker who had strayed into a mined area; (1958) Constable V. Bradford – arrest of an armed man in Tunbridge Wells.

Queen's Gallantry Medal. Instituted in June 1974 by Queen Elizabeth II for exemplary acts of bravery. Typically awarded to members of the police, fire and ambulance services, it was first awarded to three men who displayed outstanding courage and complete disregard for personal safety when an attempt was made to kidnap Princess Anne in The Mall, London.

> (1975) Inspector R. Neville, Sergeant Kelso and Constable Bryant. For the rescue of a man from the River Thames; (1993) Constable E. Tanner, shot when tackling an armed robber in Tankerton when off duty.

Queen's Commendation for Brave Conduct. Typically awarded for saving life and for tackling armed criminals.

> (1961) Constable Baker; (1961) Constable H. Smith; (1961) Constable Totman; (1962) Inspector Cowan; (1962) Sergeant Hollands; (1969) Sergeant D. Humphries; (1969) Constable J. Fox; (1969) Constable Gamble; (1969) Sergeant B. Cooke – see also 1971; (1970) Constable A. Baitup; (1970) Constable Morris; (1971) Inspector B. Cooke – second award; (1971) Constable Dinsdale; (1977) Inspector P. Roberts; (1977) Constable N. Bath; (1989) Constable K. Williams; (1990) Detective Constable Heath.

2. Bravery in the Armed Forces

During the First World War many Kent police officers served with distinction and the following list should be seen as illustrative, rather than exhaustive, as there may be other men whose details have not come to light in the course of the research into these forces.

First World War

Victoria Cross. Constable H. Wells (awarded posthumously). He joined the police in 1913 but rejoined his old regiment (Royal Sussex) on the outbreak of war. His platoon officer was killed during an assault at Loos in 1915 and, as the platoon sergeant, he took command and led his men forward despite heavy casualties and loss of life, including finally his own.

Serbian Order of White Eagle. Captain Chapman (Deputy Chief Constable of Kent)

King of Serbia's Gold Medal. Constable Carter

Distinguished Conduct Medal. Constable W. Robertson; Constable E. Lawrence (Canterbury City); Constable Whitehead – with clasp; Constable Dicker; Constable Grinyer

Military Cross. Constable Robertson; Constable Dicker; Sergeant Sweeney; Constable Whitehead

Military Medal. Constable Brooker (Maidstone Borough); Constable Williams (Maidstone Borough); Constable E. Lawrence (Canterbury City); Constable J. Ede (Canterbury City); Constable Whitehead; Constable T. Goodall – and bar; Constable Laming; Constable Isaac; Constable Jordan; Constable Ingram; Constable Webb; Constable Hills; Constable Castleton; Constable Ashby; Constable Ward; Constable Baddesley; Constable Ford; Constable Croucher.

Second World War

Distinguished Service Order. Constable D. Parkin.

Military Cross. Constable C. Bailey; Constable H. Burwash; Constable J. Steele.

Distinguished Flying Cross. Sergeant L. Gilmore; Constable G. Smith; Constable J. Denton; Constable W. Holman; Constable J. Bell; Constable T. Bland; Constable J. Harmston; Constable H. Hosier; Constable W. Vearrals; Constable R. Marsden; Civilian Employee C. Wilson (deceased).

Military Medal. Constable Craddock, Ramsgate Borough – who was later killed in action; Constable W. Charles; Constable D. Jordan; Constable D. MacKay; Constable L. Musgrove; Constable J. Tait; Constable P. Veale; Constable R. Walter; Constable J. Ward.

3. Honours for outstanding police service

Knight Bachelor. (1953) Major John Ferguson, CBE, Chief Constable of Kent; (1970) Richard Dawnay Lemon, CBE, QPM, Chief Constable of Kent; (2000) David Phillips, QPM, Chief Constable of Kent.

King's Police Medal for Conspicuous Devotion to Duty. (1914) Superintendent T Fowle; (1924) Chief Constable Beesley (Folkestone Borough); (1928) Chief Superintendent Ambrose; (1939) Chief Constable S.F. Butler (Ramsgate Borough); (1940) Chief Inspector Saddleton (Dover Borough); (1945) Superintendent Webb; (1945) Chief Inspector Hollands; (1945) Assistant Chief Constable R.C.M. Jenkins; (1949) Assistant Chief Constable K. Horwood; (1950) Detective Chief Superintendent F. Smeed; (1952) Chief Superintendent C. Broughton; (1954) Chief Superintendent W. Deacon.

Queen's Police Medal for Conspicuous Devotion to Duty. (1957) Major Sir John Ferguson, Chief Constable of Kent; (1960) Assistant Chief Constable N. Fowler; (1961) Chief Superintendent A. Woolgar; (1961) Chief Superintendent G. Burton; (1964) Dawnay Lemon, CBE, Chief Constable of Kent; (1966) Assistant Chief Constable J. Jenner; (1971) Eric Haslam,

Deputy Chief Constable of Kent; (1973) Chief Superintendent R. Mills; (1976) Barry Pain, Chief Constable of Kent; (1977) Assistant Chief Constable Ashley Warman; (1978); W/ Chief Superintendent M. Bishop; (1979) Det. Chief Superintendent H. Blackburn; (1980) Assistant Chief Constable M. Gibson; (1981) Frank Jordan, Deputy Chief Constable of Kent; (1983) Assistant Chief Constable H.V.D. Hallett; (1984) Chief Superintendent A. Stuart; (1991) Edward Crew, Deputy Chief Constable of Kent; (1996) Peter Hermitage, acting as Director of National Police Training with the rank of Chief Constable; (1996) A/ Assistant Chief Constable J. Blackburn;[2] (1998) Chief Superintendent C. Horton; (1999) Chief Superintendent B. Flood BA; (2000) Robert Ayling, Deputy Chief Constable of Kent.

Commander of the Order of the British Empire. (1921) Major H.E. Chapman, Chief Constable of Kent; (1921) Asst. Chief Constable Surtees; (1921) Lt. Col. H.M.A. Warde, Chief Constable of Kent; (1967) Sergeant A. Evans (Secretary of the Police Federation for England and Wales); (1979) Barry Pain, Chief Constable of Kent.

Officer of the Order of the British Empire. (1953) R.C.M. Jenkins, Deputy Chief Constable of Kent; (1953) N. Fowler, Assistant Chief Constable; (1956) K. Horwood, Assistant Chief Constable; (1971) J. Jenner, Assistant Chief Constable; (1973) E. Haslam, QPM, Deputy Chief Constable of Kent; (1987) D. O'Brien, Deputy Chief Constable of Kent.

Member of the Order of the British Empire. (1918) Det. Superintendent Ambrose; (1928) Superintendent Paramour; (1945) Major J.S. Robson, JP, Chief Supervisor, Kent Special Constabulary; (1945) Superintendent Kitchingham – as a Lieutenant Colonel in the Army; (1945) Constable A. Green – as a Lieutenant Colonel in the Army; (1945) Constable W. Sheppard – as a Major in the Army; (1945) Constable P. MacCallum – as a CSM in the Army – awarded for Gallantry. He was also awarded the RSPCA Bronze Medal for assistance in the rescue of animals from a farm in Tunbridge Wells in 1958. Sadly he died the same year; (1970) Chief Superintendent J. Cruttenden; (1985) Miss P. Fullman, secretary to the Chief Constables of Kent for many years; (1988) Chief Superintendent K. Tappenden; (1991) Superintendent D. Harding; (1994) Ms Marjorie Ravensdale, retiring Force Catering Officer; (1995) Brenda Butler, BA, Chief Commandant Kent Special Constabulary.

British Empire Medal. (1943) T/Chief Inspector R. Butcher, Folkestone Borough – for outstanding services during the war; (1953) Chief Inspector Brown; (1953) Inspector Setterfield; (1962) Constable P. Finch – for gallantry; (1971) Chief Inspector Edridge; (1974) Sergeant Baker – for gallantry in arresting an armed drunk in Sheerness; (1977) Constable W. Ely; (1978) Sergeant R. Jupp; (1979) W/Sergeant M. Court; (1981) Sergeant G. Pond; (1985) Constable Piddock; (1985) Constable Potter; (1989) Constable Maddocks; (1990) Constable N. Govett; (1991) Constable R. Bruce.

Colonial Police Medal. (1957) Sergeant Fraser – seconded to the Cyprus Police – was responsible for the capture of bomb-thrower, 'displaying initiative, intelligence and personal courage'; (1958) Chief Inspector White – seconded to the Cyprus Police – for meritorious service. In addition, in 1920 Chief Constable Reeve, Folkestone Borough, and one of his Inspectors were decorated by the King of the Belgians for their outstanding work in assisting Belgian refugees during the First World War.

It must be stressed that this list is probably incomplete and apologies are extended to any officer who has been left out. Nevertheless, it will give the reader some idea of the calibre of the police officers who served Kent in the last century.

Notes
1. All are members of the Kent County Constabulary, unless the contrary is shown.
2. The son of Detective Chief Superintendent Harold Blackburn, QPM.

SIGNIFICANT DATES

1829   Metropolitan Police formed in London – the first of the 'new police forces.

1830s   Most forces wearing the Swallow-tail type of uniform with white or blue trousers and a high hat following the Metropolitan Police pattern.

1835   Municipal Corporations Act passed, requiring Boroughs to form Watch Committees and police forces. Tunbridge Wells formed a police force under a local Act of Parliament (not being a chartered Borough until 1889) with William Morton at its head.

1836   Police forces formed in Canterbury (J. Clements), Deal (G. Hoile), Dover (H. Crosoer) and Gravesend (W. North).

1837   Police force formed in Maidstone (T. Fancett) and Rochester (T. Cork).

1838   Ramsgate police force formed.
        Police station erected in Queen Street, Dover.

1839   Rural Constabulary Act passed but not adopted in Kent. E. Correll appointed head of Dover Borough Police.

1840   Ashford appoints its first policeman.

1841   Serious affray in Canterbury involving military personnel.

1841-5 Money problems result in cuts in the strength of many police forces.

1844   James Livick appointed head of Ramsgate Borough Police. Constable Couchman of Dover Borough Police murdered.

1846   Mr Laker appointed head of Dover Borough Police.

1847   Police station opened at Rusthall for Tunbridge Wells Borough Police.

1850   Henry Redsull appointed head of Deal Police. John Rofe appointed head of Dover Borough Police.

1851   Folkestone sets up its first true Borough force under James Steer. John Coram appointed head of Dover Borough Police.

1853   Frederick White appointed head of Gravesend Borough Police. John Blundell appointed head of Maidstone Borough Police. Cyril Onslow appointed head of Tunbridge Wells Borough Police.

1856   County and Borough Police Act passed, introducing government support for local police forces and a system of government inspection. W. Martin appointed head of Folkestone Borough Police. John Tuff appointed head of Rochester City Police.

1857   Kent County Constabulary formed under Captain John Ruxton to police the whole of the County outside the areas covered by the Borough police forces.

1858   'Occurrence Books' introduced in County force. Thomas Parker appointed head of Deal Police. Gravesend Police replace frock coats with tunics.

1860   Most forces adopted the long tunic and Kent County introduced the shako hat. Romney Marsh came under the Kent County Constabulary. First County police station at Seabrook.

1861   H.C. Saunders appointed head of Canterbury City Police. Deal Police adopt the shako type of hat. Folkestone Police moved into the newly-built Town Hall.

1862   Ramsgate Borough introduced whistles to replace rattles. Rochester forms a Water Guard on the River Medway. Robert P. Davies appointed head of Canterbury City Police. J.J. Embery appointed head of Tunbridge Wells Borough Police. Margate Police replaced dress coats with tunics.

1863   J.H. Radley appointed head of Rochester City Police. Bonfire Night riots in Dartford.

1864   County police stations erected at Chatham, Cranbrook, Sevenoaks, Tonbridge and Whitstable.

1865   County police stations erected at Ashford and Northfleet. Gravesend Police adopt the helmet. Margate sergeants to wear three stripes instead of two.

1866   County police stations erected at Dartford, Sheerness and Sittingbourne. John Barnes appointed head of Maidstone Borough Police. Borough forces started to wear the helmet.

1867   County police station erected at Malling.

1868   County police stations erected at Sandwich and Kirby Lane, Canterbury.

1869   W. Gifford appointed head of Maidstone Borough Police. Dover Police adopt the helmet. County men ordered not to shave 'for health reasons'.

1870   Edward Buss appointed head of Ramsgate Borough Police. Superintendent English (Kent County) absconded to Australia with stolen property.

1872   Parish Constables abolished by Act of Parliament. Thomas Sanders appointed head of Dover Borough Police. Dover Police issued with whistles.

1873   Constable Israel May murdered at Snodland. George Berry appointed head of Gravesend Borough Police. Order not to shave rescinded.

1874   William Parker appointed head of Deal Police. John Wilshere appointed head of Folkestone Borough Police. Instructing Constables permitted to wear two stripes. Building in Charlotte Place taken into use as Ramsgate's police station.

1877   Hilder B. Capps appointed head of Deal Police. W. Broadbridge appointed head of Rochester City Police.

1878   New County police station erected at Seabrook to replace previous one.

1879   Merit Stars replaced earlier chevrons in the County Constabulary.

1880   Samuel Rutter appointed head of Folkestone Borough Police. Rochester sergeants to wear stripes for the first time. Election riots in Tonbridge.

1881   James McBean appointed head of Canterbury City Police. Dover Police moved into the Maison Dieu building.

1882   Henry Dalton appointed head of Maidstone Borough Police.

1883   John Taylor appointed head of Folkestone Borough Police.

1884   Groom constables attached to each County Division.

1885   Whistles issued to the Kent County Constabulary.

1888   Local Government Act passed, creating County Councils. Control of the County Constabulary passed from the Court of General Sessions to a Standing Joint Committee of county councillors and justices of the peace. Robert Peacock appointed head of Canterbury City Police.

1889   The police forces in Deal, Hythe, Faversham, Sandwich and Tenterden merged into the Kent County Constabulary. New County police station completed at Brompton (Gillingham).

1890   New four-wheel dog carts introduced for use by Kent County superintendents.

1891   J.C. Allison appointed head of Tunbridge Wells Borough Police. Rochester Police issued with tunics instead of frock coats.

1892   County police station erected at Lydd. John Farmery appointed head of Canterbury City Police. Walter Thornton appointed head of Gravesend Borough Police.

1893   Charles Prior appointed head of Tunbridge Wells Borough Police.

1894   Captain Ruxton retired as first chief constable of the Kent County Constabulary after 37 years, aged 77. Major H.H. Edwards appointed chief constable.

1895   Head of Maidstone Borough Police re-named 'Chief Constable'. Major Edwards, chief constable of Kent, died suddenly. Lt. Col. H.M.A. Warde appointed chief constable of Kent. County police stations erected at Herne Bay and Knockholt. Angus C. Mackintosh appointed head of Maidstone Borough Police. Roderick Ross appointed head of Ramsgate Borough Police.

1896   Detective Branch formed in the County force. Bicycles introduced in county force for some patrolling officers. Need for man with red flag to precede automobiles lifted and speed limit raised to 20 m.p.h.

1897   Kent County Constabulary ceased wearing the shako and started wearing helmets. 'Instructing constables' in the County Constabulary renamed 'corporals'. Head of Rochester Police re-named 'chief constable'. Kent County Constabulary Sports Committee formed.

1898   William B. Jones appointed head of Ramsgate Borough Police. County men forbidden to take their dogs on patrol. Broadstairs police station completed. First County Police Annual Sports Day.

1899   Heads of Folkestone and Margate Police forces re-named 'chief constable'. Harry Reeve appointed chief constable of Folkestone.

1900   All ranks in the County Constabulary ordered to attend church at least once each Sunday.

1901   Faversham Division divided into two new Divisions (Faversham and Sittingbourne). H.N.K. Knott appointed head of Dover Borough Police.

1902   Rank of corporal abolished in the County force. 'Speed traps' introduced in Kent.

1903   Alfred S. Arnold appointed head of Rochester City Police.

1904   Knickers, puttees and forage caps provided for County cycle patrols. County police station erected at Faversham.

1905   Head of Dover Police re-titled 'chief constable'.

1907   L.T. Dunk appointed chief constable of Canterbury.

1908   David Fox appointed head of Dover Borough Police. French lessons given to Margate Police. Two Folkestone constables killed by an overturning horse cab. New police station built in Palace Avenue, Maidstone for the Borough Police.

1909   All Borough forces to wear a crown on the collar. Forces encouraged to form small mounted sections.

1912   One rest day in 14 granted to constables, sergeants and inspectors. Harry Thurley appointed chief constable of Gravesend.

1913   John Dain appointed chief constable of Canterbury. County men not to carry sticks or canes. New police station erected in Hythe for the County Constabulary.

1915   New cyclists cap with peak and chinstrap issued to cyclists in the County Constabulary.

1916   Samuel Butler appointed head of Ramsgate Borough Police. Kent's first detective superintendent appointed. Two policewomen appointed in Folkestone.

1917   B.H.A. Carlton appointed head of Canterbury City Police. French lessons given to six County detectives.

1918   Inspectors and superintendents to wear military style cap instead of the pill-box type.

1919   Desborough Report published, improving conditions in the police and creating the Police Federation. Ramsgate appoints its first policewoman.

1920   First chief superintendent (chief clerk) appointed to the county force. Charles Green appointed chief constable of Dover.

1921   Maidstone Borough proposes merger with the County force but not pursued. Coke riots in Ramsgate. Lt. Col. Warde retired as chief constable of Kent, replaced by Major H.E. Chapman. Major R.L. Surtees appointed the County's first assistant chief constable. Charles E. Butler appointed chief constable of Maidstone. S.A. Hector appointed chief constable of Tunbridge Wells.

1923   Captain J.A. McDonnell appointed chief constable of Canterbury. Alfred Beesley appointed chief constable of Folkestone.

1924   Home Division of the County Constabulary (Canterbury area) renamed St Augustine's Division. Alexander M. Bond appointed chief constable of Dover. Arthur G. Martin appointed chief constable of Gravesend. Rochester, Dover and Margate recruits sent to Birmingham City Police for training.

1925   Telephones installed in all rural sergeants' houses.

1926   Use of leggings in County force ceased.

1927   Guy Carlton appointed chief constable of Tunbridge Wells. Tunbridge Wells acquired a BSA motorcycle combination.

1928   Gravesend recruits sent to Birmingham City Police for training.

1929   Faversham and Sittingbourne Divisions (KCC) merged into a new Swale Division. Cavendish House, Ramsgate taken into use as the Borough police station. Gravesend Borough Police brought police boxes into use.

1930   George T. Hall appointed chief constable of Canterbury. Frank L. Bunn appointed chief constable of Gravesend. Eight motorcycles purchased for Kent rural sergeants. Folkestone Police bought a motorcycle combination. New County police station built at Deal.

1931   Bearsted Division of KCC abolished. One car and 19 motorcycles purchased by the County Constabulary for road patrol. Herbert C. Allen appointed chief constable of Rochester. Gravesend now sending recruits to the Kent County Constabulary for training. Motorcycle combinations purchased for Margate and Rochester police forces. Triumph 'Scorpion' purchased for Dover Police. Kent County Constabulary Old Comrades Association formed.

1932   County Force magazine *Patrol* introduced. Canterbury Police issued with its first motor car.

1933   Ramsgate recruits sent to Birmingham City Police for training.

1934   Cranbrook Division of KCC ceased to exist. First 12 civilian clerks appointed to the County force. Keith Webster appointed chief constable of Gravesend. 30 m.p.h. speed limit introduced in built-up areas.

1935 Site at Sutton Road purchased for new County Police Headquarters. Marshall H. Bolt appointed chief constable of Dover. Horace P. Hind appointed chief constable of Rochester. Ramsgate provided with its first motor car.

1936 Henry J. Vann appointed chief constable of Maidstone.

1937 Commander W.J.A. Willis appointed chief constable of Rochester.

1938 Rank of chief inspector created in Kent County Constabulary. Elham Division (KCC) ceased to exist.

1939 War declared; 200 First Police Reserves enrolled. New police station opened in Tunbridge Wells. Rochester Police acquired the *Pamela* launch for river patrol.

1940 Major Chapman retired as chief constable of Kent, replaced by Captain J.A. Davison New County Police Headquarters on Sutton Road, Maidstone, opened. Kenneth Horwood appointed chief constable of Rochester. German spies arrested on Romney Marsh by Kent officers. Police station built at Ladywell, Dover for the Borough Police and severely damaged in an air raid.

1941 Last County police horse disposed of. Marshall H. Bolt left Dover Police – temporarily replaced by H.A. Saddleton, pending amalgamation. Alfred Beesley resigned as chief constable of Folkestone. Replaced by R.C.M. Jenkins. Women's Auxiliary Police Corps formed.

1942 Captain Davison, chief constable of Kent, committed suicide.

1943 All the police forces in Kent amalgamated into the Kent County Constabulary. Sir Percy Sillitoe appointed chief constable of the combined force. Traffic Department set up under Superintendent Deacon on transfer from Glasgow.

1944 Miss Denis de Vitre appointed Kent's first woman inspector.

1946 Sir Percy Sillitoe resigned as chief constable of Kent on appointment to the War Office, to be replaced by Major (later Sir) John Ferguson. Kent County Police Driving School opened. Women's Auxiliary Police Corps disbanded. 999 Emergency call system brought into use.

1947 Deputy Chief Constable William Palmer died. ACC Jenkins appointed DCC. Parishes of Chelsfield, Cudham and Knockholt transferred to the Metropolitan Police force restructured into 12 territorial Divisions once more (A to M), plus R (Reserve) Division and a Traffic Division.

1949 Velocette LE lightweight motorcycles introduced.

1950 Triumph 'Speed Twins' issued to Traffic Department. Extensive police house building scheme started. Kent men seconded to Greece as part of the British Police Mission.

1951 Constable Alan Baxter murdered. Information and wireless room in operation from attic at Force Headquarters. First 40 Police Cadets employed. First woman detective appointed. New-style open necked tunics issued, with collar and tie for summer wear. First Kent police dog (Justice) acquired.

1952 Advanced driving courses started at Force Driving School. New police station built on Castle Hill, Rochester to replace the old City police station.

1953 Serious floods in North Kent. Major Ferguson, chief constable of Kent, knighted.

1955 Old type tunics with 'dog-collar' neck withdrawn. Open-neck tunics now worn all year. Kent officers seconded to the Cyprus Police.

1956 Norman 'Nippy' mopeds introduced. Constable Rooney killed by terrorist in Cyprus.

1957 Centenary of the Kent County Constabulary. End of National Service.

1958 Lt. Col. Geoffrey White appointed chief constable of Kent.

1960 New-style belted tunics with four pockets introduced. Flashing blue lights fitted to patrol cars.

1961 Sudden death of Lt. Col. White, chief constable of Kent. New police station started at Margate.

1962 (Sir) Richard Dawnay Lemon appointed chief constable of Kent.

1964 Police Act passed by Parliament but Kent unaffected. Opportunity taken to reorganise the force, reducing the number of territorial divisions by three. 'Mods and Rockers' riots in Margate. New police stations opened at The Brook, Chatham and Cross Street, Sheerness. First traffic wardens in Kent appointed.

1965 First firearms course for police at the Small Arms School, Hythe. New police stations opened at Northfleet and Old Dover Road, Canterbury. Operations Room moved from the attic to ground-floor accommodation at Force Headquarters.

1966 New police stations opened at Rochester and Sittingbourne. First personal radios in use.

1967   New police station opened in Cranbrook. Mr Frank Dewhirst appointed the first civilian senior administrative officer.

1968   Commencement of relations with the French Police.

1967   Reports of the Home Office Working Parties on Police Manpower, Equipment and Efficiency published. Unit Beat Policing introduced. Special Patrol Group formed. 'Breathalyser' introduced.

1970   Dawnay Lemon, chief constable of Kent, knighted.

1971   Memoranda ceased to be published. Format of General Orders changed.

1972   First Force welfare officer appointed.

1973   New Sevenoaks police station opened.

1974   Force reorganised to follow the reorganisation of local government. Now only seven Divisions. District Commands (East/West Kent) abolished and a centralised command structure introduced. Barry Pain appointed chief constable of Kent. New Dartford police station opened. Traffic garage built at Coldharbour, Maidstone. Sexual Discrimination Act spelt the end of the Police Women's Branch as a separate entity. Police National Computer came on line. 'Families Day' organised to replace the former 'Sports Days'.

1975   IRA bomb exploded at *Hare & Hounds* public house, Maidstone. New Gravesend police station opened.

1976   *Alexandra II* launch purchased.

1977   Police Open Day held at Force Headquarters for the Queen's Silver Jubilee celebrations. Kent Police Band formed.

1978   Kent took over responsibility for policing the Channel Ports from the Metropolitan Police.

1979   Edmund Davis Report brings considerable improvements in pay and conditions.

1980   Kent Police officers to Rhodesia to oversee the elections there.

1981   Recruitment to Cadet Force ended.

1982   Chief Constable Barry Pain appointed commandant of the National Police College. DCC Francis Jordan appointed chief constable of Kent. Police launches *Marina* and *Alexandra* sold.

1984   Police and Criminal Evidence Act passed. Miners' strike resulting in major disorders. Maidstone police station refurbished.

1985   Further reorganisation; now only five Divisions and Traffic Division reduced to three Areas. Promotion Boards for chief inspectors introduced. Southborough police station closed. Computer terminals in every police station.

1987   Devolution of financial matters and training on to sub-divisions. Promotion Boards introduced for superintendents. Kent hit by the 'Hurricane'. Loss of the *Herald of Free Enterprise* off Zeebrugge.

1988   New Operations Centre opened.

1989   Paul Condon appointed chief constable of Kent. Royal Marines bandsmen killed by IRA in Deal.

1990   Armed Response Vehicles introduced.

1991   European Liaison Unit formed.

1992   Force divided into 13 Territorial Areas instead of Divisions, plus a Traffic Area. Publication of the 'Sheehy Report'.

1993   (Sir) John David Phillips appointed chief constable of Kent. New police station opened at Longport for the Channel Tunnel.

1994   Abolition of rent and certain other allowances under the 'Sheehy Report'. Channel Tunnel opened. Central Tactical Support Unit formed. Integrated Communications System introduced. Police Museum opened in Chatham Historic Dockyard. Operational Information System introduced, replacing the old Occurrence Books.

1995   Town centre constables introduced. GENESIS force-wide IT system came on line.

1996   'Operation Stack' introduced to hold lorries when industrial action in France meant long delays in crossing the Channel. Hythe police station closed. Chatham police station converted into a dedicated custody suite. All police enquiry desks closed from 10 p.m. to 8 a.m.

1998   Firearms and Tactical Skills Centre opened at Force Headquarters, replacing firearm ranges at Canterbury and Rochester. Tonbridge police station demolished and new station erected on same site.

1999   Ramsgate police station closed. Work began on new Force Communications Centre at Force Headquarters. All remaining traffic wardens transferred to the local authorities.

2000   Former Orion Insurance offices taken into use as police station for Folkestone. David Phillips, chief constable of Kent, knighted.

NOTES

INTRODUCTION, PP.XV-XVII

1. *The Royal Commission for the purpose of inquiring as to the best means of establishing an efficient constabulary force in the counties of England and Wales.* BPP 1939, xc, pp.104-5. (Henceforth referred to as the *Chadwick Report*).
2. J.S. Cockburn (ed.), *Calendar of Assize Records: Kent Indictments, Elizabeth I* (London, HMSO, 1979), No.2617.
3. e.g. 23 Edward III, c.7 ; 7 Richard II, c.5, and 12 Richard II, c.2.
4. 14 Eliz. I, c.5.
5. E.P. Thompson, 'The Moral Economy of the English Crowd in the 18th century' in *Past and Present*, 50, 1971.

1 THE EARLY DAYS 1800-1857, PP.1-28

1. C. Emsley, *The English Police – a Political & Social History* (Hemel Hempstead, Harvester Wheatsheaf, 1991), p.4.
2. Frank W. Jessup, *A History of Kent* (London, Darwen Finlayson, 1958), p.154.
3. *Parliamentary Debates*, VII, 803.
4. Letter from Sir Robert Peel to John Wilson Croker, 10 October 1829.
5. *Report of the Committee on the Police Service of England, Wales and Scotland*, London (HMSO), 1967.
6. L. Poole, 'The Canterbury Police – 1836-1888', unpublished MLitt thesis, University of Kent at Canterbury, 1974.
7. *Kentish Gazette*, 26 January 1836.
8. *Kentish Gazette*, 8 March 1836.
9. Many of the members of the Watch Committee were in fact magistrates so there was little conflict.
10. *Kentish Gazette*, 12 March 1910, p.5.
11. Dover Borough Watch Committee Minutes, 7 January 1840, p.47.
12. This is interesting in that John Rofe was dismissed from the Walsall position following complaints about the efficiency of the force. The Dover authorities appear to have been merely concerned that he was in good health. No reason is given for his resignation after just one year, raising a question as to whether this was entirely voluntary.
13. An application from his widow for financial assistance was turned down as 'the Watch Committee had no power to render her any pecuniary assistance'.
14. Watch Committee Minutes, 11 December 1856.
15. Hythe Town Archives, Ref. 1428.
16. *Maidstone Gazette*, 8 March 1836.
17. Peter Clark and Lyn Murfin, *The Making of a Modern County Town*, pp.149, 150.
18. Newman only lasted three months before he was dismissed for allowing a prisoner to escape.
19. *Municipal Corporations Report*, 1834, p.1025.
20. Select Committee on Police Superannuation, Q 3234.
21. Report of the Select Committee on the Police of the Metropolis, *Parliamentary Papers*, 1834, xvi, pp.418-19.
22. See Robert Hughes, *The Fatal Shore* (London, Collins Harvill, 1987).
23. E. Chadwick, 'Preventive Police: Organization and Preventive Action', in *London Review* 1, 1829.
24. S.E. Finer, *Sir Edwin Chadwick. His Life and Times* (1952), p.127.
25. Carolyn Steedman, *Policing the Victorian Community: The formation of English provincial police forces, 1856-1880* (London, Routledge & Kegan Paul, 1984), pp.18-19.
26. Chadwick manuscripts, University College Library, London.
27. Steedman, *op. cit.*, p.20.
28. It is of interest to note that Captain John Hay Ruxton was a member of this Committee.
29. Gifford resigned shortly afterwards and was replaced by Gilbert who was moved from Tunbridge because of his insolvency.
30. Not spelt as 'Tonbridge' until later.
31. With the exception of the Metropolitan Police being in overall command, this concept of regional police forces is something which, a century and a half later, is still very much on the cards.
32. The *Chadwick Report*, p.iii.
33. A small borough was regarded as one with fewer than 100,000 inhabitants. At the time only seven boroughs outside London had populations of this magnitude.
34. The principal justice of the peace in the county who has nominal custody of the records of the Commission of the Peace. This is usually, as here, the Lord Lieutenant of the county, the Viscount Sydney.

2 A COUNTY FORCE AT LAST 1857-1888, PP.29-64

1. Sir John Nott-Bower, *Fifty Years a Policeman* (London, Arnold, 1926).
2. *Kent Times Chronicle*, 29 April 1897 (obituary).

3. Chief Constable's Letter Books, CPO1/1/2.
4. This officer went sick shortly after his appointment and died in August 1857. He was replaced at Cranbrook by Superintendent English from the Ashford Division.
5. Replaced by Superintendent Colman from the Elham division.
6. Although this was the principle adopted, in fact the Home, Malling and Sevenoaks Divisions only had one sergeant until 1867 and Tunbridge Division only had one sergeant until 1859.
7. Chief Constable's Letter Book, QGPa8.
8. *Ibid.*, CPO1/1/5.
9. *Ibid.*, CPO1/1/5.
10. Higgler – a hawker or pedlar.
11. The latter term survived into the next century and beyond to describe the handbolts and truncheon issued to each officer.
12. Letter of 4 May 1857 to Hebbert & Co.
13. Chief Constable's Letter Books: CPO1/1/2.
14. Roy Ingleton, *Arming the British Police* (London, Frank Cass, 1997), p.35.
15. H.O. 45.6811.
16. This instruction was amended in 1901 to require a suspended member to remain at his station (i.e. his home) until the case against him had been dealt with.
17. This man would undoubtedly have been dealt with much more severely had it not been for the poor standard of the report submitted by his superintendent which the chief constable criticised in the strongest terms.
18. In 1855, 'Mr. Trow's premises in King Street' were hired and became the town's police station.
19. At this time the justices were holding their courts in various places, including public houses, such as the *Royal Oak*, in Bearsted.
20. The Bearsted Division was based at Wrens Cross, Maidstone while the Elham Division had the use of the new police station at Seabrook.
21. A magistrates court was added in 1904.
22. *Folkestone Chronicle*, 11 May 1878.
23. Lady Day was the traditional day for the annual appointment of parish constables.
24. One of the original constables, PC Rye, was permitted to continue with his former trade but was disciplined for sleeping on duty and resigned in 1838.
25. Increased to 5ft. 9in. in 1882.
26. *Kentish Gazette*, 19 June 1864.
27. *Kentish Gazette*, 5 October 1869.
28. 'The Canterbury Police 1836-1888', unpublished thesis by L. Poole, University of Kent at Canterbury, 1974.
29. *Rules, Regulations and Directions for the Government and Instruction of the Police Force of the Borough of Dover,* 1858.
30. Watch Committee Minutes for 24 September 1856.
31. *Idem*, 11 December 1956.
32. *Dover Express*, 17 March 1860.
33. *Folkestone Observer,* 13 July 1861.
34. The Police Committee, formed under the Ramsgate Improvement Act of 1838, changed its title to Watch Committee in October 1860.
35. W.H. Bishop, 'Ramsgate Borough Police Force', *Bygone Kent*, Vol. 13, No.10, pp.577-83.
36. Not until 1880 were the Rochester sergeants issued with stripes on their arms, 'like the London Police'.
37. It is interesting to note that as recently as September 1998 new instructions were given regarding the issue of Pedlars' Certificates.
38. Gordon Church, 'A Victorian Country Copper' in *Bygone Kent*, Vol.13, No.7, p.393 *et seq.*
39. Extract from the Minutes of the Poor Law Board, circulated by the chief constable of Kent in 1862.
40. *Folkestone Chronicle*, 11 November 1865.
41. Gordon Church, *op. cit.*
42. Chief Constable's General Orders, CPO1/17/1.
43. Gordon Church, *op. cit.*
44. Chief Constable's Letter Books.
45. Gordon Church, *op. cit.*
46. To put this killing into perspective, it has to be pointed out that, in that year (1873), no fewer than five constables were killed in places as far apart as Northumberland and London, Cheshire and Salford. One hundred years later, only two police officers were killed on duty in 1973, one shot in Devon and one killed by a vehicle in London.
47. Regina v English, 1871, QCs5.
48. General Orders CPO1/17/3.
49. There appears to be no explanation for this apparent leniency at a time when justice was normally extremely severe.

3 TOWARDS GREATER PROFESSIONALISM 1888-1943, PP.65-129

1. *The Hythe Reporter*, 11 March 1922.
2. Majors Baynes, Lushington, Mayne and Stratford. Only Major Otway Mayne appears to have had any subsequent success, being appointed chief constable of Buckinghamshire two years later.
3. *Kent Police Centenary* (Kent County Constabulary, Maidstone, 1957), p.41.

4.   General Order of 30 May 1904.

5.   They thus became 'detective constables' for the first time.

6.   This restriction was temporarily suspended during the Great War.

7.   Oral history.

8.   Memorandum of 8 August 1904.

9.   Memorandum 215/12.

10. Home Office circular 214312, 15 September 1911.

11. Although in June 1856 a large number of special constables was appointed by the county justices, to keep the peace along the line of the East Kent Railway during the progress of the work. This, of course, was before the County force was formed and when the rural areas were still policed by the parish constables.

12. Section 1 of the 1831 Act provided that special constables could only be appointed where a riot, tumult or felony had taken place or was reasonably expected. Similarly, constables appointed under the Municipal Corporations Act could only act when so required by a justice's warrant which could only be issued when the justices considered that the ordinary borough police force was insufficient to maintain the peace.

13. Seth, R., *The Specials: The Story of the Special Constabulary in England, Wales and Scotland* (London, Victor Gollancz, 1961), pp.85-6

14. *Daily Mail*, 23 October 1914.

15. Memorandum of 17 November 1916.

16. The 'Reserve Force of Voluntary Special Constables'.

17. *Chatham Observer*, 27 July 1914, p.7.

18. Statutory Rules and Orders 1920 No.1484.

19. Given this definition it is even more difficult to understand the reason for re-naming the Kent Divisions as 'Areas' in the 1990s.

20. Ambrose had been the force's first detective superintendent (1915-1919) before taking charge of the administration of the force.

21. *Op. cit.*

22. Roy Ingleton, *The Gentlemen at War : Policing Britain 1939 to 1945* (Maidstone, Cranborne Publications, 1994), p.188.

23. General Orders, 25 April 1900.

24. Forage caps were issued to superintendents in 1900 but do not appear to have replaced the traditional 'pill box'.

25. General Order of 29 January 1896.

26. Memorandum 198/11.

27. This early car, with its shiny brass radiator, was affectionately known as the 'Flying Bedstead'.

28. No figures are available for the boroughs although it is known that there were six fatalities in Maidstone in 1919 and three the following year.

29. *Police*, July 2000, p.24.

30. *Kent Police Centenary* (Kent County Constabulary, Maidstone, 1957), p.45.

31. Authorised by an Order in Council on 28 September 1939.

32. Police and Firemen (War Service) Act, 1939.

33. A W Cockerill, *Sir Percy Sillitoe* (London, W.H. Allen, 1975).

34. For a more detailed account of this incident, see Roy Ingleton, *The Gentlemen at War*, pp.110-12.

35. Replaced by Sergeant Cash who was eventually promoted to superintendent.

36. Home Office Letter No.163219/10 of 15 April 1909 contained the recommendations of the Select Committee on this matter.

37. *Kentish Gazette*, 12 March 1910, p.5.

38. Chief Constable's Report for 1918.

39. Outside London, Dover suffered the most attacks (by air and Cross-Channel shelling) – a total of 125. Third (after Great Yarmouth) came Folkestone with 83 attacks, Margate came 10th with 70 and Ramsgate 16th with 63.

40. *The Vote*, 28 August 1914.

41. It is not clear what became of the latter officer since, in November 1916, the Watch Committee minutes refer to the resignation of a Constable C. Kirby.

42. Sergeant Floydd was well-known in the town as a powerful champion swimmer.

43. It is quite possible that Rodman or another officer was appointed as detective constable prior to this but the records for the town's Watch Committee are incomplete with a gap between 1865 and 1873.

44. Coincidentally, when Ross left Bradford he was replaced by Joseph Farndale who had previously been the chief constable of Margate.

45. At this salary the post was presumably part-time.

46. It seems likely that this man's condition had been brought to the attention of the Home Department by the HMI following an inspection of the force.

47. Watch Committee Minutes A254.

48. This was known as Lord Derby's scheme.

49. There are many retired officers who can remember doing traffic duty at the busy and complex junction at the bottom of Star Hill, Rochester, certainly up to the 1950s, if not beyond. Other 'hot-spots' included Strood High Street's junction with North Street and the Corporation Street end of Rochester bridge.

50. Probably the MG PA four-seater model, purchased second-hand as mentioned in the manufacturer's records.

51. Not the infamous Captain Bailey!

52. One of these was possibly the MG PA model, BKP293, which was supplied on the understanding that it would be

returned to the makers for modification once it had been run in. These modifications included moving the pedals nearer the centre of the car, presumably because of the drivers' rather large feet!

4 A UNITED FORCE 1943-2000, PP.130-170

1. Crash helmets, of the 'Corker' type, were not introduced until the 1950s.
2. Named after the Duchess of Kent.
3. Believed to be 28 TA models, plus the saloons referred to previously.
4. Since demolished and replaced by the headquarters of the SAGA organisation.
5. Like Kent, the East and West Sussex forces and the various borough forces in Sussex were all compulsorily amalgamated as a war-time measure in 1943 but, unlike Kent, they reverted to their previous form after the war.
6. The tin trunk in question may be seen at the Kent Police Museum in Chatham Historic Dockyard.
7. The chief constable of Kent issued a warning in October 1989 that personnel convicted of driving with excess alcohol – on or off duty – would normally be dismissed from the force and that drinking on duty was a disciplinary offence.
8. This was before the Sexual Offences Act, 1967 made homosexual acts between consenting adult males legal.
9. The first County First Aid team was formed in 1951 to compete in the National Pim Trophy competition.
10. R.C.M. Jenkins died in March 1973.
11. Norman Fowler enjoyed a long retirement, dying in March 2001 at the age of 97!
12. Coincidentally, these ages and heights are almost exactly the same as existed in the Maidstone Borough force in 1904.
13. Chief Superintendent Brice (as he had then become) retired on an ill-health pension in April 1981 and died just four days later.
14. It is interesting to note that this new station was erected almost opposite the place where the original Chatham lock-up stood in Military Road (now occupied by the Pentagon Centre).
15. Only 57,000 of these were classified as requiring urgent police attention.
16. In fact, UHF radios had a very limited range and were subject to screening by tall buildings, etc.
17. Gallagher's treatise on Cross-Channel Liaison later earned him his PhD.
18. The last person in charge of the Women Police, Chief Superintendent Margery Bishop, QPM, retired in 1981, since when women have held a number of senior ranks (up to and including ACC) in the force.
19. Chief Constable's Annual Reports for 1986, 1987, 1989.
20. Chief Constable's Annual Report for 1977.
21. Command and Control for 21st century.
22. Another Kent senior officer, Peter Hermitage, was appointed Director of National Police Training in 1996, embracing the command of the Police Staff College, as it was now known.
23. Motorways plus A229, A249 and A299.
24. The difficulties were less where the Belgians were concerned since many of them spoke and understood the English language very well.
25. Chief Constable of Kent's Report for 1993.
26. Jonathan Hoare, 'Back to the Future … Maybe' in *Police,* January 2001, p.25.
27. Because of some doubt as to the veracity of a witness at the trial, a re-trial was ordered and held towards the end of 2001where Stone was again found guilty.
28. Ken Hyder, 'Commuter Belt Crime Lords', *Police Review,* 28 May 1999, pp.22-3.

INDEX

Figures in **bold** refer to illustration page numbers. † Indicates a death in action.